国际结算与融资
International Settlement and Finance

赵 薇 编著
Zhao Wei

东南大学出版社
·南京·

内 容 提 要

国际结算是商业银行主要的中间业务之一。本书对商业银行国际结算业务中涉及的票据、国际结算和融资的方法以及单据等三大内容进行了全面系统的论述。本书用英文撰写,涉及大量的国际银行业务术语,不仅是一本有实用价值的国际结算教材,而且是一本国际银行业务英语阅读教材。本书可以作为高校金融和国际贸易专业的双语教学教材,也可供从事银行国际结算业务工作的人员阅读。

图书在版编目(CIP)数据

国际结算与融资:双语版:汉、英/赵薇编著. —2版. —南京:东南大学出版社,2015.8(2024.1重印)
 ISBN 978 - 7 - 5641 - 5983 - 2

Ⅰ. ①国… Ⅱ. ①赵… Ⅲ. ①国际结算—汉、英 ②国际金融—融资—汉、英 Ⅳ. ①F831

中国版本图书馆 CIP 数据核字(2015)第 198109 号

国际结算与融资

出版发行:	东南大学出版社
社　　址:	南京市四牌楼2号　邮编:210096
出 版 人:	江建中
网　　址:	http://www.seupress.com
经　　销:	全国各地新华书店
印　　刷:	广东虎彩云印刷有限公司
开　　本:	652mm×960mm　1/16
印　　张:	21
字　　数:	411 千字
版　　次:	2015 年 8 月第 2 版
印　　次:	2024 年 1 月第 3 次印刷
书　　号:	ISBN 978 - 7 - 5641 - 5983 - 2
定　　价:	39.00 元

本社图书若有印装质量问题,请直接与营销部联系。电话:025 - 83791830

Acknowledgements

This book reflects my 19 years of teaching to undergraduate students in the Department of Finance and Insurance at Nanjing University. Not only has it benefited from the students' feedback but also from lots of literature and materials I have referred to. Thus, I should thank all the authors who have been listed or missed in the references.

I am most grateful to Liu Guoqiang who was the manager of the International Department of the Bank of Communications in Nanjing and offered me a chance of getting to know what the practice was in 1996. I am grateful to Johan Bergamin, a consultant in trade and commodity finance with the ING Bank Barings Amsterdam back in 1999 who provided me with some valuable resources for my teaching and the book. I would like to thank my former graduate student Liu Kun who currently works in the Jiangsu Branch of the Export-Import Bank of China and has been helping me with materials and even added a few segments in Chapter 10. I would also like to thank my former graduate students Zhang Xiaochen and Jiang Yalin for their assistance in collecting some materials and Liu Kun for proofreading the whole book.

I would like to thank my two former classmates at Nanjing University, Wu Ping and Jia Yun, for their time and efforts in proofreading the book and preface for grammatical fixes which make the book read smoothly. I should also thank Ms. Zhou Ju, the editor from the Southeast University Press for her hard working in proofreading the book.

My special thanks are extended to Professor Pei Ping, Associate Dean of the School of Business at Nanjing University, for writing a preface for the book.

Preface

As an important component of foreign-related economic activities, international settlement possesses the characteristics of being theoretical and operational. In institutes of higher learning, international settlement has been one of the important compulsory courses on economics and business administration curriculum, especially in finance and trade specialties. Thus, selecting or writing a good textbook is of great importance to classroom teaching and the construction of finance and trade specialties. Especially since China entered the World Trade Organization (WTO), its foreign-related economic activities have increased both in volume and complexity, the contents of international settlement have been constantly enriched and renewed, and the specific operation procedures and expressions have tended to be internationally standardized. Therefore, there is a great demand for talents who not only have a good command of knowledge in international settlement but also are proficient in conducting international settlement operations in English. Moreover, the Ministry of Education encourages some specialties in higher learning institutes, such as finance specialty, to practice bilingual teaching in some courses. The publication of this English edition of *International Settlement and Finance* not only marks a new stage of bilingual teaching and learning in the Department of Finance at Nanjing University, but also helps promote bilingual teaching and learning in economics and business administration specialties in China, and hence contributes to the training of internationalized professional talents.

Some claim that English textbooks for specialty courses should be directly imported from the United States or other developed countries. It may not be a bad option, but I do not think that it is the best one available. Speaking as someone who once studied and obtained a degree in Europe, was a Fulbright professor and visiting professor in the United States and other developed countries for some time, has engaged in teaching and researching in finance for 20 years, and translated some American textbooks in finance, I am of the opinion that the high costs of importing English textbooks from developed countries matter, but only secondarily. What matters most is that the contents of such books are to some extent not applicable to the practical conditions in China and that some of the contents are not even international but with "local colors" and "local accents". Of course, writing textbooks solely based on Chinese conditions and in Chinese does little good to the training of internationalized professional talents. The best option is for Chinese professors who are good at English, who have mastered relevant theories and knowledge and possess international perspectives to write English edition textbooks in relative specialties. The reason is simple: they understand international customs and practices as well as domestic conditions; they know what to convey to students and how, and can express their thoughts accurately in English.

Associate Professor Zhao Wei's academic records are highly impressive. She had an M. A. in English Language and Literature from Nanjing University, studied economics and business administration under American professors at Nanjing University—the Johns Hopkins University Center for Chinese and American Studies, studied as a visiting scholar in the Joint Educational Program in Economics in the Faculty of Economics and Business Administration at Tilburg University of the Netherlands, and obtained a Ph. D. in management at Nanjing University. She has engaged in teaching Spoken English, Financial English and International Settlement for 19 years. I have sat in on her classes conducted in English, and personally witnessed the positive feedback from students on her teaching. I have also heard her interpreting when she accompanied the two Nobel Laureates Lawrence Klein and Michael Spence on their visit to the School of Business at Nanjing University. I have read some of her academic papers published in core journals such as the *World Economy*. Her academic levels in finance and English, especially her exactness in and devotion to work, are appraised highly by both faculty and students. It should be said that she is best-suited to write an English edition of *International Settlement and Finance*, as evidenced by the enormous success enjoyed by the former English edition in 2003. The textbook results from years of diligent English study and bilingual teaching and research. The characteristics of this textbook can be summarized as follows: (1) The basic framework and main contents are internationally acceptable and at the same time reflect Chinese theories and practices in international settlement; (2) The textbook lists many domestically and internationally seen documents used in international settlement and elaborates on major operation procedures; (3) The important concepts and terms are explained in Chinese with a glossary of terms; (4) The English used in this textbook is a "working language" acceptable to both Chinese and foreigners in conducting international settlement operations, and the language is relatively smooth.

I hope that the new version textbook will receive high ratings from readers upon publication and that Associate Professor Zhao Wei would be given an opportunity to perfect this book in her future teaching and researching.

Pei Ping
At An Zhong Building
Nanjing University
July 2014

Contents

Acknowledgements 1

Preface 1

1 Introduction 1

1.1 International settlement vs. trade finance 1
1.2 The evolution of international settlement 3
From cash settlement to non-cash settlement 3
From direct payment to indirect payment 4
From simple price terms to complex price terms 5
From paper documents to electronic documents 7
1.3 Electronic communication and payment systems 10
SWIFT 10
BOLERO 12
CHIPS 13
CHAPS & Faster Payment 14
Fedwire® Funds Service, Fedwire Securities Service and National Settlement Services 15
TARGET and TARGET2 17
CNAPS 18
1.4 Players, roles and risks in international trade payments
.... 19
Exporter 19
Importer 20
Banks 21

1.5 Types of payment techniques ... 21
Consignment ... 22
Open account ... 22
Documentary collections ... 23
Letters of credit ... 23
Guarantees/standby letters of credit ... 23
Payment in advance ... 23
Factoring ... 26
Forfaiting ... 26

1.6 Related laws, customs and practice ... 27
Laws on negotiable instruments ... 27
International customs and practice for collections, documentary letters of credit, standby letters of credit, guarantees and international factoring ... 27
International conventions on bills of lading ... 28

1.7 Correspondent bank ... 30
Correspondent bank agreement ... 30
Control documents ... 30

2 Negotiable instruments ... 39

2.1 Characteristics and functions of negotiable instruments ... 40
Negotiability ... 40
Unconditional promise or order to pay ... 40
Requisite in form ... 41
Non-causative nature ... 41
Functions of negotiable instruments ... 43

2.2 Negotiable instrument laws ... 43

2.3 Parties to a negotiable instrument ... 45
Drawer ... 45
Drawee ... 46

	Payee	46
	Indorser	47
	Acceptor	48
	Guarantor	48
	Holder	49
	The relationship of the parties to negotiable instruments	51
2.4	**Bills of Exchange**	53
	Definition	53
	Essential items required in a bill of exchange	55
2.5	**Acts related to a bill of exchange**	62
	Issue	62
	Indorsement	63
	Presentment or presentation	67
	Acceptance	68
	Payment	70
	Dishonour	72
	Protest	73
	Notice of Dishonour	76
	Right of recourse	77
	Guarantee or aval	78
	Acceptance for honour supra protest	81
	Payment for honour supra protest	83
	Classification of bills of exchange	84
2.6	**Promissory Notes**	85
	Definition	85
	Essential items of a promissory note	86
	Joint notes vs. joint and several notes	87
	Types of promissory notes	89
	Differences between bills of exchange and promissory notes	90
2.7	**Cheques**	92

  Definition ……… 92
  Essential items of a cheque ……… 93
  Types of cheques ……… 93
  Differences between cheques and bills of exchange ……… 99

3 Remittance ……… 100

3.1 Definition ……… 100

3.2 Parties to a remittance ……… 101
  Remitter ……… 101
  Remitting bank ……… 101
  Paying bank ……… 102
  Payee or beneficiary ……… 102

3.3 Types of remittance ……… 102
  Mail transfer ……… 102
  Telegraphic transfer ……… 103
  Demand draft ……… 104

3.4 Reimbursement of remittance cover ……… 105

3.5 The cancellation of remittance ……… 106

3.6 Application of remittance in international trade ……… 107
  Cash in advance ……… 107
  Open account ……… 108

3.7 Trade finance under remittance ……… 109
  Financing under T/T ……… 109
  Credit insurance and bank financing ……… 110

3.8 Other methods of remittance ……… 110
  Credit card ……… 111
  PapPal ……… 112
  Western Union and MoneyGram ……… 113
  Cheque payment ……… 114

4 Collection ……… 115

4.1 Definition ……… 115

4.2 Basic parties to a collection ········· 117
    Principal ········· 117
    Remitting bank ········· 118
    Collecting bank ········· 118
    Presenting bank ········· 119
    Drawee ········· 120
    Collection instruction ········· 121
    The relationship between the basic parties ········· 122

4.3 Types of collection ········· 123
    Clean collection ········· 123
    Documentary collection ········· 123
    Procedures of a documentary collection transaction ········· 124

4.4 Terms of releasing documents ········· 125
    Documents against payment (D/P) ········· 125
    Documents against acceptance (D/A) ········· 126

4.5 Liabilities and disclaimers of banks under a collection ········· 127
    Banks have no obligation to handle a collection ········· 127
    Disclaimer for acts of an instructed party ········· 128
    Disclaimer on documents received ········· 128
    Disclaimer on effectiveness of documents ········· 128
    Disclaimer on delays, loss in transit and translation ········· 129
    Banks do not deal with the goods, services or other acts ········· 129

4.6 Financing provided by banks under a collection ········· 129
    Financing provided by the remitting bank to the exporter ········· 130
    Financing provided by the collecting bank to the importer ········· 132

4.7 Problems frequently arising from a collection ········· 134

The problems of using D/P at a fixed period after sight ················· 134

Problems related to insurance ············· 136

Negative events that may occur to the exporter ········· 137

5 Letters of credit ················· 139

5.1 Definition ················· 139

5.2 Characteristics of a documentary credit ········· 141

A written undertaking on the part of the issuing bank ················· 141

Independent of the sales contract ············· 142

Exclusively dealing with documents ············· 142

5.3 Parties to a letter of credit ················· 143

Applicant ················· 143

Issuing bank ················· 145

Beneficiary ················· 146

Advising bank ················· 147

Confirming bank ················· 148

Paying bank/accepting bank ············· 150

Negotiating bank ················· 150

Claiming bank ················· 151

Reimbursing bank ················· 152

5.4 Stages to a documentary credit operation ········· 153

Stage 1: The importer applies to its bank for a documentary credit ················· 153

Stage 2: The issuing bank reviews the importer's application for credit and issues a documentary credit ············· 154

Stage 3: The advising bank advises the credit to the seller ················· 155

Stage 4: The exporter examines the credit, prepares for the

required documents and submits the documents to the nominated bank ⋯⋯ 156

Stage 5: The issuing bank examines the documents and pays or reimburses the negotiating bank ⋯⋯ 158

Stage 6: The importer redeems the documents from the issuing bank and picks up the goods against the bills of lading from the shipping company ⋯⋯ 159

5.5 Contents of a documentary credit ⋯⋯ 159
    Items on the credit itself ⋯⋯ 159
    Items on draft ⋯⋯ 160
    Items on goods, shipping documents and transport ⋯⋯ 160
    Other items ⋯⋯ 160

5.6 The examination of a documentary credit ⋯⋯ 163
    The examination by the advising bank ⋯⋯ 163
    The examination by the exporter ⋯⋯ 171

5.7 Types of credit ⋯⋯ 175
    Irrevocable credit ⋯⋯ 175
    Confirmed irrevocable credit ⋯⋯ 175
    Sight payment credit ⋯⋯ 176
    Acceptance credit ⋯⋯ 177
    Deferred payment credit ⋯⋯ 179
    Negotiation credit ⋯⋯ 180
    Straight credit ⋯⋯ 182
    Anticipatory credit ⋯⋯ 183
    Green clause credit ⋯⋯ 184
    Transferable credit ⋯⋯ 185
    Back-to-back credit ⋯⋯ 188
    Revolving credit ⋯⋯ 189
    Reciprocal credit ⋯⋯ 190

5.8 Trade finance provided by banks ⋯⋯ 192
    Finance provided to the exporter ⋯⋯ 192

	Finance provided to the importer	197
5.9	Letters of credit vs. other payment methods	200

6 Standby letters of credit ... 202

6.1 Definition ... 202
Origin ... 202
UCP 600 vs. ISP 98 ... 203
Definition by ISP 98 ... 203

6.2 Characteristics of a standby letter of credit ... 204
Clean credit ... 204
Financial obligation ... 205
Non-financial obligation ... 205
Irrevocable form ... 205
Duration and amount ... 206
Payment procedures ... 206

6.3 Parties to a standby letter of credit ... 206
Applicant ... 206
Issuer ... 208
Beneficiary ... 209
Transferree beneficiary ... 209
Confirmer ... 210

6.4 Types of documents required in a standby letter of credit ... 210
Demand for payment ... 211
Statement of default or other drawing event ... 211
Negotiable documents ... 211
Legal or judicial documents ... 212
Other documents ... 212
Examination of the documents ... 213

6.5 Types of standby credit ... 214
Performance standby ... 214

　　　　　Advance payment standby ·· 214
　　　　　Bid bond/tender bond standby ·· 214
　　　　　Counter standby ··· 215
　　　　　Financial standby ··· 215
　　　　　Direct payment standby ·· 215
　　　　　Insurance standby ·· 216
　　　　　Commercial standby ··· 216
　　6.6　**The problems arising by making a standby subject to UCP**
　　　　　·· 216
　　　　　When a copy bill of lading is required ································ 216
　　　　　When partial payment is used ·· 217

7　Letters of guarantee ·· 218

　　7.1　**Definition** ·· 218
　　　　　Demand guarantee ·· 218
　　　　　Contract guarantee ··· 219
　　7.2　**Characteristics of a demand guarantee** ························ 220
　　7.3　**Basic parties to a demand guarantee** ·························· 220
　　7.4　**Direct and indirect guarantees** ······································ 222
　　7.5　**Types of guarantee** ·· 222
　　　　　Tender guarantee/bid bond ·· 223
　　　　　Performance guarantee ··· 223
　　　　　Repayment guarantee ··· 223
　　　　　Advance payment guarantee ·· 223
　　　　　Maintenance guarantee ·· 223
　　　　　Retention money guarantee ··· 224
　　　　　Counter guarantee ·· 224
　　7.6　**Contents of a guarantee** ··· 225
　　　　　Basic contents of a guarantee ··· 225
　　　　　Additional clauses of a guarantee ·· 226
　　　　　Basic contents of a counter guarantee ································· 231

8 International factoring ... 239

8.1 Origin and legal framework ... 239
Origin ... 239
Legal framework ... 240

8.2 What is factoring? ... 241

8.3 The procedures of international factoring ... 242

8.4 Types of factoring ... 243
Maturity factoring and financed factoring ... 243
Disclosed factoring and undisclosed factoring ... 244
Single factoring and co-factoring ... 244

8.5 Services provided to the exporter by a factor ... 245
Credit investigation of buyers ... 245
Credit protection ... 246
Collection and management of receivables ... 247
Finance ... 247

8.6 The role of factoring in international trade ... 248

8.7 Risks faced by factors ... 249
Credit risks ... 249
Operational risks ... 250
Legal risks ... 250

8.8 Factoring in China ... 251

9 International forfaiting ... 257

9.1 Origin and evolution ... 257

9.2 What is forfaiting? ... 259
Parties to the forfaiting transaction ... 261
Required Documents ... 261
Aval or guarantee ... 262
Costs ... 262
Application and tenors ... 263

9.3　**The mechanics of a forfaiting transaction** ⋯⋯⋯⋯⋯⋯⋯⋯ 264
　　　The underlying trade contract ⋯⋯⋯⋯⋯⋯⋯⋯⋯⋯⋯⋯⋯⋯ 264
　　　The forfaiting proposal ⋯⋯⋯⋯⋯⋯⋯⋯⋯⋯⋯⋯⋯⋯⋯⋯⋯ 265
　　　Terms and conditions ⋯⋯⋯⋯⋯⋯⋯⋯⋯⋯⋯⋯⋯⋯⋯⋯⋯⋯ 267
　　　Summary of the procedures of forfaiting ⋯⋯⋯⋯⋯⋯⋯⋯⋯ 270
9.4　**Forfaiting vs. other trade financing methods** ⋯⋯⋯⋯⋯⋯ 271
　　　Forfaiting vs. officially supported export credits ⋯⋯⋯⋯⋯ 271
　　　Forfaiting vs. factoring ⋯⋯⋯⋯⋯⋯⋯⋯⋯⋯⋯⋯⋯⋯⋯⋯⋯ 272
9.5　**Forfaiting in China** ⋯⋯⋯⋯⋯⋯⋯⋯⋯⋯⋯⋯⋯⋯⋯⋯⋯⋯⋯⋯ 272

10　Documents used in international trade payments

⋯⋯⋯⋯⋯⋯⋯⋯⋯⋯⋯⋯⋯⋯⋯⋯⋯⋯⋯⋯⋯⋯⋯⋯⋯⋯⋯⋯⋯⋯⋯⋯ 274

10.1　**Types and functions of documents** ⋯⋯⋯⋯⋯⋯⋯⋯⋯⋯⋯ 274
　　　Basic documents and additional documents ⋯⋯⋯⋯⋯⋯⋯⋯ 274
　　　Financial documents and commercial documents ⋯⋯⋯⋯⋯ 274
　　　Representing the title to the ownership of the goods
　　　⋯⋯⋯⋯⋯⋯⋯⋯⋯⋯⋯⋯⋯⋯⋯⋯⋯⋯⋯⋯⋯⋯⋯⋯⋯⋯⋯⋯ 275
　　　Evidencing the fulfillment of obligations ⋯⋯⋯⋯⋯⋯⋯⋯⋯ 275
10.2　**Draft(s) drawn under a letter of credit** ⋯⋯⋯⋯⋯⋯⋯⋯⋯ 275
　　　Characteristics of drafts drawn under a letter of credit
　　　⋯⋯⋯⋯⋯⋯⋯⋯⋯⋯⋯⋯⋯⋯⋯⋯⋯⋯⋯⋯⋯⋯⋯⋯⋯⋯⋯⋯ 276
　　　Examination of the draft(s) drawn under a letter of credit
　　　⋯⋯⋯⋯⋯⋯⋯⋯⋯⋯⋯⋯⋯⋯⋯⋯⋯⋯⋯⋯⋯⋯⋯⋯⋯⋯⋯⋯ 276
　　　The most frequently found discrepancies with drafts
　　　⋯⋯⋯⋯⋯⋯⋯⋯⋯⋯⋯⋯⋯⋯⋯⋯⋯⋯⋯⋯⋯⋯⋯⋯⋯⋯⋯⋯ 278
10.3　**Commercial invoices** ⋯⋯⋯⋯⋯⋯⋯⋯⋯⋯⋯⋯⋯⋯⋯⋯⋯⋯ 278
　　　Contents of a commercial invoice ⋯⋯⋯⋯⋯⋯⋯⋯⋯⋯⋯⋯ 278
　　　Other invoices ⋯⋯⋯⋯⋯⋯⋯⋯⋯⋯⋯⋯⋯⋯⋯⋯⋯⋯⋯⋯⋯ 280
10.4　**Transport documents** ⋯⋯⋯⋯⋯⋯⋯⋯⋯⋯⋯⋯⋯⋯⋯⋯⋯⋯ 284
　　　Marine bills of lading ⋯⋯⋯⋯⋯⋯⋯⋯⋯⋯⋯⋯⋯⋯⋯⋯⋯⋯ 284
　　　Basic parties to a bill of lading ⋯⋯⋯⋯⋯⋯⋯⋯⋯⋯⋯⋯⋯ 285

　　　　　　Main contents of a bill of lading ················· 286
　　　　　　Types of bills of lading ························ 286
　　　　　　The most frequently found discrepancies with a bill of lading
　　　　　　　··· 290
　　　　　　Other transport documents ····················· 291
　　10. 5　**Insurance documents** ······················· 295
　　　　　　Types of marine cargo transport insurance ········ 295
　　　　　　Examining an insurance policy under a letter of credit
　　　　　　　··· 296
　　　　　　The most frequently found discrepancies with an insurance
　　　　　　document ······································ 300
　　10. 6　**Other documents** ·························· 305
　　　　　　Certificates of origin ··························· 305
　　　　　　Inspection certificate ··························· 309
　　　　　　Packing list and weight list ···················· 309
　　　　　　Cable copy ···································· 309
　　　　　　Beneficiary's statement ························· 309
　　　　　　Shipping company's certificate ················· 310
　　　　　　Certificate of analysis ························· 310
　　　　　　Certificate of weight ··························· 310
　　10. 7　**Examination of documents under documentary credits**
　　　　　　　··· 310
　　　　　　Examination of documents with reference to the documentary
　　　　　　credit ··· 311
　　　　　　Examination of documents with reference to the UCP
　　　　　　　··· 312
　　　　　　Examination of documents with reference to one another
　　　　　　　··· 312

References ··· 313

1 Introduction

1.1 International settlement vs. trade finance

Before we start, it is necessary for us to distinguish the two concepts: *international settlement* and *trade finance*①. What is the difference between the two? Actually, they reflect the two aspects of the intermediate businesses② related to international trade payments in commercial banks. The former focuses on such traditional methods as remittance, collection and letter of credit③, whereas the latter refers to the financing activities offered by banks under both traditional methods and so-called innovated financing methods. In fact, the term a bank chooses as the name of its department dealing with such banking activities implies the business focus of the department. Although most foreign banks prefer trade finance or similar expressions to name the equivalent departments, most Chinese banks have been using international settlement department, foreign department, or similar expressions to describe the equivalent departments, in which banking activities are usually divided into traditional international settlement methods and innovated trade finance methods.

In China, the term of *international settlement* is perceived as financial activities of settling the claims and debts④ among countries. Since most of the claims and debts are generated from transactions in international trade, it is natural that *international settlement* mainly deals with commercial

---

① international settlement: 国际结算; trade finance: 贸易融资
② intermediate business: 中间业务
③ remittance: 汇款; collection: 托收; letter of credit: 信用证, 可以简称为 L/C
④ claims and debts: 债权和债务

settlements and consists of international trade settlement and non-trade settlement①. International trade settlement refers to the financial activities arisen from international commercial transactions while international non-trade settlement from the financial activities generated in the course of other economic, political or cultural contacts among countries. In other words, the payments for visible trades② fall into the category of international trade settlement while the payments for services or the transfers of funds among countries belong to international non-trade settlement. Services rendered across borders are paid in such forms as insurance premium, freight, postage, cable charge, bank commission, etc③. Transfers of funds include overseas remittances, educational expenses and inheritance④.

Trade finance is related to international trade. Banks may assist or support the transactions of international trade in various forms. For instances, when an exporter requires the importer to prepay for the goods shipped, the importer faces the risk of non-delivery⑤ by the exporter. Then, the exporter's bank may provide a bank guarantee or a standby⑥ on behalf of the exporter in favor of the importer. On the contrary, when an exporter sells goods to an importer on open account(O/A)⑦, the exporter may face the risk of non-payment by the importer. The importer's bank may provide a bank guarantee or a standby on behalf of the importer in favor of the exporter. Other forms of trade finance are international factoring and forfaiting⑧. In the former, the exporter sells its accounts

---

① international trade settlement：国际贸易结算；international non-trade settlement：国际非贸易结算

② visible trade：有形贸易

③ insurance premium：保险费；freight：运费；postage：邮费；cable charge：电报费；bank commission：银行手续费

④ overseas remittances：海外汇款；educational expenses：教育费用；inheritance：遗产

⑤ non-delivery：不交货

⑥ bank guarantee：银行保函；standby：standby letter of credit，备用信用证

⑦ open account(O/A)：赊销

⑧ factoring：保理；forfaiting：福费廷

receivable① to a factor② (usually a bank in mainland China) under a factoring contract, and in the latter the exporter transfers its negotiable instruments (bills or notes)③ to a forfaiting company (usually a bank in mainland China) without recourse④. With the innovation of trade finance, banks now engage in various forms of trade finance for its clients under traditional international settlement methods, including T/T financing⑤.

1.2 The evolution of international settlement

*From cash settlement to non-cash settlement*⑥

Before the 6th century B. C., goods were exchanged between traders in different countries on a barter basis⑦. By the 5th century however emerged cash settlement, using a medium of exchange⑧, such as precious metals⑨. The coins were measured and exchanged by weight and fineness⑩ among trading countries for settling international debts. Hence precious metals in the forms of coins, bars or bullions⑪ were shipped among the trading countries, but this method was risky and expensive.

From the 13th century A. D. on, bills of exchange were created and non-cash settlement appeared and the bill of exchange market began to develop. By the end of the 18th century, banks had begun to engage in

---

① accounts receivable：应收账款
② factor：保理商
③ negotiable instruments：流通票据；bills：bills of exchange，汇票；notes：promissory notes，本票
④ without recourse：没有追索权,追索权是指票据持有人在遭到退票或拒付时所拥有的向背书人和出票人索回票款的权利
⑤ T/T financing：电汇项下的融资
⑥ cash settlement：现金结算；non-cash settlement：非现金结算
⑦ on a barter basis：在易货贸易的基础上；barter：barter trade,物物交换,易货贸易
⑧ medium of exchange：交换媒介
⑨ precious metals：贵金属
⑩ weight and fineness：重量和纯度
⑪ coins, bars and bullions：金币、金条和金块

foreign exchange transactions and international payments could be settled by transferring funds through accounts maintained with these banks. Original non-cash settlement is portrayed in Figure 1.1.

In the flowchart, we suppose that A a New York importer wants to purchase US $1 million worth of cotton from B a Tokyo exporter and C another Tokyo importer wants to buy US $1 million worth of corn from D another New York exporter. Then, the payment procedures should be:

(1) D draws a draft worth US $1 million for his exports and transfers it to A for US $1 million;

(2) A pays US $1 million to D;

(3) A transfers the draft to B as payment for his imports;

(4) Upon receipt of the draft, B presents the draft to C for payment;

(5) After verifying the draft, C makes payment to B.

This kind of settlement through transferring bills of exchange was much safer than shipping precious metals from a country to another. It is the original bills of exchange that have gradually evolved into modern ones frequently used today.

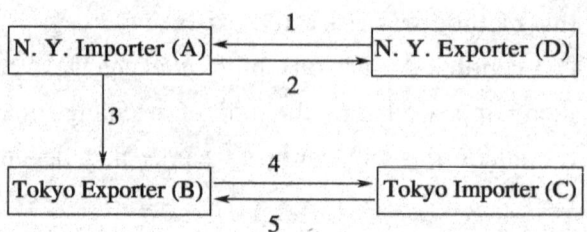

Figure 1.1 Flowchart of original non-cash settlement[①]

From direct payment to indirect payment[②]

Originally, direct payment is based on barter or cash basis, i.e., a seller makes payment directly to a buyer. It was the main method of settling debts in the earliest years of international trade. With the growth of cross border

---

① 王丽丽主编,《国际结算》,北京：中国金融出版社,1996年,第4页
② direct payment：直接支付；indirect payment：间接支付

trade and further division of labor①, carriers②, insurers and bankers all established their independent organizations at home and abroad. Particularly, with adequate funds and high credit, banks not only had maintained their establishments at home and abroad but also had built up extensive correspondent banking relationships③ with foreign banks. With their capability of understanding the conditions of trade and foreign exchange controls④ in different countries, banks naturally began to serve as intermediaries⑤ facilitating international settlement between sellers and buyers and finally developed into indispensably important financial intermediaries in international trade payments. Please find the initial intermediary role of a bank in an international transaction in Figure 1.2.

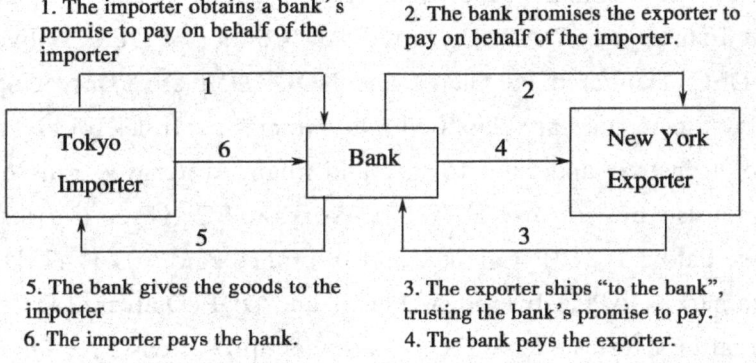

Figure 1.2 Flowchart of the intermediary role of a bank

*From simple price terms to complex price terms*⑥

Originally, international trade payments were settled on simple price terms, such as cash on delivery⑦, cash on shipment, cash with order, cash

---

① division of labor：劳动分工
② carriers：承运人
③ correspondent banking relationship：代理行关系
④ foreign exchange controls：外汇管制
⑤ intermediary：中介
⑥ price term：价格条款
⑦ cash on delivery：COD，交货付现

before shipment, etc. Nowadays however international trade payments are conducted in more complex price terms. The *Incoterms*® (International Rules for the Interpretation of Trade Terms)①, one of the publications by International Chamber of Commerce(ICC)②, is internationally recognized and used worldwide in international and domestic contracts for the sale of goods. Its latest version is *Incoterms*® 2010, which came into effect on January 1, 2011. Traders are recommended to use Incoterms 2010 after 2011, but they still can choose *Incoterms*® 2000 or any earlier versions so long as the specified version is incorporated into the contract.

There are some changes in *Incoterms*® 2010 rules. First of all, the number of rules has been reduced from 13 to 11. Two new terms—DAT (Delivered at Terminal) and DAP (Delivered at Place)—replaced the previous four terms—DAF (Delivered At Frontier), DES (Delivered Ex Ship), DEQ (Delivered Ex Quay) and DDU (Delivered Duty Unpaid).③ Secondly, the 11 rules are classified into two classes—rules for any mode or modes of transport and rules for sea and inland waterway transport. The former consists of 7 terms—EXW (Ex Works), FCA (Free Carrier), CPT (Carriage Paid To), CIP (Carriage and Insurance Paid to), DAT (Delivered At Terminal), DAP (Delivered At Place) and DDP (Delivered Duty Paid); and the latter 4 terms—FAS (Free Alongside Ship), FOB (Free On Board), CFR (Cost and Freight) and CIF (Cost Insurance and Freight).④

---

① Incoterms: International Rules for the Interpretation of Trader Terms:《国际贸易术语解释通则》

② International Chamber of Commerce ICC: 国际商会

③ DAT(Delivered At Terminal): 目的地交货; DAP(Delivered At Place): 所在地交货; DAF(Delivered At Frontier): 边境交货; DES(Delivered Ex Ship): 目的港船上交货; DEQ(Delivered Ex Quay): 目的港码头交货; DDU(Delivered Duty Unpaid): 未完税交货

④ EXW(Ex Works): 工厂交货; FCA(Free Carrier): 货交承运人; CPT(Carriage Paid To): 运费付至; CIP(Carriage and Insurance Paid to): 运费及保险付至; DDP(Delivered Duty Paid): 完税后交货; FAS(Free Alongside Ship): 船边交货; FOB(Free On Board): 船上交货; CFR(Cost and Freight): 成本加运费; CIF(Cost Insurance and Freight): 成本、保险费加运费

From paper documents to electronic documents

International settlements involve various documents, including commercial invoices, marine bills of lading, insurance policies, packing lists, certificates of inspection, certificates of origin, etc.① Among these documents, marine bills of lading are the most important ones. By issuing bills of lading, the carrier acknowledges that the specified goods have been received from the shipper and have been shipped on board and will be transported to a named place for delivery to the consignee. Originally, bills of lading were in simple contents and forms and served merely as cargo receipts and carriers in different countries had different rules or laws governing their practices. With the development of maritime transportation industry, the existence of different rules concerning bills of lading made it inconvenient to transport goods across borders. On August 25, 1924 in Brussels, Belgium, representatives from 26 countries signed on a convention—the International Convention for the Unification of Certain Rules of Law Relating to Bills of Lading, i. e., The Hague Rules②. In February 1997, the number of countries having joined the Convention was 88.

Today, a full set of original marine bills of lading simultaneously evidence cargo receipt, transport contract and title to the goods.③ Because of the feature of being the title to the goods, possessing the full set of original bills of lading means controlling the title to the goods. What's more, bills of lading are negotiable instruments in a broad sense. Owing to such features, bills of lading make it convenient and possible for banks to get involved in international trade in the process of documenting and

---

① commercial invoice：商业发票；marine bill of lading：海洋运输提单；insurance policies：保险单；packing lists：包装单，装箱单；certificate of inspection：检验证书；certificate of origin：原产地证明

② The International Convention for the Unification of Certain Rules of Law Relating to Bills of Lading：《统一提单若干法律的国际公约》,简称《海牙规则》(The Hague Rules)

③ cargo receipt：货物收据；transport contract：运输合同；title to the goods：货物的所有权

assisting and settling debts as financial intermediaries.

Electronic documents in international trade originated with the extensive usage of computers. Since the software systems were not uniform and the formats of data were not the same, it was not convenient for them to exchange or communicate their data. More work would be needed in processing and restoring the data. In order to solve the problem, a uniform data platform was required. In 1975, the Transportation Data Communication Committee[①] in the United States issued TDCC—the first professional EDI (Electronic Data Interchange)[②] standard in transportation. Following that, more industries developed their own standards, such as WINS in warehousing, VICS(US) and TRADACOMS (Europe) in retailing, DISH in maritime transportation, AIAG(US) and ODETTE(Europe) in auto industry.[③] It is EDI that has enabled the possibility of using electronic documents among the participants in international trade. Although EDI has been widely used in various industries, the mostly used areas are E-commerce and maritime transportation. Different from traditional paper bills of lading, electronic bills of lading mean that the data of the specified goods transportation will be transferred among the shippers, the carriers, the consignees, the banks and the customs.

In addition to electronic bills of lading, a new concept—electronic

---

① The Transportation Data Communication Committee：TDCC，美国的运输数据通信委员会

② EDI(Electronic Data Interchange)：电子数据交换；According to the Rules for Electronic Bills of Lading issued by Comite Maritime International(CMI) in 1990, EDI means Electronic Data Interchange, i. e. the interchange of trade data effected by teletransmission. October 22, 2011, See http：//comitemaritime. org/Rules-for-Electronic-Bills-of-Lading/0,2728,12832,00. html

③ "电子数据交换"，维基百科，October 22，2011，参见 http：//zh. wikipedia. org/wiki/电子数据交换. WINS in warehousing：仓储业的电子数据交换平台 WINS；VICS (US) and TRADACOMS(Europe) in retailing：零售业的电子数据交换平台 VICS(美国)和 TRADACOMS(欧洲)；，DISH in maritime transportation：海洋运输业的电子数据交换平台 DISH；AIAG(US) and ODETTE(Europe) in auto industry：汽车业电子数据交换平台 AIAG(美国)和 ODETTE(欧洲)

letters of credit—appears. An electronic letter of credit does not refer to a letter of credit that can be received via the Internet; instead, all the procedures of letter of credit are handled through electronic means, including opening the letter of credit, advising the letter of credit, delivering the documents, examining the documents and effecting payment.① At that time, the relatively mature electronic platform for electronic letters of credit was Bolero. net, a joint venture by the T. T. Club (Through Transport Mutual Insurance Association Ltd.) and SWIFT (Society for Worldwide Interbank Financial Telecommunication)② in 1999. Bolero stands for Bill of Lading Registry Organization③. It was the first company to be able to deliver the eUCP④ compliant solution and now has a number of corporate customers presenting documents to their banks electronically. It provides electronic communication channel and application solutions for the management of export letters of credit, import letters of credit, guarantees, documentary collections and supply chain finance.⑤ As a project of the EU⑥ to study feasibility of electronic bills of lading, Bolero. net supports all the participants in international trade, including importer, exporter, bank, insurance company, carrier, port

---

① opening the letter of credit: 开出信用证; advising the letter of credit: 通知信用证; delivering the documents: 交付单据; examining the documents: 审核单据; effecting payment: 实施付款

② Bolero. net: Bolero 是一个优化复杂的国际贸易链的云平台, 从银行到海运承运人等贸易链中的公司客户可以进入该平台管理和完成他们的融资和贸易业务; T. T. Club(Through Transport Mutual Insurance Association Ltd.): T. T. 俱乐部(联运互保俱乐部), 1968 年成立于伦敦; SWIFT: 环球银行同业金融电讯协会, 国际银行间非盈利性的合作组织, 总部设在比利时的布鲁塞尔, 成立于 1973 年

③ Bill of Lading Registry Organization: 提单注册组织

④ eUCP: UCP 是《跟单信用证统一惯例》(*Uniform Customs and Practice for Documentary Credit*) 的简称, eUCP: 《UCP 电子交单增补》(*UCP Supplement for Electronic Presentation*), 最新版本 eUCP 1.1, 跟 UCP600 配套

⑤ export letters of credit: 出口信用证; import letters of credit: 进口信用证; guarantees: 保函; documentary collections: 跟单托收; supply chain finance: 供应链融资; 参见 Solution overview, Bolero, October 22, 2011, http://www.bolero.net/en/solutions/Overview.aspx.

⑥ EU: European Union 欧盟

agency, customs and inspection institution to transmit and exchange electronic documents and data. All the participants are subscribers of the system and subject to the *BOLERO Rule Book*.① Some famous foreign banks have registered with the system. Similar systems include Tradecard, CCEWeb and CMI.②

With the development of electronic bills of lading and electronic letters of credit, people are concerned about the future of the currently widely used letters of credit. Will electronic letters of credit replace traditional ones? The answer is not certain. At present, the two are developing at parallel lines and electronic letters of credit are still faced with legal barriers when using internationally.

1.3 Electronic communication and payment systems

SWIFT

SWIFT is the abbreviation of the Society for Worldwide Interbank Financial Telecommunication. It is a cooperative society established in 1973 by European bankers under Belgium laws and owned and controlled by its shareholders. Its governance consists of a board of 25 independent directors and the executive committee.③ SWIFT is neither a payment nor a settlement system, but a "global provider of secure financial messaging services."④ It not only provides a speedy and safe communications platform for its customers but also plays a role in bringing the financial community together to shape market practice, define standards and consider solutions to issues of mutual interest. Since a large and growing number of systemically important payment systems have become dependent on

---

① subscriber: 订购者; BOLERO Rule Book:《BOLERO 规则手册》

② Tradecard: 美国纽约市电子商务公司开发的电子信用证处理系统; CCEWeb: 加拿大电子商务公司开发的电子信用证处理系统; CMI: 民间规则性质的电子商务系统

③ governance: 治理, 治理结构; board: board of directors, 董事会; executive committee: 执行委员会

④ 参见 SWIFT, October 25, 2011, http://www.swift.com

SWIFT, the central banks of the Group of Ten countries agreed that SWIFT should be subject to cooperative oversight by central banks.[①]

Each type of message is a condition of wire transfer. The messages are preset and referred to by category numbers called MT numbers. For example, MT800's deal with Traveler's Cheques, and MT300's deal with Foreign Currency Exchanges.[②] Each type of message or condition in each category is preset as well. For instance, there are 89 different messages available under the category MT500[③]. This does not include the occasional sub code[④]. Additionally, certain phrases are allowable but must be short and to the point, not exceeding a certain number of letters and acceptable under SWIFT standards. Each MT category has its own manual of standards. Depending on the size of the financial institution, each department is only familiar with the MT manual that pertains to wire transfers made by that department. A SWIFT message consists of the name and code of the originating bank[⑤], the date and time, the address and code of the receiving bank, the name and internal code of the officer initiating the transmission[⑥], the names and account numbers of the accounts involved in the transfer, a description of the asset being transferred, the MT category of the transmission and acceptable, standardized phrases as described above.

Originally, about 250 member banks in West Europe and North America joined it, but its membership has been growing. The Bank of China has been a member of SWIFT since 1983. By 1990s, other Chinese banks, such as the Bank of Communications, the Industrial and

---

① central banks：中央银行；Group of Ten：十国集团；参见 *Annual Review* 2010. SWIFT. October 25, 2011, http://www.swift.com/about_swift/publications/annual_reports/annual_review_2010/SWIFT_AR2010.pdf

② MT800's deal with Traveler's Cheques：MT800 用于旅行支票销售及清算；MT300's deal with Foreign Currency Exchanges：MT300 用于外汇兑换确认

③ MT500：登记指标，用于证券市场

④ occasional sub code：临时子码

⑤ originating bank：发送 SWIFT 信息的银行

⑥ internal code of the officer initiating the transmission：发起信息传递的职员的内部代码

Commercial Bank of China, the Agricultural Bank of China and so on were all SWIFT members. At present, its members include more than 9,700 banking organizations, securities institutions and corporate customers from 209 countries.

SWIFT is a highly sophisticated message switching or communication system and goes into operation 24 hours per day, seven days a week, delivering a very high level of online performance to its members. As a cooperative automatic world communication system, SWIFT's aim is to enable its member banks to transmit among themselves inter-payments, statements and other messages, facilitate and accelerate their operations.

BOLERO

Bolero stands for the Bill of Lading Registry Organization. Bolero was founded jointly by T. T. Club and SWIFT to be a "neutral, trusted third party" with the aim to "develop an open and legally certain platform to deliver paperless trading between buyers, sellers, financial institutions and logistics service providers[①] anywhere in the world." It is an "electronic communication channel" that enables "trade finance collaboration for corporates, commodity traders and banks globally." Bolero provides electronic communication channel and application solutions for the management of export letters of credit, import letters of credit, guarantees, documentary collections and supply chain finance. The core technology lies in its unique infrastructure—Bolero Open4Trade[②], which is designed specifically to enable the secure, guaranteed exchange of trade information and contractually binding trade documents. Although SWIFT is a co-owner of Bolero, Bolero is independent of SWIFT service. The Core Messaging Platform of Bolero was specifically for electronic collaboration of trade documents.

Initially, Bolero aimed at the large corporations and their banks as

---

① logistics service providers：物流服务提供者；logistics：物流

② infrastructure：基础设施；Open4Trade：Bolero 的核心信息平台（Core Messaging Platform） their customers, but now corporations of different sizes are using the services of Bolero. Its customers consist of corporate customers, commodity partners, banks and financial institutions. Corporate customers now are primarily in engineering, construction, technology and other project-based manufacturing industries where L/Cs and/or Guarantees are in general use, such as ABB, Heymans, IHC Merwede, Konecranes, ThyssenKrupp, Outotec, Nokia Siemens Networks, Siemens, Stora Enso, Nokia, Wartsila and MAN. Its commodity partners include large-, smaller- and medium-sized traders in the industries of energy, metals, chemicals and agriculture. Representative commodity trader customers include: Glencore, Noble Group, Louis Dreyfus, Kolmar, Nidera and Metinvest. Bolero has a large number of bank customers across all major global regions, including HSBC in Hong Kong, Standard Chartered in Singapore, Commonwealth Bank in Australia and New Zealand, QNB in Qatar, RBS and Lloyds TSB in UK, Rabobank, ING, ABN-AMRO, National Borg and FORTIS in the Netherlands, Deutsche Bank and West LB in Germany, KBC in Belgium, Zurcher Kantonalbank, Credit Suisse and UBS in Switzerland, Unicredit Bank in Italy, Santander in Spain, DnB NOR in Norway, SEB and Handelsbanken in Sweden, Pohjola and Nordea in Finland and Bank of America in US.[1]

CHIPS

CHIPS stands for Clearing House Inter-bank Payment System[2], which was established by The Clearing House[3] in New York in 1970. The concept for CHIPS dates back to 1966 when The Bank Conference of the New York Clearing House Association(Predecessor to The Clearing House)[4] identified

---

[1] 参见 Bolero, October 23, 11, http://www.bolero.net/en/company/overview.aspx

[2] CHIPS: 交换银行相互收付系统

[3] The Clearing House was established in 1853 and owned by 20 of the largest banks in the United States. Now it is the leading private sector provider of payments settlement and clearing services to financial institutions worldwide.

[4] The Bank Conference of the New York Clearing House Association: 纽约清算所协会银行大会; predecessor: 前身

the need to provide a quicker and more efficient alternative to official cheques used for interbank payments. As part of a feasibility study on automating such payments, a computer system test was performed to determine whether electronic signals could act as a proxy for the paper transfer of funds between banks. This successful experiment became the Clearing House Interbank Payments System.① Today, the system has grown to be one of the largest private payment systems in the world and currently over 95% of cross-border US dollar payments and half of all the domestic US dollar payments are made via CHIPS.

On April 6, 1970 when CHIPS was first put online, the number of participants was 9 and total dollar amount settled was USD547,615,444. The largest number of participants in CHIPS was in the year of 1986, that is, 140 participants, with total dollar amount of USD106,583,481,092. Until September 2011, the number of participants was 50 while the total dollar amount reached to 306,627,548,062.② The 50 participants are banks from all over the world, including two banks from China—the Bank of China and the Bank of Communications. It now has a network of 50 leading financial institutions from 22 countries and is responsible for 95% of all international US dollar clearings.

CHAPS & Faster Payment

CHAPS stands for Clearing House Automated Payment System③. CHAPS Sterling and Faster Payments④ are the two important electronic payment systems of CHAPS Company. CHAPS Sterling is an electronic bank-to-bank same-day value payment made within the UK in sterling as well as one of

---

① 参见 CHIPS Celebrates 40th Anniversary Milestone. Press Release, New York, April 6, 2010. October 28, 11 from http://www.chips.org/press_releases/pressReleaseDocs/070431.pdf

② 参见 CHIPS Annual Statistics From 1970 to 2011. October 28, 11 from http://www.chips.org/docs/000652.pdf

③ CHAPS:交换银行自动收付系统

④ CHAPS Sterling and Faster Payments:CHAPS 英镑和快速支付

the largest real-time gross settlement(RTGS) systems① in the world. It has 15 member banks and around 400 financial institutions utilizing agency arrangements② through direct members for their Sterling RTGS payment requirements. In 2007, the Sterling amount processed through CHAPS was about 7 trillion.

The Faster Payments is the first new payments service introduced in the UK for more than 20 years. Thirteen banks and building societies were founding members of the new service and other financial institutions are able to join the system or have access to the system through agency arrangement with a member.

Fedwire® Funds Service, Fedwire Securities Service and National Settlement Services

The Federal Reserve Banks③ operate three wholesale payment services: Fedwire® Funds Service, Fedwire Securities Service and National Settlement Service. ④

Fedwire Funds Service is a real-time gross settlement system to settle funds electronically between banks. It links the Federal Reserve Board of Governors, the 12 Federal Reserve Banks and the 25 branches, the U.S. Treasury Department and other federal agencies. In 2008, about 7,300 participants made Fedwire funds transfers. ⑤Depository institutions utilize it to send funds to other institutions for their own business purposes or on behalf of their customers. It is mainly used for the purchase and sale of federal funds, the purchase, sale and financing of securities transaction, the disbursement or repayment of loans, the settlement of cross-border U.S. dollar commercial transactions and the settlement of real estate

---

① real-time gross settlement(RTGS) systems: 实时总结算系统
② agency arrangements: 代理协议
③ Federal Reserve Banks: 美国联邦储备银行
④ Fedwire® Funds Service: 美联储资金转账系统; Fedwire Securities Service: 美联储证券转账系统; National Settlement Service: 全国结算系统;参见 Fedwire and National Settlement Services. October 28, 2011, http://www.newyorkfed.org/aboutthefed/fedpoint/fed43.html
⑤ http://www.federalreserve.gov/paymentsystems/fedfunds_about.htm

transactions and other high-value, time-critical payments. The Treasury and other federal agencies use it extensively to disburse and receive funds.

The Fedwire Securities Service provides issuance, settlement and transfer services for U.S. Treasury securities and other government-related securities. The Federal Reserve Banks in their capacity as fiscal agents facilitate the issuance of book-entry securities to participants in the Federal Securities Service. Participants may maintain multiple Fedwire securities to settle secondary market trades—including open market operations—to move collateral used to secure obligations and to facilitate repurchase agreement (repo) transactions. The Fedwire Securities Service processes securities transfers on an individual, or gross, basis in real time and the transfer of the securities and the related funds (if any) is final and irrevocable when made. Access to the Fedwire Securities Service is limited to depository institutions and a few other entities, such as the Treasury, government-sponsored enterprises, state treasurers and limited-purpose trust companies that are members of the Federal Reserve System. Nonbank brokers and dealers typically hold and transfer their Fedwire securities through depository institutions that are Fedwire participants and that provide specialized government securities clearing services.

The National Settlement Service is a multilateral settlement service used by clearing houses, financial exchanges and other clearing and settlement groups. It is available to depository institutions[①] that settle for participants in clearing houses, financial exchanges and other clearing and settlement groups. Settlement agents, acting on behalf of those depository institutions in a settlement arrangement, electronically submit settlement files to the Federal Reserve Banks. Files are processed on receipts and entries are automatically posted to the depository institutions' Federal Reserve accounts. It provides an automated mechanism for submitting settlement files to the Federal Reserve Banks, improves operational efficiency and reduces settlement risk to participants by granting settlement finality on settlement day. It also enables Federal Reserve Banks to manage

---

① depository institutions：存款机构

and limit risk by incorporating risk controls that are as robust as those used in the Fedwire Funds Service.

TARGET and TARGET 2

TARGET stands for Trans-European Automated Real-time Gross Settlement Express Transfer system and was the real-time gross settlement system of the euro before TARGET2.① The TARGET system was the first-generation RTGS system for the euro, commenced operations on January 4, 1999 following the launch of the euro. It was built by linking the different RTGS structures at the national level. On November 2007 when TARGET2 system was launched, TARGET consisted of 17 national RTGS which were interlinked to provide a technical framework for the processing of payments across national borders in the European Union (EU). TARGET2 replaced TARGET system completely in May 2008.

Although TARGET had successfully operated over a number of years, it had proved to have some shortcomings or challenges. The decentralized structure of TARGET multiplied the local technical components and thus increased the maintenance and running cost. With the enlargement of the EU, new member states were expected to connect to the system, thereby increasing the number of TARGET components. This led to the redesign of the system.

The migration from TARGET to TARGET2 included three steps. The first step is when TARGET2 started operations on November 19, 2007, the first group of countries—Austria, Cyprus, Germany, Latvia, Lithuania, Luxembourg, Malta and Slovenia—migrated to the Single Shared Platform (SSP). The second step was on February 18, 2008 when the second group—Belgium, Finland, France, Ireland, the Netherlands, Portugal and Spain—migrated to TARGET2. The last step was on May 19, 2008, the final

---

① TARGET: the Trans-European Automated Real-time Gross Settlement Express Transfer system, 第一代跨欧洲自动实时总结算支付系统

② TARGET 2: 第二代跨欧洲自动实时总结算支付系统

③ About its forerunner TARGET1. European Central Bank, Eurosystem. October 30, 2011 from http://www.ecb.int/paym/t2/target/html/index.en.html

group—Denmark, Estonia, Greece, Italy, Poland and the European Central Bank migrated to TARGET2. The new system has a single technical platform—the SSP. Three Eurosystem central banks—the Banca d'Italia, the Banque de France and the Deutsche Bundesbank—jointly provide the SSP for TARGET2 and operate it on behalf of the Eurosystem.③

CNAPS

CNAPS stands for China National Automatic Payment System①, which was designed and operated by the People's Bank of China (PBOC). China's modern payment systems consist of CNAPS (the core), the intra-systems of commercial banks (the basis) and local intra-city commercial paper exchanges. CNAPS has two layers of processing centers: National Processing Center (NPC) and Capital City Processing Center (CCPC).② NPC is linked with CCPC with a special network. Policy banks and commercial banks are the major participants in the payment system. Policy banks and commercial banks may use intra-systems to link to CNAPS through CCPC locally or through its head office linking to local CCPC. To make it convenient for small- and medium-sized financial institutions to settle debts, rural cooperatives are allowed to set up their own remittance system to link to CCPC locally or through their head office linking to local CCPC. City commercial banks may develop their own bank draft clearing system and transfer funds based on the CNAPS.③

Currently, CNAPS has over 1,600 direct participants and over 90,000 branches and sub-branches of banks are linked with it. CNAPS is also linked with China Foreign Exchange Trading System, China Bond Comprehensive Business System, China Uni-pay Information Processing System, City Commercial Bank Draft Processing System, RMB clearing

---

① China National Automatic Payment System: 中国现代化支付系统

② National Processing Center(NPC) and Capital City Processing Center(CCPC): 国家处理中心和省会城市处理中心

③ 中国现代化支付系统,百度百科, October 30, 2011 from http://baike.baidu.com/view/1035980.html? fromTaglist

banks in Hong Kong and Macau.① The payment of funds may be transferred from one account to another within a minute, realizing the real-time settlement among banks in China. In 2010, CNAPS was improved and now the PBOC is developing the second-generation payment system with the large-amount payment system, the small-amount payment system and the online interbank clearing system as the main application systems.②

1.4 Players, roles and risks in international trade payments

There are three basic players in international trade—exporter, importer and financial intermediary. Obviously, each player has its own motivations and needs different from each other. As a player, say, a financial intermediary, it is important to understand the differences in the desires of the exporter and importer and seek appropriate solutions to allow the highest possible mutual satisfaction among all the players.

Exporter

What an exporter concerns most is to receive payment as soon as possible. Undoubtedly, its aim is to maximize cash flows by prompt payment of the buyer for the goods supplied and minimize non-payment risks of the buyer by carefully choosing more protective or safer payment methods. However, competitive pressures force the exporter to trade off between risks and benefits. So, it is not uncommon for large and well-financed firms to use more liberal trade terms, even open account term, as competitive advantages.

In selecting a payment technique, an exporter need consider four aspects:

---

① China Foreign Exchange Trading System: 中国外汇交易系统; China Bond Comprehensive Business System: 中国债券综合业务系统; China Uni-pay Information Processing System: 中国银联信息处理系统; City Commercial Bank Draft Processing System: 城市商业银行银行汇票处理系统; RMB clearing banks in Hong Kong and Macau: 香港和澳门的人民币清算银行

② 中国现代化支付系统的发展,中国人民银行,November 2, 2011 from http://www.pbc.gov.cn/publish/zhifujiesuansi/903/2010/20100910134943002421899/20100910134943002421899_.html

protection, convenience, cost and commercial competitiveness.① Protection refers to the safety of a payment technique, i.e., the payment technique can protect the exporter against the risk of non-payment by the importer. Meanwhile, the exporter need consider the technique's convenience and availability at a reasonable cost. Additionally, the exporter has to compare the technique it offers to those offered by its rivals to ensure the competitiveness of his technique. In a seller's market, an exporter can dictate payment terms, but in a buyer's market, an exporter may have to concede to less protected payment terms in order to sell its products. Thus, in selecting a payment technique, an exporter is faced with trade-offs among these four criteria. Typically, a payment technique that offers a high degree of protection against non-payment will be more costly and more cumbersome than alternative techniques that offer less protection.

To illustrate in detail, the exporter has to take the following risks into consideration in selecting a payment technique: (1) commercial risks: the deterioration in the importer's operations and sales will result in insufficient cash flow to pay the exporter; (2) financial risks: the inability of the importer to obtain the necessary financing to complete the asset conversion cycle; (3) political or country risks: the risks of occurrence of events, say, societal upheavals, will disrupt the importers' ability to generate cash flow; (4) risks in control of title to the goods: the ability of the exporter to retain control over the title to the goods until the importer pays; (5) transfer risks: the buyer cannot convert its soft currency into a hard currency or has no access to hard currency due to exchange control or exchange shortage in the importer's country to repay the exporter.②

Importer

What an importer concerns most is to receive the goods as ordered and pay

---

① protection: 安全性; convenience: 方便性; cost: 成本; commercial competitiveness: 商业竞争力

② commercial risk: 商业风险; financial risk: 财务风险; political or country risk: 政治或国家风险; risk in control of the title to the goods: 控制货权的风险; transfer risk: 支付风险

for the goods as late as possible. Its aim is to seek guarantee that the goods purchased will meet the specified level of quality and quantity in the original order. Like the exporter, the importer will try to obtain the most favorable payment method to maximize its own cash flows. Yet, its size and importance to the exporter will be an element for the exporter to consider in accepting a proposed payment method.

From the viewpoint of importer in selecting a payment technique, the major risk for it to consider in selecting a payment technique is that the goods that are shipped will not meet the terms and conditions of the original sales contract or order.

Banks

As a financila intermediary in international trade, the bank's role is to assist the exporter and the importer in documenting, implementing and financing. Banks provide various payment and financing methods for its clients. From the perspective of the exporter, banks can provide traditional settlement methods, such as remittance, collection, letters of credit and various trade financing methods including financing under traditional settlement methods.

The bank's motivation is to maximize its revenues through providing its payment or financing products and services. However, it must weigh its revenue objectives against operational risks inherent in most payment or financing products as well as credit risks of its clients.[1]

1.5 Types of payment techniques

The main payment techniques in international trade consist of consignment, open account, documentary collections, letters of credit, standby letters of credit, guarantees and payment in advance.[2] With the development of international trade and further involvement of banks in trade finance, factoring and forfeiting have become increasingly important so that banks

---

[1] operational risk: 操作性风险; credit risk: 信用风险
[2] consignment: 寄售; payment in advance: 预付货款

today dare not take the chance not to attach importance to them.

Consignment

Under consignment, an exporter (consignor) enters into a consignment agreement with a foreign distributor①, by which the exporter ships the goods to the foreign distributor that will sell the goods for the exporter on a best effort basis. After the goods have been sold, the foreign distributor will deduct its commission and fees out of the proceeds of sale and remits the rest to the exporter.

Under the consignment agreement, the foreign distributor is the trustee of the goods and the exporter is the real owner. Therefore, the exporter will have to be responsible for the freight, insurance, warehouse, import duties, etc. and undertake all the risks and losses incurred to the goods. Thus, before selecting such a payment method, the exporter should carefully investigate the market conditions in the importing country, select creditworthy distributors and even require a bank guarantee when possible to protect against the risks.

Open account

Under an open account payment agreement, the importer agrees to pay the exporter at an agreed time and in an agreed manner. Usually, there are no strict contracts or documentation required between the two parties. Thus, before such an agreement is entered into, there must be a long, successful and profitable relationship between the importer and the exporter. In addition, the exporter should thoroughly check the buyer's creditworthiness to ensure the buyer to have a good to excellent credit rating.

Open account terms usually fix a due date by stating the number of days from a specific date such as the invoice or shipping date. Yet, it is common for the buyer to wait until the goods arrive before paying, regardless of the due date. It is important for the exporter to ensure the prompt arrival of the goods. Since open account terms tie up the exporter's capital and

---

① distributor：分销商

involve risks, the exporter had better seek foreign credit insurance or bank guarantees for protection.

Documentary collections

Under documentary collections, prior to the receipt of the goods, the importer is required to either pay for the goods or accept a draft, which evidences indebtedness. A bank is involved in the handling of the documents between the two parties.

Letters of credit

A letter of credit is a document issued by a bank at the request of the importer and in favor of the exporter. It represents the issuing bank's promise to pay a specified amount of money upon the receipt of certain documents within a specified period of time, provided the documents have fulfilled the terms and conditions of the credit.

Since the issuing bank is normally a foreign bank, it is advisable that the exporter should request the importer to confirm the letter of credit. If the issuing bank arranges for its correspondent bank in the exporter's country to confirm the letter of credit, this means that the letter of credit bears double guarantee by both the issuing bank and the confirming bank.

A letter of credit is based on the bank credit, hence a safer payment technique for the exporter than a documentary collection.

Guarantees/standby letters of credit

A guarantee is an irrevocable undertaking by which the issuing bank holds itself financially liable for the consequences of non-performance of the obligations by the applicant to the beneficiary. A standby letter of credit is similar to a guarantee and mostly used in cases where the buyer requests a trade transaction on an open account basis. In the United States, banks use standby letters of credit in more cases, while banks outside the United States will issue a bank guarantee.

Payment in advance

Payment in advance is certainly the most favorable way of getting paid from the exporter's viewpoint, for there is no risk at all. What's more, the exporter has immediate or advance use of the money. However, it is risky to the importer. This is why most starting exporters will unlikely obtain the term of payment in advance. Only in very rare cases where the buyer desperately needs the products that the exporter is selling and no alternative sources of supply exist, will perhaps the buyer be prepared to make payment in advance.

In above-mentioned payment techniques, the greatest areas of bank involvement are documentary collections, letters of credit, guarantees and standby letters of credit. The bank's role in consignment, O/A and payment in advance is limited to clearing. The roles of the three players in international trade settlement are portrayed in Table 1.1.

Table 1.1 The roles of players in international trade settlement

Payment technique	Exporter	Importer	Banks		
			Money transfer	Document handling	Payment guarantee
Remittance (cash in advance or open account)	Sending the invoice to the buyers after delivery	Arranging for payment according to the invoice	x		
Documentary collection	After delivery, having the agreed documents sent to the buyer's bank	Pay/accept at the bank against the documents presented.	x	x	
Letter of credit	After delivery, presenting complying documents to the issuing bank	To have the letter of credit issued according to contract	x	x	x
Guarantee/ standby letter of credit	After delivery, claiming compensation in the case of default by the importer	To have the guarantee or standby letter of credit issued according to the contract	x	x	x

Source: Anders Grath. (2008). *The Handbook of International Trade and Finance*. London and Philadelphia: Kogan Page, p. 31.

As discussed, risk and cost are the two driving factors for the exporter to trade off in choosing payment techniques. Open account arrangement is the least costly but offers virtually no credit protection for the exporter. On the contrary, cash in advance or bank guarantee well protects the exporter against credit risks but is costly and relatively inflexible in implementation.

Figure 1.3 and Table 1.2 illustrate the relative risks of different payment techniques discussed above.

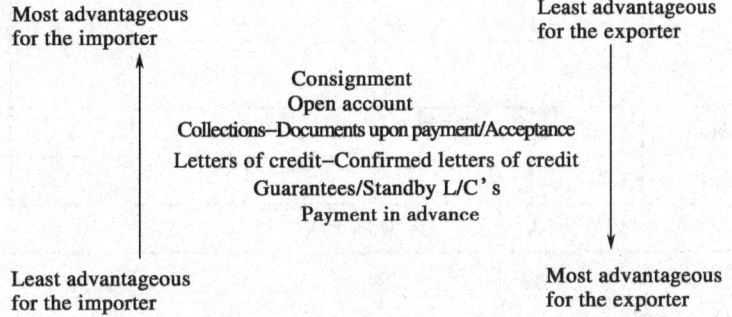

Figure 1.3 Comparison of traditional payment techniques[①]

Table 1.2 Risk matrix of payment techniques[②]

Type of risk	Credit risk	USD billing exchange risk	Foreign currency billing exchange risk	Transfer risk	Political risk
Risk scale *	1—7	1—2	1—5+	1—2	1—3
Cash with order/cash in advance/credit card	1	1	1	1	1
Confirmed irrevocable letter of credit	2	1	1	1	1
Irrevocable letter of credit unconfirmed	3	2	2	2	2

---

① John Bergamin. *Payment Techniques in Trade Finance*, ING Barings. April/May 1999. p. 16

② John S. Gordon. *Export/Import Letters of Credit and Payment Methods: Making Payments in International Trade*, Second Edition. Global Training Center, Inc. 2002. p. 1-32

Continued

Type of risk	Credit risk	USD billing exchange risk	Foreign currency billing exchange risk	Transfer risk	Political risk
Revocable letter of credit	4	2	3	2	3
Sight draft documentary collection	4	2	3	2	3
Time draft documentary collection	5	2	4	2	3
Open account	6	2	4+	2	3
Consignment	7	2	5+	2	3
* Risk scale: 1 = least risk, 7 = most risk					

Factoring

Factoring has now become a widely accepted payment technique in trade finance. By entering into a factoring contract, the exporter sells its accounts receivables to a factor on a non-recourse basis. Before purchasing any accounts receivables from the exporter, however, the factor need investigate the buyers' creditworthiness. Only when the amount of the receivables is within the approved limit will the factor buy it and assume the credit risk of buyers. Details will be discussed in Chapter 8.

Forfaiting

Forfaiting refers to the discounting of bills or notes by a forfaiter without recourse to the exporter. As a highly flexible payment technique, forfaiting allows the exporter to grant attractive credit terms to its foreign buyers, without tying up cash flow or assuming the risks of possible late payment or default. At the same time, the exporter is fully protected against interest rate, commercial and political risks. Details will be found in Chapter 9.

1.6 Related laws, customs and practice

Many laws and rules have been formed and play active roles in standardizing settlement transactions. Customs and practice are not laws but still complied by and referred to as the basis of conducting settlement transactions by international banks. Therefore, it is important to understand the related international customs and practice relating to international trade settlements.

Laws on negotiable instruments

There are two major negotiable instrument laws: the Convention Providing a Uniform Law for Bills of Exchange and Promissory Notes(Geneva, 1930) and the UK Bills of Exchange Act of 1882[①]. Since the United States plays such an important role in the world that its law on negotiable instruments should be attached importance. The Article 3 of the US Uniform Commercial Code of 1962[②] is about negotiable instruments.

International customs and practice for collections, documentary letters of credit, standby letters of credit, guarantees and international factoring

For collection, documentary letter of credit, standby letter of credit, guarantee and factoring, applicable international customs and practice are

---

　　① Convention Providing a Uniform Law for Bills of Exchange and Promissory Notes (Geneva, 1930):《关于统一汇票和本票法律的公约》(日内瓦,1930 年); the UK Bills of Exchange Act of 1882:《英国 1882 汇票法案》

　　② US Uniform Commercial Code of 1962:美国 1962 年修订的《统一商法典》

as follows respectively:①

(1) Uniform Rules for Collection(URC), ICC Publication No. 522

(2) Uniform Customs and Practice for Documentary Credit(UCP), ICC Publication No. 600;

(3) eUCP(v. 1.1)—UCP Supplement for Electronic Presentation(v. 1.1);

(4) In ternational Standard Banking Practice (ISBP) for the Examination of Documents under Documentary Credits 2007 Revision for UCP 600, ICC Publication No. 681;

(5) International Standby Practice 98 (ISP 98), ICC Publication No. 590;

(6) Uniform Rules for Demand Guarantees(URDG), ICC Publication No. 758;

(7) Uniform Rules for Contract Guarantees(URCG), ICC Publication No. 325; and

(8) FCI General Rules for International Factoring, 2010 Revision.

International conventions on bills of lading

The Hague Rules was the first international convention for the Unification of Certain Rules of Law Relating to Bills of Lading, which was concluded on August 25, 1924 by the countries including Germany, Argentina, Belgium, Chile, Cuba, Denmark and Iceland, Spain, Estonia, the United

---

① Uniform Rules for Collection(URC), ICC Publication No. 522:《托收统一规则》, 国际商会第 522 号出版物; Uniform Customs and Practice for Documentary Credit(UCP), ICC Publication No. 600:《跟单信用证统一惯例》, 国际商会第 600 号出版物; eUCP(v. 1.1)—UCP Supplement for Electronic Presentation(v. 1.1):《UCP 电子交单增补》, 1.1 版本; International Standard Banking Practice(ISBP) for the Examination of Documents under Documentary Credits 2007 Revision for UCP 600, ICC Publication No. 681:《跟单信用证项下审核单据的国际标准银行实务》, 2007 年为 UCP600 修订, 国际商会第 681 号出版物; International Standby Practice 98(ISP 98), ICC Publication No. 590:《国际备用信用证实务》, 简称 ISP98, 国际商会第 590 号出版物; Uniform Rules for Demand Guarantees(URDG), ICC Publication No. 758:《见索即付保函统一规则》, 国际商会第 758 号出版物; Uniform Rules for Contract Guarantees(URCG), ICC Publication No. 325:《合约保函统一规则》, 国际商务第 325 号出版物; FCI General Rules for International Factoring, 2010 Revision: 国际保理联合会的《国际保理通则》, 2010 年修订

States of America, Finland, France, the United Kingdom, Ireland, the British Dominions beyond the seas, India, Hungary, Italy, Japan, Latvia, Mexico, Norway, Netherlands, Peru, Poland, Portugal Romania, Serbia, Croatia and Slovenia, Sweden and Uruguay.①

In 1968, the Hague Rules were amended by the Brussels Amendments—The Protocol to Amend the International Convention for the Unification of Certain Rules of Law relating to Bills of Lading②. After the amendments, the Rules became the Hague-Visby Rules③. It is noted that not all the member countries of the Hague Rules have accepted the amendments.

Under the Hague-Visby Rules, a carrier has far greater bargaining power than the shipper, thus most developing countries thought they are not on the same level playing field. On March 31, 1978, the United Nations Conference on the Carriage of Goods by Sea adopted a new set of rules governing the international marine shipment—the United Nations International Convention on the Carriage of Goods by Sea.④ The Convention was an attempt to form a uniform legal base for the transportation of goods on oceangoing ships. Since the Conference was held in Hamburg, Germany, the Convention was called the Hamburg Rules. The United Nations kept the Convention open for signature by all states until April 30, 1979.⑤ The Convention finally came into force on November 1, 1992 and has been ratified by 34 countries.⑥

---

① http://www.admiraltylawguide.com/conven/haguerules1924.html

② Brussels Amendments—The Protocol to Amend the International Convention for the Unification of Certain Rules of Law Relating to Bills of Lading:《布鲁塞尔议定书》,即《关于修订统一提单若干法律规定的国际公约的议定书》

③ the Hague-Visby Rules:《海牙-维斯比规则》

④ the United Nations Conference on the Carriage of Goods by Sea: 联合国海洋货物运输大会; the United Nations International Convention on the Carriage of Goods by Sea:《联合国关于海洋运输货物的国际公约》,即 Hamburg Rules,《汉堡规则》; http://en.wikipedia.org/wiki/Hague-Visby_Rules

⑤ http://treaties.un.org/pages/ViewDetails.aspx?src=TREATY&mtdsg_no=XI-D-3&chapter=11&lang=en

⑥ http://en.wikipedia.org/wiki/Hamburg_Rules

1.7 Correspondent bank

When the demographic and economic characteristics do not make it profitable for a domestic bank to open a foreign branch, a correspondent bank will enable it to offer banking services in a foreign country. A correspondent bank is a financial institution that acts as an agent for another bank, providing services and products in an area which the other bank does not operate in.

Correspondent bank agreement

A correspondent bank agreement takes place when one bank performs a transaction on behalf of another bank. It is used for various types of financial transaction, such as payments or electronic transfers, foreign currency exchanges, investments and loans. To establish a correspondent banking relationship, two banks concerned conclude a correspondent banking agreement, exchange their control documents, and fix the schedule of terms and conditions[①].

Before concluding an agreement, the two banks concerned investigate each other's creditworthiness and relevant financial policies in the respective countries. Only when the two banks accept each other's credit rating, operation style and financial status, will they sign a correspondent banking agreement and exchange control documents.

Control documents

Control documents are authorized signatures, telegraphic test keys, the schedule of terms and conditions and SWIFT authentic keys. Authorized signatures are used to authenticate messages, letters, remittance, letters of credit, etc. addressed by a bank to its correspondent bank. A bank's signatures book contains facsimiles of signatures of authorized officers. For

---

① control documents：控制文件；authorize signature：印鉴,有权签字的人的签字字样；telegraphic test keys：电报密押；schedule of terms and conditions：费率表

instance, without an authorized signature, a bank draft will not be paid by the drawee bank.

Telegraphic test keys are code arrangements that enable the banks to receive cables from other banks to verify the genuineness of the cables or telexes. The codes are strictly confidential. Although there is no standard form for test keys, a test key generally consists of a series of tabulated numbers, perhaps one for the day of the month, another for the day of the week, another for the month of the year, another for the amount and another for the currency. The indicated numbers are totaled and the total number precedes the text of the message. The receiving bank verifies the number to confirm if the cable or telex is received from the particular bank.

Schedule of terms and conditions is a list of service fees that a bank should charge its overseas correspondent bank when providing correspondent services, such as the commission for advising a letter of credit, handling a collection item, etc.

SWIFT authentic key[①] is used between SWIFT member banks for authenticating all messages to be transmitted through SWIFT.

---

① SWIFT authentic key: SWIFT 验证押

Specimen of a schedule of terms and conditions

Correspondent Bank Terms and Conditions[①]

Effective: January 1, 2014

General Terms and Conditions for Correspondent Bank Accounts and Services

Notes and Interpretation

All services offered remain subject to…Bank's ability to provide such services based on legal, regulatory and internal policy requirements and standards.

All rates shown in this schedule are subject to change without prior notice unless otherwise agreed by…Bank.

Unless otherwise instructed, payments expressed in a foreign currency are payable at…Bank's buying rate for demand drafts on the country of the currency on the date the payment is processed.

Additional charges may apply in certain circumstances to cover any out-of-pocket expenses or for additional actions required to carry out any services. Where additional charges other than out-of-pocket expenses are to be charged,…Bank will provide you with notice of those charges and they will become effective immediately unless otherwise required by law or regulation.

Account Services

Accounts are available in Canadian and United States dollars.

Account maintenance	Subject to arrangement
Statements	Subject to arrangement
Drafts drawn on your account	Subject to arrangement
Servicing of cheques/drafts with no MT110 instructions on file (The issuance of SWIFT MT110s is required for ALL cheques/drafts drawn on your account)	$ 30

---

① CIBC. Correspondent Bank Terms and Conditions. Retrieved August 21, 2014 from https://www.cibc.com/ca/pdf/correspondent-banking/terms-and-conditions.pdf; CIBC: Canadian Imperial Bank of Commerce (加拿大帝国商业银行), 参见 https://www.cibc.com

Stop Payments on your drafts/cheques:

Via MT111	$ 15
Via Sundry SWIFT	$ 30

Miscellaneous:

Account Balance reporting with prior arrangement	$ 15
Credit Information	$ 50 per report
Audit Confirmation	$ 25 per report

Investigations:

Under 3 months	Free
3—6 months	$ 50
Over 6 months	$ 75

Payment Processing

All payment processing is centralized with ··· Bank Payment & Treasury Operations group in Toronto. SWIFT is our preferred method of receipt of payment instructions. Payment instructions should be sent to:

···Bank, Toronto
SWIFT···

Payments to Financial Institutions in Canada should contain the branch address and transit number where the beneficiary maintains their account. To allow a SWIFT MT103 Customer Transfer to be processed straight through, the Canadian Sort Code should be included in Field 57D. This 9-digit Canadian Sort Code is a unique code that identifies the correct financial institution and branch of account. The identifier code '//CC' must precede the Financial Institution Number and the Branch Transit Number where the beneficiary has an account.

//CC-Auto Routing Code
4 Digits-Financial Institution Number
5 Digits-Branch Transit Number
E. g. //CC00100XXXX-···Bank Main Branch

···Bank may, at its discretion, convert any payments to Financial Institutions in Canada into Canadian or United States dollars.

To guarantee same day value for payments to points in Canada, ... Bank must receive your instructions prior to the following times (unless otherwise agreed by ... Bank in writing):

All Customer Payments	16:30 hrs. ET
All Financial Institution Transfers	16:30 hrs. ET
All Financial Institution Transfers on our books	18:00 hrs. ET
All Foreign Currency payments (except U.S. dollars)	15:00 hrs. ET (value day − 1)
Cancellations/Amendments for Same Day Value Payments	Best-efforts basis
Cancellations/Amendments for Future Value Payments	17:00 hrs. ET (value day − 1)

Instructions received after these times will be executed on a best-efforts basis. Fully qualified payments can be processed on a straight-through basis until the close of Canada's Large Value Transfer System at 18:00 hrs. ET.

Customer Payments (charges "BEN") Payments of less than $50 charges are waived	$15 (deducted from proceeds)
Customer Payments (charges "OUR")	Subject to arrangement
Customer Payments (charges "OUR" with 71G)	As per arrangements (Min. $15)
Financial Institution Transfers for credit to an account with our Bank	Subject to arrangement
Financial Institution Transfers for credit to an account with another	Bank Subject to arrangement

Note: For United States dollar payments, charges are deducted in USD. Charges for Foreign Currency wire payments are deducted using the Canadian dollar equivalent.

Payments Outside Canada (any currency)	$20
Bulk Payment Service	Subject to arrangement
Amendment or cancellation instructions	$25
Inquiries due to incorrect tests	$25
Inquiries due to insufficient/incorrect details to effect payment	$25

Deposits—Cash Letters

Deposits may be sent to ... Bank for all cheques drawn on Canada in CAD or USD, for immediate credit to your ... Bank account, subject to final payment. Other currencies will be handled on a collection basis, unless prior arrangements have been made.

Deposits for immediate credit to your account on our books without advice of ultimate payment and with full recourse in the event of dishonour for any reason	Subject to certain conditions and prior arrangements
Encoded Cash Letter deposit slips	Free
Cheques in any currency returned unpaid	$ 10 per cheque
SWIFT MT456 (Advice of Return) for items returned unpaid of $ 2,500 or more	$ 7 per advice issued

Cash Letter parcels should be addressed to:

[Address...]

Attention: Cheque Processing

Clean Cheque Collections

Clean Cheques: includes drafts and traveller's cheques.

For credit to your ... Bank account (Includes SWIFT MT400 advice)	0.125% Min. $ 40, Max. $ 175 per cheque
For other methods of settlement	0.125% Min. $ 50, Max. $ 175 per cheque

Clean Cheque Collections should be addressed to:

[Address...]

Attention: Clean Cheque Collections

Note: Your attached letter to ... Bank must include the following instructions: "Enclosed find [Clean Collection item particulars] and credit the proceeds after final payment under advice to us. This Collection is subject to the Uniform Rules for Collections, International Chamber of Commerce, Publication No. 522."

Documentary Credits

For USD and CAD transactions, fees quoted are in the currency of the transaction. For all other currencies, fees are collected based on the Canadian dollar equivalent at ... Bank's prevailing rate of exchange.

Notes:
- Where reimbursement for payment of sight drafts on us, or maturing term drafts bearing our acceptance, is to be obtained by redrawing or claiming by mail or cable on another bank, interest from date of payment to date of receipt of cover will be for your account.
- Our out-of-pocket expenses, where applicable, are for your account.
- ... Bank may charge beneficiaries or potential beneficiaries of your credits such additional fees as it may agree with such beneficiaries or potential beneficiaries from time to time and may, in advance of any presentation of documents under your credits, agree to perform the functions which you request that ... Bank perform under those credits and to discount instruments and payment obligations arising thereunder. In no event however, will any fees or expenses that ... Bank charges to beneficiaries or potential beneficiaries be for your account notwithstanding any practice among banks or any provision of the Uniform Customs and Practice for Documentary Credits, 1993 revision or any subsequent revision thereof to the contrary, unless you otherwise agree.

For advising your credits	$ 50
When pre-advised	Add $ 25
For confirming your credits	Rates on application(Min. $ 150)
Amendments	$ 50
Document Examination	0.125%(Min. $ 125)
Negotiation/ Payment	Rates on application(Min. $ 200)
Acceptance/ Deferred Payment Commission	Rates on application(Min. $ 125)
Reimbursement	$ 100
Transfer	0.1875%(Min. $ 250)
Credits cancelled at your request or credits expiring unutilized	$ 50
Discrepancy Fee	$ 50
Assignment of Proceeds	0.1%(Min. $ 150)
Tele-transmission fees	$ 20

Documentary Collections

For USD and CAD transactions, fees quoted are in the currency of the transaction. For all other currencies, fees are collected based on the Canadian dollar equivalent at ... Bank's prevailing rate of exchange.

Notes:
- Where a collection remains open for longer than six (6) months, or where any exceptional amount of work is involved, an additional charge may be levied.
- Partial settlement of a collection will be regarded as a separate item.
- In the case of items payable with charges, no deduction will be made for commission unless payment of the charges is refused, then commission at the rates eligible will be deducted.

Documentary Collections or Clean Bills of Exchange—documents or bills of exchange against payment, acceptance, delivered free or returned unpaid/unaccepted	0.25% (Min. $100, Max. $250)
Shipment by air or parcel post consigned to the Bank	$50
Indorsements of ocean Bills of Lading consigned to the Bank	$50
Amendments and/or extension of due dates	$75 each occasion
Tele-transmission fees for all wires/cables/payments, etc	$20
Preparation of promissory notes, bills of exchange, letters of undertaking, trust receipts, etc	$100 each item
Any other special handling request	Rates on application

Documentary Collections should only be directed to… Bank's Trade Finance Centres or as… Bank may otherwise advise in writing. We will not be responsible for items sent to any other location.

Trade Finance Centres

Strategically located across Canada, our Trade Finance Centres (TFCs) are fully qualified to handle all of your Documentary Credits and Documentary Collection requirements. Documentary Credits and Documentary Collection transactions should be sent directly to the local TFC or to any other location as… Bank may advise in writing.

Toronto	Montreal	Vancouver
Address…	Address…	Address…
SWIFT…	SWIFT…	SWIFT…
Fax:…	Fax…	Fax…

… Bank's Global Banking and Trade Solutions Contact Information
　　[Address…
　　Phone…
　　Fax …
　　SWIFT…
　　E-mail…]

Terms and Conditions

These General Terms and Conditions for Correspondent Accounts and Services are in addition to the … Bank Correspondent Bank Accounts and Services Operating Terms and Conditions applicable to your account(s) (including the … Bank Correspondent Bank Account Agreement) and any other written agreement you enter into with … Bank. For a copy of all such terms applicable to your account(s), please speak to your Relationship Manager or contact … Bank Global Banking and Trade Solutions at the above address.

2 Negotiable instruments

In a broad sense, negotiable instruments mean any commercial titles to ownership, including bills of lading, insurance policies, warehouse warrants[①], etc. In a narrow sense, negotiable instruments specifically refer to bills of exchange, promissory notes and cheques. This chapter focuses on the narrow-sense negotiable instruments.

According to the Uniform Commercial Code of the United States, a negotiable instrument is "an unconditional promise or order to pay a fixed amount of money to the bearer[②] or to order on demand or at a definite time[③]." In other words, a negotiable instrument is a written document that contains an unconditional promise by the drawer to pay the payee or an unconditional order by the drawer to the drawee to pay the payee a fixed amount of money at a definite time.[④] Be they bills of exchange, promissory notes or cheques, negotiable instruments have two characteristics in common: (1) representing a unilateral promise or order to pay a fixed amount of money to the instrument's legitimate holder[⑤] and (2) being transferable or negotiable[⑥].

---

① warehouse warrants：仓单
② bearer：来人
③ on demand：见索即付；at a definite time：在确定的时间
④ drawer：出票人；drawee：付款人,受票人；payee：收款人
⑤ a unilateral promise or order to pay a fixed amount of money to the instrument's legitimate holder：单方面付款给票据合法持有人的承诺或指示；holder：持票人
⑥ transferable：可转让的；transferability：可转让性；negotiable：可转让的,可流通的；negotiability：可转让性

2.1 Characteristics and functions of negotiable instruments

Negotiability

The first feature of negotiable instruments is that they are capable of being transferred or negotiated. Negotiability means that negotiable instruments can be passed on from person to person by mere delivery or by indorsement and delivery①.

Negotiability or transferability is the right embodied in negotiable instruments, yet it depends on the order of the drawer or the indorser. For instance, a bill of exchange may be transferred by mere delivery if it is made payable to bearer②; a bill of exchange may be transferred by both indorsement and delivery if it is made to a named person or order③; and a bill of exchange is not allowed to be transferred if it is made payable to a named person only④. In the first and second cases, the bill of exchange can be further transferred if the transferor or indorser⑤ does not forbid the further transfer in the indorsement; otherwise, it will not be transferred.

Unconditional promise or order to pay

Negotiable instruments contain unconditional orders or promises to pay a fixed amount in money at a definite time. For instance, the drawer of a bill of exchange unconditionally orders the drawee to pay a fixed amount of money to the payee at a definite time; the drawer (or maker⑥) of a

---

① by mere delivery or by indorsement and delivery：仅凭交付或者凭背书和交付；delivery：交付；indorsement：背书

② if it is made payable to bearer：如果票据的收款人（抬头）是来人

③ if it is made to a named person or order：如果票据的收款人（抬头）是指定的人或凭其指示

④ if it is made payable to a named person only：如果票据的收款人（抬头）限制为一个指定的人

⑤ transferor or indorser：转让人或背书人；transferee：受让人；indorsee：被背书人

⑥ maker：出票人，本票和支票的出票人也可以用 maker 来表示

promissory note unconditionally makes promise to pay the payee a fixed amount at a definite time; and the drawer (or maker) of a cheque unconditionally orders the drawee bank① to pay a fixed amount of money to the payee at a certain time. The order or promise must not be conditional; or the negotiable instrument will be invalid.

*Requisite in form*②

Negotiable instruments must contain essential items required by relevant negotiable instrument laws. Different countries have different laws on negotiable instruments, yet the essential items required are quite similar. In general, negotiable instruments must contain the following items: (1) The name of a negotiable instrument, say bill of exchange, promissory note or cheque; (2) Unconditional order or promise to pay; (3) A fixed amount of money, representing the value of the instrument; (4) The date of issue and payment③; (5) The name and place of the drawer, the payee and the drawee; and (6) The signature of the drawer.

In addition, all the acts relating to negotiable instruments, such as issue, indorsement, acceptance, guarantee, payment, enforcing right of recourse and so forth④ must be done according to the stipulations specified in the relevant negotiable instrument laws. However, since there is no uniform negotiable instrument law in the world, the law of the country where a particular act happens will be used to judge the appropriateness of the act.

*Non-causative nature*⑤

Non-causative nature of negotiable instruments means that, once issued, a negotiable instrument exists independent of the commercial relationship

---

① drawee bank：付款行，支票的付款人是银行，因而用 drawee bank 来表示
② requisite in form：要式性，即票据的票面须完整合格
③ date of issue and payment：出票和付款日期；issue：出票
④ all the acts relating to negotiable instruments, such as issue, indorsement, acceptance, guarantee, payment, enforcing right of recourse and so forth：所有与票据相关的行为，如出票、背书、承兑、保证、付款、行使追索权等；acceptance：承兑；right of recourse：追索权
⑤ non-causative nature：无因性

from which it is originated. Obviously, there must be a reason for a negotiable instrument to be issued or transferred. For instance, when a drawer draws a bill of exchange on a drawee, there must be a commercial or financial relationship between the drawer and the drawee (with the accommodation bills① as an exception), say the seller-buyer relationship. However, when the payee transfers the bill to a transferee, the transferee will not mind how the bill was generated and his only concern is whether the bill is valid, i.e., whether in a qualified form and contains the essential items required by the relevant negotiable instrument law.

Even if the underlying relationship that has generated the instrument is invalid or has infirmity②, it will not affect the validity of the negotiable instrument. In this case, when presenting the instrument to the drawee for payment, the legitimate holder of the instrument need not prove the reason for payment and the drawee may not defend to refuse to pay to the bona-fide holder③. Suppose that A the buyer draws a bill to B the payee and the seller in this case and B the payee indorses and delivers the bill to C for settling the debt he owes to C. When C presents the bill to the drawee for payment, he needs not prove the seller-buyer relationship between A and B and the borrower-lender relationship between B and C. Even if the relationship between A and B no longer exists or has infirmity, C still has the right to enforce payment so long as the indorsement can prove his position as a holder. It is the non-causative nature that allows negotiable instruments to possess the feature of negotiability.

In addition to above four characteristics, a negotiable instrument represents a certain amount of money or asset ownership and the rights and liabilities of related parties to the instrument will be determined only by what is written on the instrument, without referring to any other facts or acts outside the instrument.

---

① accommodation bill：融通汇票
② infirmity：弱点，缺陷
③ bona-fide holder：善意的持票人

Functions of negotiable instruments

Negotiable instruments can be used as payment, credit or financing instruments[①]. The basic function of negotiable instruments is to serve as substitutes for money for settling debts. Negotiable instruments themselves have no value, but the parties to them offer the credit basis for them to serve as payment instruments. Thus, another function of negotiable instruments is to serve as credit instruments. When a seller delivers goods to a buyer and if the buyer cannot pay immediately, the buyer may issue a promissory note to the seller. In this case, the debt is evidenced by the promissory note, which specifies the details of the debt, especially the date of payment. If the buyer does not want to hold the instrument until its maturity, it may discount it with a transferee.

One more function of negotiable instruments is financing. In the case of an accepted bill of exchange[②], the holder can discount it in money market because both the drawer and the acceptor guarantee the payment for the instrument at due date. If the acceptor is creditworthy, the bill will be even more acceptable.

2.2 Negotiable instrument laws

Negotiable instrument laws include the laws directly or indirectly relating to negotiable instruments. This subsection discusses the laws directly dealing with negotiable instruments.

As early as the end of the 19th century, France, Germany and the United Kingdom all had established respective laws on negotiable instruments and thus appeared the so-called three different bodies of laws on negotiable instruments. Among them, the first established was the French law and many European countries such as Belgium, the

---

① payment, credit or financing instruments: 支付、信用或融资工具

② an accepted bill of exchange: 承兑汇票, 经由付款人承兑过的远期汇票; acceptor: 承兑人, 付款人(drawee)承兑后成为承兑人

Netherlands, Portugal and Latin American countries were under its influence. The German law on negotiable instruments was developed many years later and countries such as Austria, Hungary, Switzerland, Sweden, Denmark, Japan, Norway, Poland, ex-Soviet Union, Turkey and Yugoslavia were under its influence. The British law on negotiable instruments covered some countries such as Canada, India, the United States, Australia and New Zealand.

Since the co-existence of different laws on negotiable instruments caused inconvenience to cross-border trades, a conference on forming a uniform law on negotiable instruments was held in Geneva in 1930. Delegates from about 30 countries participated in it, but most of them came from the continent of Europe. The result of the conference was the passage of the Geneva Uniform Law[1]. Since then, countries under the influence of both German and French laws have adopted the Geneva Uniform Law by revising their domestic laws accordingly. The United Kingdom did not send delegates to the conference and has not yet joined the Geneva Convention. Therefore, there exist two major laws on negotiable instruments and the two representative documents are the Convention Providing a Uniform Law for Bills of Exchange and Promissory Notes(Geneva, 1930) and the UK Bills of Exchange Act 1882.

The United States has its own law on negotiable instruments, i.e., the Article 3 of the US Uniform Commercial Code. Due to the importance of the United States in international trade, its negotiable instrument law has been attached great attention by international traders and bankers. China has not participated in the Geneva Convention, either. In international trade settlements, however, China refers to the Geneva Uniform Law and has enacted its own negotiable instrument law—The Negotiable Instrument Law of the People's Republic of China[2] in 1995.

Having recognized the inconvenience caused by the co-existence of

---

[1] the Geneva Uniform Law:《日内瓦统一法》

[2] The Negotiable Instrument Law of the People's Republic of China:《中华人民共和国票据法》

different negotiable instrument laws, the United Nations had also attempted to unify them and drafted the Convention Providing a Uniform Law for International Bills of Exchange and International Promissory Notes and the Convention Providing a Uniform Law for International Cheques①. On December 9, 1988, the Conventions were adopted on the 43rd General Assembly of the United States held in New York and kept open for signatures by all states until June 30, 1990. According to the stipulations in the Conventions, they will be valid only after at least 10 countries have approved or joined in it. At present, the convention has not yet become valid, only with 3 signatories (Canada, the United States of America and Russian Federation) and 5 parties of accession or ratification (Gabon, Guinea, Honduras, Liberia and Mexico).②

2.3 Parties to a negotiable instrument

Drawer

A drawer is the person who issues the instrument. The drawer of a bill is the person who draws the bill and orders the drawee to pay; the drawer of a promissory note is the person who makes the promise to pay; and the drawer of a cheque is the person who writes the cheque and orders the drawee bank to pay.

What is liability of the drawer? Let's look at the drawer of a bill. When issuing a bill, the drawer engages that on due presentment the bill will be paid by the drawee on demand or accepted and paid at maturity as

---

① the Convention Providing a Uniform Law for International Bills of Exchange and International Promissory Notes and the Convention Providing a Uniform Law for International Cheques: 联合国《关于统一国际汇票、本票法的公约》和《关于统一国际支票法的公约》

② Chapter X International Trade and Development, retrieved on March 7, 2013 fromhttp://treaties.un.org/pages/ViewDetails.aspx?src=TREATY&mtdsg_no=X-12&chapter=10&lang=en

specified in the bill①. If the bill is dishonoured by non-payment or non-acceptance②, the drawer will compensate the holder or any indorser who has been compelled to pay the bill, provided that the requisite proceedings on dishonour are duly taken. In a sense, the drawer guarantees the payment in issuing an instrument.

Drawee

A drawee is the person who is to pay. The drawee of a bill of exchange is the person that is ordered to pay; the drawee of a promissory note is the drawer(maker) who promises to pay; and the drawee of a cheque is the drawee bank which is ordered to pay.

The payment by the drawee is unconditional. But if the payee does not make due presentation for payment, the drawee may refuse to pay. Moreover, according to the US Uniform Commercial Code, "the drawee is not liable on unaccepted draft③", which means that if it is a usance bill④ and the drawee of the bill refuses to accept the bill, then the drawee is not obliged to pay. So, in case of a usance bill, the presentation for acceptance by the payee or holder is an important and indispensable act.

Payee

A payee is the person to whom the drawee is ordered to pay. As the only obligee⑤, the payee has the right to ask the drawee to pay and has the right of recourse to the indorsers and drawer if the instrument is dishonoured by non-payment or non-acceptance. Moreover, when an instrument is made payable to the payee's order, the payee has the right to transfer the

---

① on due presentment the bill will be paid by the drawee on demand or accepted and paid at maturity as specified in the bill：在适时提示时，汇票的付款人将见票即付或者承兑，并在到期日付款；presentation：提示，一种票据行为；maturity：到期日

② dishonoured by non-payment or non-acceptance：拒绝付款或拒绝承兑；dishonour：拒付，退票；non-payment：不付款；non-acceptance：不承兑

③ draft：这里指汇票，即 bill of exchange

④ usance bill：远期汇票，英国汇票法案中用此术语来表示远期汇票

⑤ obligee：票据上的债权人；obligor：票据上的债务人

instrument by indorsement and delivery. When the instrument is made payable to bearer, the payee may transfer it by mere delivery.

The three basic parties to negotiable instruments are drawer, drawee and payee. Bills of exchange and cheques are three-party instruments while promissory notes two-party instruments. In some cases, one party may take on the roles of more than one. For example, the UK Bills of Exchange Act 1882 stipulates that a bill may be drawn payable to or to the order of the drawer, or it may be drawn payable to or to the order of the drawee. In the former case the drawer and the payee are the same while in the latter case the drawee and the payee are the same. The UK Bills of Exchange Act 1882 also stipulates that, where in a bill the drawer and the drawee are the same or where the drawee is a fictitious person① or a person not having capacity to contract, the holder may treat the instrument either as a bill of exchange or as a promissory note.

Indorser

An indorser is the person who makes indorsement on the back of an instrument. The payee or holder may sign his name on the back of the instrument and transfer it to a transferee. The payee or holder who has signed his name on the back of the instrument and transferred it is called indorser whereas the person to whom the instrument was transferred is indorsee. To an indorsee, all indorsers before him are his prior parties and, to an indorser, all indorsees after him are his subsequent holders②.

By indorsing an instrument, the indorser guarantees to his subsequent parties that at the time of indorsement the instrument is valid, that he has good title to it, that on due presentment it will be accepted or paid as specified. If it is dishonoured he will compensate the holder or subsequent indorsers who have been compelled to pay, provided that the requisite proceedings on dishonours be duly taken.

---

① fictitious person: 虚构的人
② prior parties: 前手; subsequent holders: 后手

Acceptor

An acceptor only appears in the case of usance bills. Sight bills[①], promissory notes and cheques have so acceptors. An acceptor is the drawee who has accepted a usance bill. By acceptance, the drawee becomes acceptor. The UK Bills of Exchange Act 1882 has stipulated the liabilities of the acceptor. By accepting a bill, the acceptor engages that he will pay the bill according to the tenor[②] of his acceptance. By accepting a bill, the acceptor cannot deny to a holder in due course[③] the existence of the drawer, the genuineness of his signature and his capacity and authority to draw the bill. If a bill is payable to the drawer's order, the acceptor cannot deny the drawer's capacity to indorse but does not guarantee the genuineness or validity of his indorsement. If a bill is payable to the order of a third party, the acceptor cannot deny the existence of the payee and his capacity to indorse, but does not guarantee the genuineness or validity of his indorsement.

Guarantor

According to the Convention Providing a Uniform Law for Bills of Exchange and Promissory Notes(Geneva, 1930), the guarantor[④] is "the giver of an 'aval[⑤]' who is bound in the same manner as the person for whom he has become guarantor". Once a guarantor pays a bill, he has the right against the person guaranteed and against those who are liable to the person guaranteed on the bill. Typically, a guarantor is not a party already liable to the instrument and the party guaranteed can be any obligor on the instrument.

---

① sight bill：即期汇票
② tenor：期限
③ holder in due course：正当持票人
④ guarantor：保证人,担保人
⑤ aval：保证,担保

Holder

The Convention Providing a Uniform Law on Bills of Exchange and Promissory Notes(Geneva, 1930) defines the holder as the possessor of a bill if he establishes his title to the bill through an uninterrupted series of indorsements①. Such a possessor is the lawful holder. The UK Bills of Exchange Act defines a holder as a payee, indorsee or bearer of a bill or note who is in possession of it. A bearer means the person in possession of a bill or note which is payable to bearer.

A holder for value② is a person who possesses an instrument for which value has been given by himself or by some other person prior to him. Valuable consideration may be given in the forms of money, goods or services. If the holder of a bill has a lien③ on it, he is deemed to be a holder for value.

The UK Bills of Exchange Act 1882 defines a holder in due course as a holder who has taken a bill, complete and regular on the face of it, under the following conditions: (1) that he became the holder of it before it was overdue and without notice that it had been previously dishonoured, if such was the fact; (2) that he took the bill in good faith④ and for value and that at the time the bill was negotiated to him he had no notice of any defect in the title of the person who negotiated it.

The US Uniform Commercial Code defines a holder in due course as a holder of an instrument if (1) the instrument has no forgery or alteration⑤; and (2) the holder took the instrument for value, in good faith, without notice that the instrument is overdue or has been dishonoured or any default⑥, without notice that the instrument contains an unauthorized signature or has been altered.

---

① an uninterrupted series of indorsements: 连续背书
② holder for value: 付对价持票人; value: 对价; valuable consideration: 对价
③ lien: 留置权, 扣押权
④ in good faith: 善意地; in bad faith: 恶意地
⑤ forgery or alteration: 伪造或篡改
⑥ default: 违约

A holder in due course is also called a bona-fide holder. A holder for value may or may not be a holder in due course, but a holder in due course must be a holder for value. The following example will illustrate the position of a holder in due course and the difference between a holder for value and a holder in due course.

Suppose that A the drawer issued a usance bill on B and delivered it to C the payee. C presented the bill to B the drawee for acceptance and B the drawee accepted the bill and then delivered it to C. C, after indorsing it blankly, lost the bill. By chance, D picked it up and transferred it to E for value, for the bill had been blankly indorsed and could be transferred by mere delivery. Since E the transferee had taken the bill in good faith and for value without noticing the defect of D's title to the till, E is a holder in due course. When the bill becomes due, E the holder has the right to present it to B the acceptor for payment. In the event of dishonour, E has the right to sue A, B, C and D. The defect in the title of this instrument was on the part of D. E's title is not affected because E is the holder in due course.

In the same example, suppose E further gave the bill to his daughter F as a birthday present. Since F did not give any value for the bill to E, F is not a holder in due course, but still a holder for value for his prior party E has given the value for the bill. In the event of dishonour, F will have the right to sue A, B, C, D, but not E.

How to establish whether a man acted in good faith or bad faith? From the past legal decisions in the United Kingdom, there is a principle. That is, in order to prove his good faith, a transferee of a bill must be able to show that he acted honestly and had no knowledge of any defect in the title of the transferor and he even did not suspect of such a defect. One cannot think a transferee is in bad faith just because ordinary people can suspect because a man may act carelessly or display little intelligence in that circumstance. So long as the transferee did not deliberately blind himself to any suspicious fact, his good faith will not be doubted.[1]

---

[1] Dudley Richardson. *Guide to Negotiable Instruments and the Bills of Exchange Acts*, seventh edition. London: Butterworths, 1983: 21-22

The relationship of the parties to negotiable instruments

Sight bill

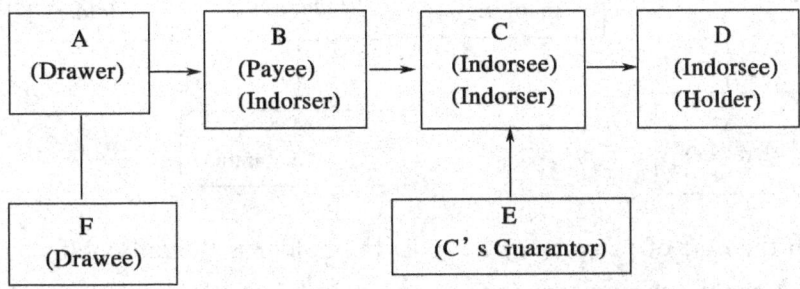

In the case of sight bill, D the holder is the only obligee on the bill while A the drawer, B the payee/indorser, C the indorsee/indorser and E the guarantor are all obligors, among whom A the drawer is the principal obligor, primarily liable for payment and B, C and E are secondary obligors, secondarily liable for payment. E is C's guarantor in this case, although it may be any obligor's guarantor.

Usance bill

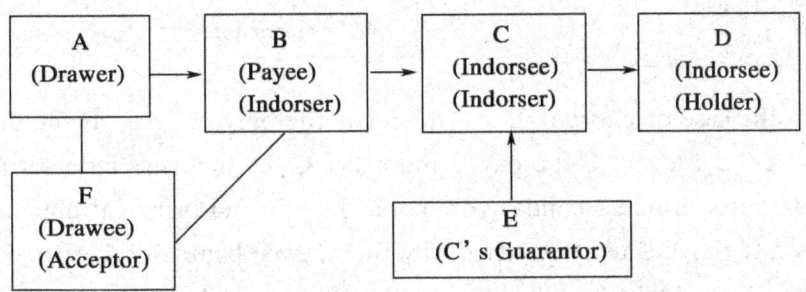

In the case of usance bill, D the holder is the only obligee of the bill. Before acceptance, F the drawee is the secondary obligor and A the drawer the principal obligor. After acceptance, F the acceptor becomes the principal obligor while A the drawer, B the payee/indorser, C the indorsee/indorser and E the guarantor are all secondary obligors. Although after acceptance F the acceptor becomes the principal obligor, if F dishonours the accepted bill, the obligee has the right to enforce his right of recourse against C, E, B and finally to A for payment.

Promissory note

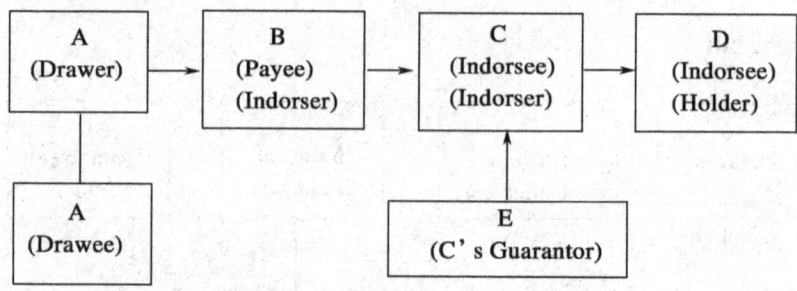

In the case of promissory note, D the holder is the only obligee of the note. A the drawer/drawee is the principal obligor. B the payee/indorser, C the indorsee/indorser and E the guarantor are secondary obligors.

Cheque

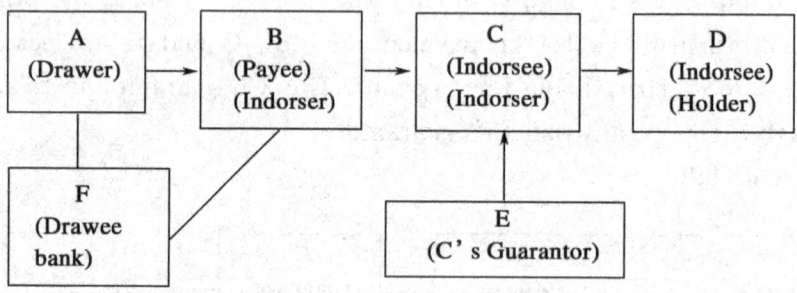

In the case of cheque, D the holder is the only obligee. F the drawee bank, A the drawer, B the payee/indorser, C the indorsee/indorser and E the guarantor are all secondary obligors. There is no principal obligor in a cheque. If the cheque is certified[①] by the drawee bank, the certified bank will be the principal obligor and all other secondary obligors will be discharged from their liabilities.

---

① certified cheque：保付支票

2.4 Bills of Exchange

Definition

Different laws have different ways of defining bills of exchange, but the contents are to some extent similar. The UK Bills of Exchange Act 1882 defines a bill of exchange as "an unconditional order in writing addressed by one person to another, signed by the person giving it, requiring the person to whom it is addressed to pay on demand or at a fixed or determinable future time a sum certain in money to or to the order of a specified person or to bearer."①Countries and areas such as Ireland, Cyprus, Hong Kong, India, Israel, Malaysia, Pakistan, Philippines, Singapore, Sri Lanka, Australia, Fiji, New Zealand and Tonga are all under the influence of the UK Bills of Exchange Act 1882. Thus, their respective definitions about bills of exchange are to a greater extent identical to one another.

The Convention Providing a Uniform Law for Bills of Exchange and Promissory Notes(Geneva, 1930) defines a bill of exchange by stipulating its essential items as: (1) the term "bill of exchange" inserted in the body of the instrument and expressed in the language employed in drawing up the instrument; (2) an unconditional order to pay a determined sum of money; (3) the name of the person who is to pay; (4) a statement of the time of payment; (5) a statement of the place where payment is to be made; (6) the name of the person to whom or to whose order payment is to be made; (7) a statement of the date and of the place where the bill is issued;

---

① an unconditional order in writing addressed by one person to another, signed by the person giving it, requiring the person to whom it is addressed to pay on demand or at a fixed or determinable future time a sum certain in money to or to the order of a specified person or to bearer: 一人向另一人签发的、要求受票人在见票时或在可以确定的将来日期无条件地支付一定的金额给指定的人或者按照指定的人的指示付款或者支付给来人的书面指示

and (8) the signature of the person who issues the bill (drawer).① More than 40 countries all over the world are under the influence of the Geneva Uniform Law, such as Germany, Denmark, Finland, France, Greece, Iceland, Italy, Leichtenstein, Luxembourg, Malta, the Netherlands, Norway, Portugal, Spain, Sweden, Switzerland, Turkey, Indonesia, Poland, Japan, Korea and so on.

Regardless of the different ways of defining a bill of exchange, a bill of exchange is a three-party negotiable instrument containing the drawer (the person giving the order to pay), the drawee (the person to whom the order is addressed) and the payee (the person to whom the sum certain in money is paid).

It should be noted that the US Uniform Commercial Code uses the term "draft" to name the bill of exchange. It considers an instrument which is an order as a draft. The Negotiable Instrument Law of the People's Republic of China also uses draft to refer to a bill of exchange and considers it as drawn by the drawer who orders the drawee to pay unconditionally at sight or the specified date a certain sum of money to the payee or holder. The draft in the law refers to bank draft and commercial draft.

---

① (1) the term "bill of exchange" inserted in the body of the instrument and expressed in the language employed in drawing up the instrument:票据上标有"汇票"字样并以开具票据的语言表示;(2) an unconditional order to pay a determined sum of money:无条件支付一个确定金额的指示;(3) the name of the person who is to pay:付款人名称;(4) a statement of the time of payment:表明付款时间;(5) a statement of the place where payment is to be made:表明付款地点;(6) the name of the person to whom or to whose order payment is to be made:收款人名称;(7) a statement of the date and of the place where the bill is issued:表明汇票的出票日期和地点;(8) the signature of the person who issues the bill(drawer):签发汇票的人(出票人)的签名

Essential items required in a bill of exchange

Specimen of a sight bill

Exchange for US $ 1,000.00　　　　　　　　　　Shanghai, March 5, 2003 At sight pay to the order of ABC Bank the sum of one thousand US dollars only value received. To: The … Bank 　　　New York, USA 　　　　　　　　　　　　　　　　　　　For China … Import & Export Co. 　　　　　　　　　　　　　　　　　　　　　　（Authorized Signature）

Specimen of a usance bill

Exchange for US $ 1,000.00　　　　　　　　　　Shanghai, March 5, 2003 At 30 days after sight pay to the order of ABC Bank the sum of one thousand US dollars only value received. To: The … Bank 　　　New York, USA 　　　　　　　　　　　　　　　　　　　For China … Import & Export Co. 　　　　　　　　　　　　　　　　　　　　　　（Authorized Signature）

The word "Exchange"

Usually the word "Exchange" is clearly indicated on the face of a bill of exchange. The UK Bills of Exchange Act 1882 has no specific requirement for it, but the Convention Providing a Uniform Law for Bills of Exchange and Promissory Notes(Geneva, 1930) expressly states that the term "Bill of Exchange" be inserted in the body of a bill and expressed in the language employed in drawing up the bill. In practice, in order to distinguish a bill of exchange from a promissory note or a cheque, it is recommended that the term "Bill of Exchange" be indicated on the face of a bill of exchange.

An unconditional order to pay a fixed amount of money

Both the UK Bills of Exchange Act 1882 and the Convention Providing a Uniform Law for Bills of Exchange and Promissory Notes(Geneva, 1930) stipulate that a bill of exchange contain an unconditional order to pay a certain sum of money. The UK Bills of Exchange Act 1882 considers a bill invalid if it does not specify the value given.

The proper way of expressing an unconditional order to pay is "Pay…" or "Please pay …". Sentences like "If the goods meet the requirements, please pay A Co. $1 000." or "I should be pleased if you would kindly pay …" are not unconditional orders, but requests. ①

Furthermore, "Pay £100 out of the proceeds of sale of my farm Haslemere" is not valid because the proceeds of sale in fact might not amount to £100 and thus there would not be enough money to pay.

Then, what is the difference between the following two payment orders: (1) "Pay from my No. 2 A/C to Mary Maltby the sum of £10." (2) "Pay Mary Maltby the sum of £10 and debit my No. 2 A/C."② Based on the UK Bills of Exchange Act 1882, the second one is valid while the first not. The reason is that the No. 2 account might not have enough money to cover the £10.

Name and address of the drawee

The name and address of the drawee must be reasonably clear and definite. Only when the name and address are clear and definite will the payee or holder be able to find the drawee and present the bill for payment or acceptance. The UK Bills of Exchange Act 1882 states that "a bill may be addressed to the two or more drawees whether they are partners or not." If there are two drawees, it is proper to write "To A and B", not "To A or B." "To A and B" means A and B will be liable for the payment jointly and severally. If the drawer and drawee are the same person or the drawee is fictitious, the bill may be considered either a promissory note or a bill of exchange at the holder's option.

The signature of the drawer

Without the signature of the drawer, no bill of exchange is valid. The drawer may be an individual or a legal entity. If it is an individual, the person himself signs the bill. If it is a legal entity, the authorized person signs for or on behalf of the entity. The general manager of a company will probably have the authority to sign on behalf of the company while an office boy is most unlikely to have such authority. If the office boy does so,

---

① 在 pay 之前加上 please 仍然是无条件支付的指示

② from my No. 2 account 和 debit my No. 2 account 的区别在于前者是有条件的，后者是无条件的

the signature will be unauthorized. If a bill is signed by R. Johns, the attorney on behalf of James Harrison, his client, it is expressed as "Per pro James Harrison, R. Johns, attorney."

The signature of the drawer is used to authenticate the genuineness of a bill of exchange①. Forged signature② of the drawer makes the bill invalid. For example, A stole B's cheque book, forged B's signature to a cheque for £10 and got C to cash it for him. C now becomes the victim of the fraud. He cannot sue B on the cheque for B did not sign on it. His remedy only lies against A(if A can be found) for what it is worth. Suppose C presented the cheque to the drawee bank and obtained the payment, the drawee bank was unable to debit B's account with it, for the bank's only authority for debiting the account was B's genuine signature. The drawee bank would lose the money unless the forgery was immediately discovered after payment and C was quickly advised of the discovery before he could alter his position on the strength of receiving payment.

Date and place of issue

Both the date and place of issue are important items to a bill of exchange. If not dated, a bill is rendered invalid by the UK Bills of Exchange Act 1882. The importance of the date of issue lies in that it can be used to determine the expiry date. For instance, the Convention Providing a Uniform Law for Bills of Exchange and Promissory Notes (Geneva, 1930) stipulates that the validity period for a sight bill should be "one year from the date of issue". Moreover, the date of presentment and the date of acceptance (if it is a usance bill) should not be prior to this date and the date of issue is also used to calculate the due date when a bill is payable at, say, 30 days after date.

The place of issue is also crucial because whether an international bill is valid or not depends on the local law of the issuing place. If there is no indication of such a place, the place where the drawer resides is considered the place of issue.

---

① authenticate the genuineness of a bill of exchange：验证汇票的真实性
② forged signature：伪造的签名

Name of the payee

The payee is the person to whom a bill of exchange is payable. Since a bill may be payable to a named person only, a named person or order or bearer, there are three different ways of writing the payee on a bill.

Restricted order[①] A bill may be payable to a named person only or to a named person not transferable. A bill with a restricted order is non-negotiable and thus cannot be transferred to another person. The ways of writing such an order include: (1) "Pay A Co. only." (2) "Pay A Co. not transferable." (3) "Pay A Co." plus "Not Transferable" on the face of the bill.

Demonstrative order[②] A bill may be made payable to the order of a specified person or to a specified person without any words indicating the prohibition of further transfer. Examples are: (1) "Pay A Co. or order." (2) "Pay to the order of A Co." (3) "Pay A Co." and no words like "Not Transferable" can be found on the face of the bill. A bill with any one of the three orders may be further transferred by the payee.

Payable to bearer[③] A bill may be made payable to bearer without a specific person as the payee. For examples: (1) "Pay bearer." (2) "Pay A Co. or bearer." In this way, the bill may be transferred by mere delivery.

The UK Bills of Exchange Act 1882 stipulates that the payee must be named or otherwise indicated in a bill with reasonable certainty if the bill is not payable to bearer. A bill may be made payable to two or more payees jointly, or it may be made payable in the alternative to one of two or one or some of several payees. A bill may also be made payable to the holder of an office for the time being. Where the payee is a fictitious or non-existing person the bill may be treated as payable to bearer.

Tenor

Tenor refers to the due date of a bill on which the drawee or the acceptor should effect payment. Based on the tenor, we can divide bills

---

① restrictive order：限制性性抬头，出票人(drawer)限制收款人(payee)进一步转让票据

② demonstrative order：指示性抬头，出票人(drawer)指示付款人(drawee)付款给收款人(payee)或按照收款人的指示(the order of payee)付款，收款人可以进一步转让该票据

③ payable to bearer：来人抬头，收款人(payee，即 bearer)可以仅凭交付转让票据

into two types: sight bills and usance bills. Sight bills are payable on demand while usance bills payable at a fixed or determinable future date.

Payable on demand When a bill is expressed to be payable at sight, on demand or on presentation, the bill is a sight bill. The UK Bills of Exchange Act 1882 considers a bill in which no time for payment is expressed as a sight bill. When an accepted or indorsed bill is overdue, it shall be deemed as payable on demand by the acceptor or indorser. For a sight bill, if the holder duly presents the bill for payment, the drawee should immediately effect the payment.

Payable at a fixed period after sight[①] A bill may be made payable at "30 days after sight", "60 days after sight" or "three months after sight", etc. When a bill is payable at a fixed period after sight, the holder first presents the bill to the drawee for acceptance and then presents the accepted bill to the acceptor for payment on the due date. The due date is calculated based on the accepting date.

Payable at a fixed period after date[②] A bill may be made payable at "30 days after date", "60 days after date", "three months after date", etc. When a bill is payable at a fixed period after date, the due date of the bill is calculated based on the date of issue. However, the holder is recommended to present the bill for acceptance first and then present the accepted bill for payment on the due date. By acceptance, the drawee becomes the acceptor, i.e., the principal obligor of the bill.

Payable on or at a fixed period after the occurrence of a specified event which is certain to happen, though the time of happening may be uncertain[③] A bill may be made payable at "60 days after the bill of lading

---

① payable at a fixed period after sight: 见票后定日付款，如"见票后30天付款"，"见票后3个月付款"

② payable at a fixed period after date: 出票后定日付款，如"出票后30天付款"，"出票后3个月付款"

③ Payable on or at a fixed period after the occurrence of a specified event which is certain to happen, though the time of happening may be uncertain: 在一个具体事件发生后定日付款,尽管事件发生的时间尚不确定，如"提单日后60天付款"(60 days after the bill of lading date)

date", "60 days after the presentment of documents" or "three months after the death of A". In the last case, "death" is deemed to be a specified event because the death of a living man is inevitable and a certain future event. However, a tenor like "three months after Mary gets married" is not proper, for Mary may keep single all her life. Marriage is a contingency, so it will make the bill invalid even if it really happens some day. It is also recommended that the holder present a bill with one of the tenors for acceptance first to ascertain the drawee's liability of payment on the bill.

Then, what are the rules for calculating the due date of a bill?

First of all, if the due date happens to be a non-business day, the paying date will be the succeeding business day.

Second, when the two words "*after*" and "*from*" are used with a date, do they have any difference? Previously, they were perceived to be different, but now UCP 600 and ISBP 681 both specify that the two words using before a date are construed as both excluding the date mentions. For example, 10 days after March 1 and 10 day from March 1 has the same due date, i.e., March 11.[①]

Third, the month in the tenor of a bill is the calendar month[②]. For instance, if the tenor of a bill is one month after date and the issuing date is March 1, 2013, the paying date should be April 1, 2013. With the same issuing date, if the bill is payable at five month after date, the due date should be August 1, 2013.

Again, suppose that a bill is payable at one month after sight and the accepting date is January 31, 2013, the due date should be February 28, 2013. If it was a leap year, the due date should be February 29. With the same accepting date, if the bill is payable at five month after sight, the due date should be June 30, 2013.

---

① 值得注意的是，UCP600 和 ISBP 681 均规定：10 days after March 1 和 10 days from March 1 的到期日都是 3 月 11 日，均不包括 3 月 1 日当天。

② calendar month：日历月，如果期限是 one month after date，出票日期是 3 月 1 日，那么到期日是 4 月 1 日。如果出票日期是 2013 年 1 月 31 日，但是 2 月没有 31 日，那么到期日就是 2013 年 2 月 28 日；也就是说，当没有对应的日期时，到期的月份的最后一天即是到期日，如果是闰年，到期日则为 2 月 29 日

Sometimes a bill may be made payable at one month and half after sight and its due date will be calculated as one month plus 15 days. If the tenor is half month after sight, the due date should be calculated as 15 days after the accepting date.

Finally, the beginning of a month refers to the first day of the month, the middle of a month the 15th and the end of a month the last day, say January 31, February 28(or 29 in a leap year) or April 30, as the case may be.

Place of payment

The place of payment is the place where the holder presents the bill for payment. If there is no indication of the place of payment, the address of the drawee or the acceptor on the bill will be the place for the payee or the holder to present the bill for payment. If no place of payment and no address are specified, the payee or the holder may present the bill to the drawee's or the acceptor's place of business or home for payment.

A fixed amount of money

The amount certain in money must be clearly expressed in both words and figures and the two amounts must be the consistent. If there is a discrepancy between the sums in words and figures, according to the UK Bills of Exchange Act 1882, the sum in words will be used as the amount of the bill. Some countries customarily use the smaller one as the amount, though. According to the Law on Negotiable Instruments of the People's Republic of China, a discrepancy between the two amounts will render the instrument invalid. In addition, the amount may be paid with interest. In this case, the interest rate must be indicated clearly on the bill.

Writing

According to the UK Bills of Exchange Act 1882, the order to pay must be in a form of writing, which includes typewriting and printing. Apparently, ink is not the only medium used and therefore a bill drawn up in pencil is still valid. In practice, however, drawing a bill in pencil is usually not encouraged because of the easy opportunity for fraudulent alteration. Moreover, the UK Bills of Exchange Act does not state the maximum and minimum sizes of the writing or that the writing must be on paper or parchment only; nor do the laws of other countries. Therefore, as the late Sir Alan Herbert humorously pointed out, the order to pay could be written on the white belly of a live cow, which would be a valid bill if properly signed.

2.5　Acts related to a bill of exchange

Since most of the acts related to bills of exchange also apply to promissory notes or cheques, the acts related to negotiable instruments are discussed in this subsection.

Issue

According to the UK Bills of Exchange Act 1882, issue means "the first delivery of a bill or note, complete in form to a person who takes it as a holder".[①] Generally, the act of issue comprises two actions by the drawer: (1) to draw and sign a bill and (2) to deliver it to the payee. "Complete in form" means that the bill or note should meet the requirements of the relevant negotiable instrument law in the place of issue. Delivery means the transfer of possession actually or constructively from one person to another. In a normal way, liability on a bill arises not by mere signature but by signature plus delivery. Delivery can be actual or constructive[②], i. e., it can be the actual physical transfer of the bill or it can be some act that shows immediate intention to deliver. In the case of acceptance, even mere advice of acceptance sent by the acceptor to the person entitled to the bill will suffice for delivery.

A man may sign a bill in the capacity as the drawer, the acceptor or the indorser but with no intention of delivering the bill, or he may sign and then deliver it subject to the recipient's fulfilling a certain condition. In neither case will a valid delivery occur. In the latter case, if the recipient does not fulfill the

---

　　① issue means "the first delivery of a bill or note, complete in form to a person who takes it as a holder"：出票是指"第一次交付票面完整的汇票或本票给持票人"；issue：出票；complete in form：票面完整合格

　　② constructive delivery：推定交付，立即交付的意向亦被视为推定交付

condition, his title to the instrument will be defective by reason of non-delivery since delivery will not be completed until the condition is fulfilled. In the former case where no delivery is made at all, if a person takes a bill without authority, he will have no title just because of the absence of delivery. But the law makes an exception in favor of a holder in due course. Should such a bill be negotiated to a holder in due course, a complete and valid delivery by all prior parties will be conclusively presumed in his favor.

Suppose Brown signed some bearer cheque and left it in his desk from which it was stolen. Brown the drawer will not be liable on the grounds of non-delivery. But if the thief negotiated the cheque to a holder in due course, the holder in due course may enforce payment. It can avail Brown nothing to plead non-delivery since a valid delivery will be conclusively presumed in favor of the holder in due course.

Indorsement

Indorsement contains two actions. The payee or holder (1) signs on the back of a bill and (2) delivers it to the indorsee. As having discussed earlier, if a bill is drawn payable to a specified person only or to a specified person not transferable, the bill cannot be negotiated. If a bill is drawn payable to bearer, it can be negotiated by mere delivery without indorsement. If a bill is drawn payable to the order of a specified person, it can be negotiated by indorsement and delivery.

The UK Bills of Exchange Act 1882 prescribes the following requisites for a valid indorsement: (1) It must be written on the bill itself and be signed by the indorser. A simple signature of the indorser on the bill without additional words is sufficient. (2) It must be an indorsement of the entire bill. Partial indorsement, that is, an indorsement that purports to transfer to the indorsee only part of the amount payable, or which purports to transfer the bill to two or more indorsees severally, does not operate as a negotiation of the bill. (3) Where a bill is payable to the order of two or more payees or indorsees who are not partners, all must indorse unless the one indorsing has authority to indorse for the others. (4) Where, in a bill payable to order, the payee or indorsee is wrongly designated, or his name is spelt wrong, he may indorse the bill as therein described, adding, if he think fit, his proper signature. (5) Where there are two or more indorsements on a bill, each indorsement is deemed to have been made in the order in which it appears on the bill, until the contrary is proved. (6) An indorsement may be made in blank or special. It may also contain terms making it restrictive.

The following discusses the different types of indorsement based on the UK Bills of Exchange Act 1882, the Convention Providing a Uniform Law for Bills of Exchange and Promissory Notes(Geneva, 1930) and the US Commercial Code.

Special indorsement Special indorsement, also called indorsement in full[①], specifies the person to whom or to whose order the bill or note is to be payable in addition to the signature of the indorser. For example, suppose A is the indorser and B the indorsee. When indorsing, A may write:

"Pay to B. A(Signed)" or

"Pay to the order of B, A(Signed)".

A bill with a special indorsement is capable of being transferred only by the indorsee. The Convention Providing a Uniform Law for Bills of Exchange and Promissory Notes(Geneva, 1930) states that a holder may establish his or her title to the bill "through an uninterrupted series of indorsements." If all the indorsements are special indorsements, it will be easy to establish the legitimate holder of the bill. Special indorsements not only show a chain of indorsers but also give the holder full right of recourse against all the prior indorsers in the event of dishonour. For example, A the payee specially indorses a bill and delivers it to B the indorsee, B the indroser does the same to C the indorsee, C the indorser to D the indorsee and finally D the indroser to E the indorsee. Then, on the back of the bill, we can find the chain of indorsers and indorsees as follows:

---

① special indorsement or indorsement in full：特别背书或完全背书，背书中写明被背书人(indorsee)的名称,背书人(indorser)指示付款人(drawee)付款给指定的人(indorsee)或按照指定人(indorsee)的指示付款

"Pay to B or order   A(signed)"
"Pay to C or order   B(signed)"
"Pay to D or order   C(signed)"
"Pay to E or order   D(signed)"

In the chain of indorsements, it is easy to see that E is the last indorsee and the holder of the bill.

Blank indorsement[①] Blank indorsement, also called general indorsement, shows an indorser's signature only and specifies no indorsee. A bill blankly indorsed becomes payable to bearer.

Based on the Convention Providing a Uniform Law for Bills of Exchange and Promissory Notes (Geneva, 1930), "an indorsement may leave the beneficiary unspecified or may consist simply of the signature of the indorser." This kind of indorsement is indorsement in blank or blank indorsement. The holder has three ways to deal with a bill with a blank indorsement: (1) The holder may fill up the blank either with his own name or with the name of some other person, transferring the blank indorsement into a special indorsement. (2) The holder may indorse the bill in blank and then transfers it to another person. (3) The holder may transfer the bill to another person without filling up the blank and without indorsing it, i.e., by mere delivery. In this case, the bill is deemed to be payable to bearer.[②]

The US Commercial Code also stipulates that an instrument indorsed in blank becomes payable to bearer and may be transferred by mere delivery, or the holder may convert a blank indorsement into a special indorsement

---

① blank indorsement: 空白背书，背书中没有写明被背书人的名称，相当于空白抬头，也称为一般背书(general indorsement)

② (1) The holder may fill up the blank either with his own name or with the name of some other person, transferring the blank indorsement into a special indorsement: 持票人可以在空白背书中填写自己的名字，或者在空白背书中填写另一受让人的名字转让给另一受让人，两种方法都把空白背书转化成了特别背书。(2) The holder may indorse the bill in blank and then transfers it to another person: 持票人可以再写一个空白背书将票据转让给另一受让人。(3) The holder may transfer the bill to another person without filling up the blank and without indorsing it, i.e., by mere delivery. In this case, the bill is deemed to be payable to bearer: 持票人可以将有空白背书的票据直接转让给受让人，即仅凭交付即可转让。这里空白背书的票据相当于来人抬头的票据，仅凭交付即可转让

by writing words above the signature of the indorser identifying the person to whom the instrument is made payable.

Restrictive indorsement[①] Restrictive indorsement prohibits further transfer of the bill. For example, where an indorsement is "Pay to B only. A(signed)", then B the indorsee is the only party that has the right to present the instrument for payment and cannot further transfer it to any other person.

According to the UK Bills of Exchange Act 1882, a restrictive indorsement may merely authorize the indorsee to deal with the bill as directed but has no intent to transfer the ownership of the bill. For example, "Pay B or order for collection. A(signed)" is just an indorsement for collection. Another case is that the indorsement only vests the title in the indorsee in trust for some other person, e.g., "Pay X for account of Z. Z(Signed)".

Conditional indorsement[②] A conditional indorsement is a special indorsement with a condition for the indorsee to fulfill before the payment, i.e., the indorser is liable only if the condition is fulfilled. For examples:

"Pay to B or order upon his delivery of goods. A(signed)"

"Pay to B without recourse to me. A(signed)"

However, not all the laws allow the use of conditional indorsement. For instance, the Convention Providing a Uniform Law for Bills of Exchange and Promissory Notes (Geneva, 1930) stipulates that "an indorsement must be unconditional. Any condition to which it is made subject is deemed not to be written". The UK Bills of Exchange Act 1882 also stipulates that "where a bill purports to be indorsed conditionally the condition may be disregarded by the payer, and payment to the indorsee is valid whether the condition has been fulfilled or not."

The Negotiable Instrument Law of the People's Republic of China stipulates that the indorsement on the back of the instrument should be in

---

① restrictive indorsement：限制性背书，背书人指示付款人仅付款给被背书人，被背书人不得进一步转让票据

② conditional indorsement：有条件背书，背书人指示付款人在被背书人满足一定条件的情况下付款给被背书人

uninterrupted series, i.e., the signatures or seals by the indorsers and the indorsees must be in the sequential consistency and the indorsements be unconditional.

Presentment or presentation

A bill must be duly presented for payment if it is a sight bill, or duly presented for acceptance first and then for payment at maturity if it is a usance bill. It should be understood that a holder of a bill payable at a fixed time after date is under no obligation to present the bill for acceptance. Such a step, however, is strongly recommended. After the drawee accepts the usance bill, the drawee becomes the acceptor primarily liable for payment, hence the bill is more desirable and more likely to be paid at maturity by virtue of the acceptor's liability.

Where a bill is drawn payable at a fixed time after sight, presentment for acceptance is essential, since only when the date of "sighting" (accepting) by the drawee is ascertained will it be possible to calculate the maturity of the bill. The sooner a bill is "sighted", the sooner it will be due for payment.

The time for presentment A bill must be presented for payment or acceptance at the specified time or place. For presenting a sight bill for payment or a usance bill for acceptance, the UK Bills of Exchange Act 1882 requires that the presentment be made within a reasonable time and in business hours on a business day, whereas the Convention Providing a Uniform Law for Bills of Exchange and Promissory Notes(Geneva, 1930) requires that the period for presentment be one year. For presenting an accepted bill for payment, the former requires that the presentment be made on the due date, while the latter on the due date or within two days after the due date. If the holder fails to present for payment within the specified time, the holder will lose its right of recourse to its prior parties.

According to the Negotiable Instrument Law of the People's Republic of China, the presentment of a sight bill for payment must be done within one month after the date of issue and the presentment of a usance bill for payment within 10 days from the due date. For a bill payable at a fixed future time or at a fixed time after date, the holder must present for acceptance before the maturity. For a bill payable at a fixed time after sight, the holder should present it for acceptance within one month from the date of issue. Also, if the holder fails to do as required, it will lose its right of recourse to its prior parties.

Obviously, different laws have different stipulations on the time of presentment for payment or acceptance. The date of presentment is up to the law of the specific country where the act of presentment occurs.

The place of presentment The holder must present a bill for payment or acceptance at the place specified on the bill. If there is no such indication, the holder should present it at the drawee's business office. If the drawee has no business office, his residential house will be the place of presentment.

Acceptance

The UK Bill of Exchange Act 1882 defines acceptance of a bill as "a signification by the drawee of his assent to the order of the drawer"①. Acceptance means the drawee's agreement to pay according to the order of the drawer. The US Uniform Commercial Code states that acceptance is "the drawee's signed agreement to pay a draft as presented" and the drawee must write on the draft. According to the Convention Providing a Uniform Law for Bills of Exchange and Promissory Notes (Geneva, 1930), "an acceptance is written on the bill of exchange" and "expressed by the word 'accepted' or any other equivalent term" and signed by the drawee.

By signing his name on the face of a usance bill, the drawee becomes the acceptor and promises to pay when the bill falls due. Acceptance includes two acts by the drawee—to sign on the face of the bill and to deliver it to the person presenting for acceptance. Once the drawee signs his name on the bill and delivers it to the payee or the holder, he is known as the acceptor and primarily liable for the payment of the bill.

---

① a signification by the drawee of his assent to the order of the drawer: 付款人确认他同意按照出票人的指示付款

The UK Bill of Exchange Act 1882 specifies two types of acceptance: general and qualified.①

General acceptance A general acceptance means the acceptor agrees without qualification to the order of the drawer. It usually takes one of the following forms: (1) mere signature of the drawee; (2) signature of the drawee plus the word "accepted"; (3) signature of the drawee plus date; (4) signature of the drawee plus the word 'accepted' and the date; and (5) any of the above four plus such words as "*Payable at Lloyds Bank, Blandton*".

An example of general acceptance is as follows:

Accepted
March 1, 2002
For…Bank
Signed

Qualified acceptance A qualified acceptance is one by which the acceptor agrees to pay a bill at maturity with qualification.

The first type of qualification is a condition. Conditional acceptance means the payment to be made by the acceptor will depend on the payee or the holder's fulfillment of a certain condition as stated. For example:

Accepted
March 1, 2002
Payable providing goods fulfill the…Standard
For…Bank
Signed

The second type of qualified acceptance is partial acceptance, by which the drawee agrees to pay only part of the amount for which the bill is drawn. For instance, where the whole amount stated on the bill is $100, a partial acceptance is written as:

Accepted
March 1, 2002
Payable for the amount of $80 only
For…Bank
Signed

---

① general acceptance: 一般承兑; qualified acceptance: 限制承兑

The third type of qualified acceptance is local acceptance, by which the drawee agrees to effect payment only at a particular specified place. For example:

Accepted
March 1, 2002
Payable at Lloyds Bank, Blandton only
For … Bank
Signed

If there is no the word "only" in the above acceptance, it will be a general acceptance.①

One more qualification is related to time. If a bill is drawn payable three months after date and accepted by the drawee as payable six months after date, it is a time-qualified acceptance. By this acceptance, the drawee postpones the maturity date of the bill.

In the case that a bill is drawn on two or more drawees, the acceptance is made only by one or some of them, rather than by all of them, this acceptance is also perceived as qualified acceptance. For instance, a bill is drawn on four persons jointly and only three of them consent to accept, then their acceptance, if taken by the holder, is known as a qualified one. The three acceptors must be liable for the whole amount of the bill.

The Convention Providing a Uniform Law for Bills of Exchange and Promissory Notes (Geneva, 1930) stipulates that an acceptance is unconditional, but the drawee can restrict it to part of the sum payable. Any modification introduced by an acceptance into the tenor of the bill of exchange operates as a refusal to accept. Nevertheless, the acceptor is bound according to the terms of his acceptance.

Payment

Payment of a bill is generally made by the drawee or the acceptor, but in the event of dishonour the holder may demand payment from any prior indorser or the drawer. However, in order to discharge the liability of the

---

① 如果有 only 则表明仅仅在某家银行支付,就变成了限制性的承兑

drawee or acceptor, the payment of the amount due on a bill must be made to the holder of the instrument. Before explaining the concept of the discharge of a bill, let's see the concept of payment in due course first.

Payment in due course means payment made at or after the maturity of the bill to the holder in good faith and without notice that his title to the bill is defective.① A bill can be paid in due course by *any* party to a bill providing that party pays the holder at or after maturity in good faith and without notice that his title is defective. If the drawee or acceptor of a bill dishonors, the holder may enforce his right of recourse to ask the indorser to pay. If the indorser makes the payment to the holder at maturity in good faith, the indorser makes payment in due course. If the indorser enforces his right of recourse against its prior party the drawer and the drawer is forced to pay him, then the drawer's payment is also called payment in due course.

Then, whose payment can discharge a bill②? The UK Bills of Exchange Act 1882 stipulates that a bill is discharged by payment in due course by or on behalf of the drawee or acceptor. If one repays a loan of £10 to his or her friend, he or she discharges the indebtedness, i. e., the obligation ceases to exist and the transaction commencing with the original loan comes to an end. In the same way, a bill is discharged when the obligation it represents ceases to exist and all rights of action on the bill are extinguished. Thus, the obvious and most usual way of discharging a bill is payment in due course by the drawee or acceptor. After such payment, the whole transaction or series of transactions for which it has served as an instrument of payment are complete and settled. The bill becomes history, a mere voucher evidencing what has happened and how it has been concluded. To make certain that it remains only a voucher and will not be misused in any other way, the drawee or acceptor may cancel the signature

---

① Payment in due course means payment made at or after the maturity of the bill to the holder in good faith and without notice that his title to the bill is defective：正当付款是指在汇票到期日或之后善意地并且在没有注意到持票人的票据权利有缺陷的情况下付款给持票人；payment in due course：正当付款

② discharge a bill：清偿汇票；只有付款人或承兑人的正当付款才能清偿票据

of the drawer.

What about the payment in due course by the parties to a bill other than the drawee or acceptor? Payment in due course by an indorser or the drawer cannot discharge the bill because, if an indorser is compelled to pay the bill, he may likewise recover it from a prior indorser or the drawer and at the same time sue the acceptor for dishonour as the case may be. If the drawer is compelled to pay, he can still sue the acceptor for dishonour. The point here is that there remains a party liable on the bill and the drawer or the indorser can sue him until the drawee or acceptor makes the payment.

Moreover, payment in due course is the payment to the holder. No title to a bill can be obtained where an essential signature has been forged, the person in possession of such a bill is not even a holder and the bill in fact belongs to the person whose signature has been forged. But the person in possession of the bill may be quite ignorant of the prior forgery and deems himself to be the holder and the true owner. No matter whether he is ignorant of the forgery, he may still present the bill to the acceptor and obtain payment before the true owner discovers his loss. Then, what is the position of the acceptor? Since he has not paid the holder, he has not paid in due course. The bill is, therefore, not discharged and he can be compelled to pay again to the true owner. His only remedy is against the person he first paid. But if he pays the holder, no matter whether the latter is the true owner or not, he is not liable to the true owner.

Dishonour

Dishonour by non-acceptance[①] When a bill is duly presented for acceptance and is not accepted within reasonable or specified time, the person presenting it must treat it as dishonoured by non-acceptance. If he does not treat it as dishonoured by non-acceptance, the holder shall lose his right of recourse against the drawer and indorsers. Meanwhile, his prior parties have rights to know as soon as possible whether the drawee has accepted it or whether by reason of non-acceptance they will be called upon to pay the bill.

---

① dishonour by non-acceptance：拒绝承兑

The UK Bills of Exchange Act 1882 considers a bill as dishonoured by non-acceptance when one of the following events occurs: (1) Acceptance is refused; (2) Acceptance cannot be obtained, e. g., where the drawee cannot be found or where he deliberately avoids the presentment; and (3) The drawee is dead or bankrupt or is a fictitious person or a person not having capacity to contract by bill. Once a bill is dishonoured by non-acceptance, the holder's right of recourse against prior parties arises immediately without his having to present it for payment later. That is to say, when a bill is dishonoured by non-acceptance, the right of recourse against the indorsers and the drawer accrues to the holder and presentment for payment is not needed.

Dishonour by non-payment[①] When a bill is duly presented for payment and payment is refused or cannot be obtained, it is considered dishonour by non-payment. Dishonour by non-payment is one of the two cases: (1) The holder presents a sight bill to the drawee for payment, the drawee refuses to pay; (2) The holder presented an accepted bill to the acceptor for payment, the acceptor refuses to pay. Once a bill is dishonoured by non-payment, an immediate right of recourse against the drawer and indorsers accrues to the holder.

Protest

Once a bill is dishonoured by non-acceptance or non-payment, the holder must have the dishonour certified by a notary public within a reasonable time in order to preserve the right of recourse against its prior parties. Such a certificate is called a protest[②].

The Negotiable Instrument Law of Japan, the Convention Providing a Uniform Law for Bills of Exchange and Promissory Notes(Geneva, 1930) and the US Uniform Commercial Code all stipulate that a protest be made in the event of dishonor and before enforcing the right of recourse. The

---

① dishonour by non-payment: 拒绝付款
② protest: 拒绝证书;在遭到拒付或退票时,持票人须在规定的时间内做成拒绝证书才能行使对前手的追索权

UK Bills of Exchange Act 1882 mentions two types of bills: inland and foreign. Where an inland bill① is dishonoured, it may, if the holder thinks fit, be noted for non-acceptance or non-payment as the case may be. It means that it is not necessary to note or protest② any inland bill in order to preserve the right of recourse against the indorsers and the drawer. However, where a foreign bill is dishonoured by non-acceptance or has been accepted but is dishonoured by non-payment, it must be duly protested for non-acceptance or non-payment. If it is not so protested, the drawer and the indorsers are discharged of their liabilities. The Negotiable Instrument Law of the People's Republic of China also stipulates that the holder must present a protest as an evidence of the dishonour before enforcing its right of recourse.

Then, how to make a protest? In making a protest, the holder hands the bill to a notary public who again presents the bill for acceptance or payment, as the case may be, so as to obtain a legal proof of dishonour. If the acceptance or payment is still unobtainable, the notary public draws up a protest, evidencing the demand made to the drawee or acceptor and the answer he receives. The UK Bills of Exchange Act 1882 requires that a protest contain a copy of the bill, the signature of the notary public, the person at whose request the bill is protested, the place and date of protest, the cause or reason for protesting the bill, the demand made, the answer given or the fact that the drawee or acceptor could not be found. This form of protest is recognized by the world wide and international

---

① inland bill: 国内汇票; UK Bills of Exchange Act 1882 对 inland bill 的定义是: An inland bill is a bill which is or on the face of it purports to be (a) both drawn and payable within the British Islands, or (b) drawn within the British Islands upon some person resident therein. 凡是汇票是或者表面上是在英国岛内出票和付款的汇票,或者在英国岛内出票并以某一个居住在英国岛内的人为付款人的,就是岛内汇票。也就是英国的国内汇票,并且规定所有 inland bills 之外的汇票都是 foreign bills,即外国汇票。见 UK Bills of Exchange Act 1882 的第二部分 Bills of Exchange

② note or protest：通知做拒绝证书或做拒绝证书；note 是指汇票在过期之前或者在采取任何程序之前已经被通知即将做成拒绝证书,正式的拒绝证书可以在之后延迟做成。UK Bills of Exchange Act 1882 规定国内汇票在遭到拒付时做通知即可,无需做成拒绝证书

laws demand it as a legal proof of dishonour. Failure to obtain a protest would mean that all parties (excluding the acceptor) would be released from their liability.

The UK Bills of Exchange Act 1882 specifies two cases where even an inland bill need be protested: (1) before any bill is accepted for honour or paid for honour, it must be protested; and (2) where the acceptor becomes bankrupt or insolvent before the bill matures then, although a protest is not essential, it may be advisable 'for better security'.① In the second case, the bill can be accepted for honour as though dishonour by non-acceptance had taken place.

Since it is of little grace for the drawee when a protest is made on his dishonour, the UK Bills of Exchange Act 1882 provides for a procedure called "noting". Similar to a protest, a note is issued by a notary public. The notary public usually re-presents the bill and if the acceptance or payment is still refused, he attaches a slip of paper to the bill, showing the answer he has received from the acceptor, the date, his charges and his initials. A note is much cheaper than a formal protest.

Then how to determine the maturity date of a usuance bill that has been accepted for honour supra protest? The UK Bills of Exchange Act 1882 provides that the maturity of a bill which has been accepted for honour should be calculated from "the date of noting or protesting for non-acceptance." The Convention Providing a Uniform Law for Bills of Exchange and Promissory Notes (Geneva, 1930) also stipulates that the maturity of a bill payable at a fixed period after sight is determined "either by the date of acceptance or by the date of the protest."

As to the time of making protest, different laws have different stipulations. The Convention Providing a Uniform Law for Bills of

---

① (1) before any bill is accepted for honour or paid for honour, it must be protested: 在参加承兑人参加承兑或者参加付款人参加付款之前必须做拒绝证书；(2) where the acceptor becomes bankrupt or insolvent before the bill matures then, although a protest is not essential, it may be advisable 'for better security': 在汇票到期前承兑人破产或者丧失支付能力时，尽管拒绝证书不是必须要做的，但是明智的做法是做成拒绝证书以获得"更好的保障"；UK Bills of Exchange Act 1882 规定国内汇票在这两种情况下需要做成拒绝证书

Exchange and Promissory Notes(Geneva, 1930) states that the protest for non-acceptance should be made "within the limit of time fixed for presentment for acceptance." If in the case that the first presentment takes place on the last day of that time, the protest may nevertheless be drawn up on the next day. Protest for non-payment of a bill payable on a fixed day or at a fixed period after date or sight must be made on one of the two business days following the day on which the bill is due. In the case of a bill payable at sight, the protest must be drawn up under the same conditions as protest for non-acceptance.

The UK Bills of Exchange Act stipulates that the time of noting or protesting may be made on the day of dishonor and must not be later than the next succeeding business day. The Negotiable Instrument Law of Taiwan Province stipulates that protest for non-acceptance should be made within the time limit for presentment for acceptance while protest for non-payment must be made on the same day of dishonour or within 5 days after the date of dishonour. In the case that the holder allows deferred payment, protest for non-payment should be on the last day of the grace period or within 5 days after the last day of the grace period. The Negotiable Instrument Law of the People's Republic of China provides that the time of making a protest should be within 10 days from the date of dishonour.

Notice of Dishonour

In the event of dishonour by non-payment or non-acceptance, the holder must give notice to all the parties who remain liable on the bill that the instrument has been dishonoured.

The UK Bills of Exchange Act 1882 requires that the notice of dishonor be given to the drawer and each indorser, any drawer or indorser to whom such notice is not given is discharged and that the notice be given as soon as the bill is dishonoured and within a reasonable time after the dishonor. The Convention Providing a Uniform Law for Bills of Exchange and Promissory Notes requires that the holder give notice of dishonor to his indorser and to the drawer within the four business days following the day for protest. Every indorsee should notify his indorser of the notice he has received within the two days following the day he receives the notice and the series may go on until the drawer is notified.

Since no prescribed form of notice can be followed, any advice will do so long as the words clearly state that the bill has been dishonoured by the drawee or acceptor. To ensure that every prior party remains liable, the holder should advise all the parties when dishonour occurs. But it is equally effective if the holder gives notice to only his own transferor providing that notice is passed down through indorsers until the payee notifies the drawer.

Drawer	Payee	Indorsers	Holder	Acceptor
A	B	C. D. E. F. G	H	X

For example, where X dishonours the bill, the holder H should send individual notices to all indorsers and the drawer to preserve their liabilities on the bill. But if H only advises G of the dishonour, G gives notice to F, F to E, E to D, D to C, C to B and B to A the drawer, the same result will be achieved. In practice, the latter method is generally adopted since it is fairly certain that prior parties will pass on the notice of dishonour. Any party failing to do so would remain liable to the holder and lose his own right of recourse against the drawer and those who indorsed the bill before him. Nevertheless, a holder to be absolutely safe should give notice of dishonour to all prior parties.

Right of recourse

The UK Bills of Exchange Act 1882 entitles a holder in due course the right to sue and enforce payment against all parties liable on the bill. This is known as the right of recourse which arises in the event of dishonour. The Convention Providing a Uniform Law for Bills of Exchange and Promissory Notes (Geneva, 1930) states that the holder may exercise the right of recourse against the indorsers, the drawer and other parties liable on the instrument in case of dishonour and that the holder may recover from the person against whom he exercises his right of recourse the amount of the bill, the interest from the date of maturity, the expenses of making protest and of the notices given by the holder and other expenses.

Guarantee or aval

According to the Convention Providing a Uniform Law for Bills of Exchange and Promissory Notes(Geneva, 1930), the payment of a bill can be guaranteed by an "aval" as to the whole or part of its amount. Such guarantee can be given by a third person or even by a person who has signed as party to the bill. The guarantee or "aval" is given either on the bill itself or on an attached document.

An "aval" is made by writing the words "good as aval"[①] and signing by the giver of the "aval". The mere signature of the giver of the "aval" on the bill except the signature of the drawer or the drawee is considered as "aval". Usually, an "aval" must specify for whose account it is given. If there is no such indication, it is for the account of the drawer. The guarantor or the giver of "aval" stands surely for the debtor for whose account the "aval" is given, say the drawer, an indorser or the acceptor and assumes his indebtedness to the holder. In other words, the guarantor or the giver of "aval" is bound by the same liability of the party that is guaranteed. When the guarantor is compelled to pay, his right of recourse arises against all the prior parties of the guaranteed.

Different from the Convention Providing a Uniform Law for Bills of Exchange and Promissory Notes(Geneva, 1930), the UK Bills of Exchange Act 1882 and the Negotiable Instrument Law of P. R. China only allow a third party to serve as a guarantor.

Accommodation party According to the UK Bills of Exchange Act 1882, the accommodation party is a person who has signed a bill as drawer, acceptor or indorser without receiving value for that and for the purpose of lending his name to some other person and the accommodation party is

---

① good as aval：作为票据上的保证

liable on the bill to a holder for value.① According to the US Uniform Commercial Code, the accommodation party is the party who signs the instrument for the purpose of incurring liability on the instrument without being a direct beneficiary of the value given for the instrument. The party for whose benefit the instrument is issued for value given is called the accommodated party. It also states that an accommodation party may sign the instrument as drawer, acceptor or indorser. The Convention Providing a Uniform Law for Bills of Exchange and Promissory Notes does not mention the concept of accommodation party.

Let us look at an example: A the drawer makes out a cheque for $100 payable to B the payee, his tailor, for a suit. B specially indorses the cheque to C for wages owing to him. C further specially indorses it to his wife D as a birthday gift. Then, D specially indorses it to E her daughter as a wedding gift. E will not transfer it and becomes the ultimate holder. Even if E gave no value for the cheque, she is still a holder for value, for her prior parties, B and C, gave value in their turns for the cheque. Similarly, when the cheque was in D's possession, D was also a holder for value even if she gave no value to the cheque. In the event of dishonour, however, E in this case cannot sue D or C, since they did not receive value for the cheque. But E can sue A, the drawer and/or B, the payee, for both of them received value for transferring the cheque.

In the same example, C and D were not liable to E if the cheque was dishonoured, for they did not receive value. But C and D could not be classified as accommodation parties since they did not sign the bill with the express purpose of lending their names to someone. The US Uniform Commercial Code stipulates that an accommodation party be obliged to pay the instrument in the capacity in which the accommodation party signs. His

---

① the accommodation party is a person who has signed a bill as drawer, acceptor or indorser without receiving value for that and for the purpose of lending his name to some other person and the accommodation party is liable on the bill to a holder for value: 融通方是指作为出票人、承兑人或背书人在没有收到对价的情况下在票据上签字,出于借自己的名誉给某一个其他的人(accommodated party),融通方对付对价持票人负有债务。accommodated party: 被融通方

obligation may be enforced notwithstanding any statute of frauds and whether or not the accommodation party has received value for the accommodation. Thus, if C and D had signed the instrument with that intention they would have been liable to E.

Let us see another example: A, being pressed for money, drew a 3-month bill on his wealthy friend B with B's prior agreement and B accepted the bill, but A gave no value to B. In accepting the bill, B became an acceptor primarily liable for payment in 3 months' time. Then, A can raise money on the bill by discounting it with C immediately, hoping that in three months' time his financial stringency will disappear and that he will be able to provide B with funds to pay the bill. In this case, B has signed the bill as acceptor to accommodate A. Thus, B is an accommodation party. This method of obtaining funds employed by A is known as "kite flying" or "raising the wind".

It is essential to observe that an accommodation party is not liable to the party accommodated since the former receives no value from the latter. Thus, in the second example, when the bill matures, C can enforce payment against A and B. If A refuses to pay the bill at maturity, C may sue A or obtain the money from B. If he chooses the latter, B must pay the bill and B's payment will discharge the bill. But if B refuses to pay, A has no right to sue B since A gave no value to B in drawing the bill on B.

Accommodation bill[①] Not all bills bearing the signature of an accommodation party are accommodation bills. For example, A is the drawer, X the acceptor and B the payee. B asks C a wealthy man to indorse the bill so that the bill can easily be discounted at Bank D. If X the acceptor fails to pay, Bank D can force payment from any prior party including B the party accommodated. If it compels B to pay, then the bill is not discharged by his payment since B would still have the right to sue the acceptor for payment. In this example, the accommodation party is the indorser and the bill is not an accommodation bill. In another example, X

---

① accommodation bill: 融通汇票。只有在票据上的融通方(accommodation party)是承兑人、被融通方(accommodated party)是出票人时，该汇票才是融通汇票

accepts a bill for accommodation of A the drawer, X is the accommodation party and A the accommodated party. B is the payee, C an indorsee and D the eventual holder. If X the acceptor refuses to pay the bill at maturity, then A the drawer is in next in order of liability. If D compels A to pay, the bill is discharged since X is not liable to A. Thus the bill is discharged by payment by the party accommodated. That is to say, only when the accommodation party is the acceptor and the accommodated party is the drawer will a bill be an accommodation bill.

Acceptance for honour supra protest

According to the UK Bills of Exchange Act 1882, acceptance for honour supra protest[①] means that, if a bill of exchange has been protested for non-acceptance or for better security and is not overdue, any person, not being a party already liable on the bill, may, with the consent of the holder, by writing on the bill, accept the bill for honour of any party to the bill. A person desiring to accept for honour must indicate that he accepts the protested bill for honour of a particular party. Where an acceptance for honour does not expressly state for whose honour it is made, it is deemed to be an acceptance for honour of the drawer. As discussed earlier, based on the UK Bills of Exchange Act, where a bill payable after sight is accepted for honour, its maturity is calculated from the date of protesting for non-acceptance, not from the date of the acceptance for honour.

It can be imagined what inconvenience will be caused to all parties to a bill, particularly the drawer, when the drawee refuses to accept the bill. The holder will probably reclaim from his transferor, thus setting in motion a series of claims from transferee to transferor until the drawer eventually pays the payee. The whole process is the reverse of the original series of negotiations of the bill. In order to avoid such inconvenience, the drawer sometimes indicates a person to whom the bill should be presented "in case of need", so that the bill can be accepted by someone if the drawee fails to

---

① acceptance for honour supra protest：参加承兑，即在持票人能做成拒绝证书之后，行使追索权之前有人能参加承兑；supra protest：在做好拒绝证书的基础上

accept. Such a person is called a "referee in case of need[①]."

According to the UK Bills of Exchange Act 1882, besides "a referee in case of need", anyone that is not already liable on the bill can accept it for honour, but the holder can refuse an acceptance for honour without prejudicing himself in any way. According to the Convention Providing a Uniform Law for Bills of Exchange and Promissory Notes(Geneva, 1930), however, "the person intervening may be a third party, even the drawee or, save the acceptor, a party already liable on the bill of exchange". This means that even if a party that is already liable on the bill may intervene and accept the bill for honour.

Liability of acceptor for honour According to UK Bills of Exchange Act 1882, the acceptor for honour is liable to the holder and to the indorsers subsequent to the party for whose honour he accepts the bill in the same manner as such party. By acceptance for honour, the acceptor for honour engages that he will, on due presentment, pay the bill according to the tenor of his acceptance, if it is not paid by the drawee, provided it has been duly presented for payment and protested for non-payment and that he receives notice of these facts.

Presentment to acceptor for honour When a dishonoured bill has been accepted for honour, when it matures and before it is presented for payment to the acceptor for honour, the bill must be presented for payment to the original drawee, once again the bill has been dishonoured and a protest for non-payment is made. Before the acceptor for honour consents to pay the bill at its maturity, he must be given evidence that the bill has been presented again to the original drawee, this time for payment and that payment was refused and the bill has been protested again for non-payment.

According to the UK Bills of Exchange Act 1882, when the address of the acceptor for honour is in the same place where the bill is protested for non-payment, the bill must be presented to him not later than the day

---

① a referee in case of need：需要时可以解决问题的人,可以随时准备参加承兑的人(acceptor for honour)

following its maturity; when the address of the acceptor for honour is in some place other than the place where it was protested for non-payment, the bill must be forwarded to him not later than the day following its maturity for presentment.

Payment for honour supra protest[①]

The UK Bills of Exchange Act 1882 stipulates that, where a bill has been protested for non-payment, any party may intervene and pay it supra protest for the honour of any party liable on the bill including the drawee. The person doing so is called a payer for honour. When two or more persons offer to pay a bill for honour of different parties, the person whose payment will discharge most parties to the bill shall have the preference. When the payer for honour has paid the bill, all parties subsequent to the party for whose honour it is paid are discharged of their liabilities, then the payer for honour becomes the holder and has right to claim compensation from the party for whose honour he pays. If the holder refuses to receive payment supra protest, he shall lose his right of recourse against the party for whose honour the payment is to be made.

For example, a bill that has been accepted but dishonoured by non-payment, A is the drawer, B, C, D, E and F are indorsers and G is the holder. Suppose X offers to pay it for honour of C and G takes the payment. Then, D, E and F are discharged from liability. X, however, obtains the rights to enforce payment from C and all the parties who would have been liable to C as if C has paid the bill himself, viz., A, B and Z. In the same example, if a new person Y offers to pay for honour of the drawer, then Y's offer would have received preference over that of X since Y's payment for honour would have discharged B, C, D, E and F. To continue the same example, if G the holder had refused the offer of X to pay the bill for honour, then D, E and F would have been released from liability on the bill just as if the offer had been taken.

---

① payment supra protest: 参加付款,在持票人做成拒绝证书之后行使追索权之前参加付款; payer for honour: 参加付款人

Classification of bills of exchange

Foreign bill and inland bill

Based on the UK Bills of Exchange Act 1882, a bill both drawn and payable within the British islands or drawn within the British islands on some person residing in the British islands is an inland bill. It means that so long as the drawer and the drawee are in the British islands, the bill is an inland bill. Any other bill not satisfying the condition is a foreign bill. This classification is based on the places of issue and payment. So we can say that when the places of issue and payment are in the same country, the bill is domestic; otherwise, it is international.

Sight bill and usance bill

Bills of exchange may be drawn payable at sight, at a fixed period after sight, at a fixed period after date or at a fixed future date. Based on the tenor, bills of exchange are classified into two types: sight bills and usance bills. Sight bills are payable at sight, on demand or on presentation while usance bills are payable at a fixed or determinable future time. Sight bills are sometimes called sight drafts or demand drafts.[①] Usance bills are also called term drafts or time drafts.

Banker's draft and trader's bill[②]

Banker's draft or bank draft is drawn by a bank on another bank, i.e., both the drawer and drawee are banks. Trader's bill or trade bill is drawn by a trader on another trader or on a bank, i.e., the drawer is a trader and the drawee may be a trader or a bank. Since banker's credit is more acceptable than trader's credit, banker's drafts are more desirable than trader's bills.

---

① The UK Bills of Exchange Act 1882 用 bill of exchange 来表示汇票，而 US Uniform Commercial Code 用 draft 一词来表示汇票并认为 draft 有很多种形式，bill of exchange 是其中一种

② banker's draft and trader's bill：银行汇票和商业汇票。银行汇票的出票人和付款人均为银行；商业汇票的出票人是个人或企业，付款人则没有限制，可以是个人、企业或银行

Banker's acceptance and trader's acceptance①

Banker's acceptance is a usance bill that is drawn on a bank and has been accepted by the drawee bank while trader's acceptance is a usance bill that is drawn on a trader and has been accepted by the drawee trader. Since banker's credit is more acceptable than trader's credit, banker's acceptance is more acceptable than trader's acceptance. Nevertheless, be it trader's acceptance or banker's acceptance, it is the financial strength of the acceptor that matters.

Clean bill and documentary bill②

Clean bill is a bill without any shipping documents accompanying. Clean bills are used under clean collection in which no shipping documents are attached to the bill. Documentary bill is a bill to which shipping documents are attached. Documentary bills are often used under documentary collection or documentary credit.

2.6 Promissory Notes

Definition

The UK Bills of Exchange Act 1882 defines promissory note as "an unconditional promise in writing made by one person to another signed by the maker, engaging to pay, on demand or at a fixed or determinable future time, a sum certain in money to or to the order of, a specified person or to bearer". ③

---

① banker's acceptance and trader's acceptance: 银行承兑汇票和商业承兑汇票。如果远期汇票的付款人是银行并且由付款行(drawee bank)承兑,该汇票则成为银行承兑汇票。如果远期汇票的付款人是个人或企业并且由付款人或付款企业承兑,该汇票则成为商业承兑汇票

② clean bill and documentary bill: 光票汇票和跟单汇票。附带运输单据(shipping documents)的汇票是跟单汇票,如跟单托收和跟单信用证项下的汇票;不附带运输单据的汇票则为光票

③ an unconditional promise in writing made by one person to another signed by the maker, engaging to pay, on demand or at a fixed or determinable future time, a sum certain in money to or to the order of a specified person or to bearer: 一人(出票人)向另一人(收款人)签发的保证在见票时或在一个未来可以确定的时间支付一定的金额给指定的人(收款人)或按照指定的人的指示支付或者支付给来人的书面承诺

The Convention Providing a Uniform Law for Bills of Exchange and Promissory Notes (Geneva, 1930) stipulates that promissory note should contain: (1) The term "promissory note" inserted in the body of the instrument and expressed in the language employed in drawing up the instrument; (2) An unconditional promise to pay a determinate sum of money; (3) A statement of the time of payment; (4) A statement of the place where payment is to be made; (5) The name of the person to whom or to whose order payment is to be made; (6) A statement of the date and of the place where the promissory note is issued; and (7) The signature of the person who issues the instrument (maker).

According to the Negotiable Instrument Law of the People's Republic China, promissory note is an instrument issued by the drawer who promises to pay unconditionally at sight a fixed amount of money to the payee or holder. Thus, promissory notes stipulated in this law are payable at sight.

Promissory notes are different from bills of exchange in that promissory notes have only two basic parties—the maker and the payee. Hence promissory notes are also called two-party instruments. According to the UK Bills of Exchange Act 1882, the maker of a promissory note "engages that he will pay it according to the tenor and is precluded from denying to a holder in due course the existence of the payee and his then capacity to indorse." The maker is the drawee and the right of the holder in due course is protected against the defectiveness of his indorser.

Essential items of a promissory note

Based on the UK Bills of Exchange Act 1882, the Uniform Law for Bills of Exchange and Promissory Notes (Geneva, 1930) and other laws on negotiable instruments, promissory notes usually contain the following required items: (1) The word "promissory note" clearly indicated; (2) An unconditional promise to pay; (3) Name of the payee; (4) Place and date of issue; (5) Tenor; (6) A sum certain in money; (7) Place of payment; and (8) Signature of the maker.

Specimen of a promissory note

PROMISSORY NOTE
US＄1,000.00　　　　　　　　　　　　　　Shanghai, March 5, 2003 At 90 days after date we promise to pay ABC Company or order the sum of one thousand pounds only. 　　　　　　　　　　　　　　　　　　　　　　　　　　　For… Bank 　　　　　　　　　　　　　　　　　　　　　　　　　　　(Signed)

Joint notes vs. joint and several notes[①]

The UK Bills of Exchange Act 1882 states that a promissory note may be issued by two or more makers and the makers may be liable on the note jointly or jointly and severally. Where the makers are liable on the note jointly, the note is a joint note. Where the makers are liable on the note jointly and severally, the note is a joint and several note.

　　How to distinguish a joint note from a joint and several note? Where a note is issued by two or more makers and the unconditional promise to pay is expressed as "I promise to pay" and signed by two or more makers, the note is a joint and several note. Where a note is expressed as "we jointly and severally promise to pay" and signed by two or more makers, the note is also a joint and several note. However, where a note is expressed as "we promise to pay" and signed by two or more makers, the note is a joint note.

Specimen of a joint and several note[②]

￡200　　　　　　　　　　　　　　　　　　　Birmingham, 1 Jan 1983 I promise to pay to the order of John Davis on demand the sum of two hundred pounds. 　　　　　　　　　　　　　　　　　　　　　　　　　　　George Hallam 　　　　　　　　　　　　　　　　　　　　　　　　　　　John Douglas 　　　　　　　　　　　　　　　　　　　　　　　　　　　Charles Harrison

---

　　① joint note：出票人共同负责的本票；joint and several note：出票人共同并分别负责的本票

　　② Dudley Richardson. *Guide to Negotiable Instruments and the Bills of Exchange Acts*, seventh edition. London: Butterworths, 1983, p. 157

Specimen of a joint and several note[①]

> £1,000   Derby 1 Jan 1983
> Six months after date we jointly and severally promise to pay the bearer the sum of one thousand pounds.
>
> > Frank Scott
> > Leslie White

Specimen of a joint note[②]

> £700   Leicester 1 Jan 1983
> Ninety days after date we promise to pay William Smith or order the sum of seven hundred pounds.
>
> > James Harrison
> > John Martin
> > Florence Brown

The difference between a joint note and a joint and several note

As far as the makers are concerned, there is little difference between a joint note and a joint and several note. No matter whether the makers undertake their liability jointly or jointly and severally, each maker is *individually* liable for the full amount of the note and, if called on to pay, any of the makers must pay the holder the whole amount involved individually. After that, the maker who has made the payment can obtain from his fellow-makers whatever is their share of the liability.

However, there are some differences between the two kinds of notes. The first difference lies in that in the case of a joint note the death of a maker extinguishes the liability as far as he is concerned and the holder of the note will have no claim against the deceased maker's personal representatives.

Another difference is related to the holder's suing right. In the event of the makers' refusal to pay, the holder can sue the makers and enforce

---

① Dudley Richardson. *Guide to Negotiable Instruments and the Bills of Exchange Acts*, seventh edition. London: Butterworths, 1983, 157

② Dudley Richardson. *Guide to Negotiable Instruments and the Bills of Exchange Acts*, seventh edition. London: Butterworths, 1983, 157

payment. If the note is a joint and several note, the holder can sue each one of the makers in turn. For example, if A, B and C are the makers of a joint and several note, the holder may decide to sue A alone. He will probably win his case and obtain an order of the court against A. But supposing A becomes bankrupt immediately and pays only one penny in the pound, then the holder can sue one of the remaining makers, say B, for the amount unpaid. If the same fate overtakes B, the holder can bring a third action in court and sue C for the remainder. Of course, if he so chooses, he can sue two jointly or all three makers together.

In a joint note, however, the holder has only one right of action, i.e., he can sue in court only once. He can sue one maker alone or sue some but not all of the makers or sue all the makers together. If he fails to obtain satisfaction by his action in court, he will be allowed no second attempt. Thus, it is wise for the holder of a joint note to sue all the makers in his one action.

In other words, there is only one debt in the case of a joint note and thus only one right of action while there are as many debts as many makers in the case of a joint and several note and thus as many rights of action. But a holder is not allowed to recover more than the full amount of the note.

Types of promissory notes

Trader's note[①]

A promissory note which is made by a trader is a trader's note. A trader may be an individual or an enterprise. A trader's note may be payable on demand or at a fixed future time. Since the maker is a trader, especially when the note is made by a small enterprise, the note is not as acceptable and negotiable as a banker's note.

Banker's note[②]

A promissory note which is made by a bank is a banker's note. The bank which makes the note engages to pay on demand or at a fixed future time to or to the order of a specified person. A banker's note payable at a fixed future time is

---

① trader's note：商业本票，出票人（maker）为个人或企业
② banker's note：银行本票，出票人（maker）为银行

rarely used, though. A banker's note payable on demand is also referred to as "Cashier's Order". It can be converted into cash over the counter. Promissory notes discussed in the Negotiable Instrument Law of the People Republic of China only refer to banker's notes.

International money order①

A money order is a financial instrument issued by a bank, allowing an individual named on the order to receive a specified amount of cash on demand. So, it is a type of banker's note. International money orders are often used by those who travel around the world but do not have cheque-writing accounts.

Central banker's note②

In some western countries, central bankers are authorized to make bearer notes payable on demand with fixed amount of money. Since the makers are central banks, they are also banker's notes.

Negotiable certificates of deposit③

A certificate of deposit (CD) is an instrument containing an acknowledgment by a bank that the bank has received a certain amount of money and promises to repay it. Certificates of deposits are also notes made by banks. Usually, negotiable CDs are short-term, interest-bearing certificates issued by banks and are popular among those who like low-risk and straightforward investments. Many advisors consider CDs as safe investments suitable for diversifying portfolios.

Differences between bills of exchange and promissory notes

The basic difference between a bill and a note is that the former is an order by the drawer to the drawee to pay the payee while the latter is a promise by the maker (i.e., the drawer) to pay the payee. Obviously, bills are three-party instruments while notes two-party instruments. In spite of this, most of the acts relating to bills are relevant to notes except for those

---

① international money order: 国际小额本票
② central banker's note: 中央银行本票
③ negotiable certificate of deposit: 可流通转让的存单

related to acceptance, such as presentment for acceptance, acceptance and acceptance for honour supra protest. The differences between bills and notes are described is Table 2.1.

Table 2.1 Differences between bills of exchange and promissory notes

Bills of exchange	Promissory note
(1) An order to pay.	(1) A promise to pay.
(2) A three-party instrument.	(2) A two-party instrument.
(3) Where payable after date, a bill is generally accepted.	(3) Never accepted.
(4) Where payable after sight, a bill must be presented for acceptance to fix the maturity date of the bill. Such presentment for acceptance is necessary to render the prior parties liable.	(4) Never accepted. However, according to the Convention Providing a Uniform Law for Bills of Exchange and Promissory Notes (Geneva, 1930), the maker of a promissory note is bound in the same manner as an acceptor of a bill. A promissory note payable at a certain time after sight must be presented for the visa of the maker within the limits of time. The visa date is used to fix the maturity date of the note.
(5) A usance bill can be accepted for honour supra protest.	(5) Never accepted.
(6) Bills are drawn in a set, say two copies.	(6) Notes are made in one copy.
(7) Foreign bills need protesting on dishonour to retain the liability of prior parties.	(7) The UK Bills of Exchange Act 1882 states that, where a foreign note is dishonoured, protest is not necessary. The Convention Providing a Uniform Law for Bills of Exchange and Promissory Notes (Geneva, 1930) requires a promissory note protested in case of non-payment.
(8) Before acceptance, the drawer is primarily liable for payment, but after acceptance the acceptor becomes primarily liable for payment.	(8) The maker is the party liable primarily for payment.
(9) Where there are two or more acceptors in a bill, the acceptors are always jointly liable.	(9) Where there are two or more makers, they may be liable jointly or jointly and severally.

2.7 Cheques

Definition

The UK Bills of Exchange Act 1882 defines a cheque as "a bill of exchange drawn on a banker payable on demand."[①] It is considered as a special type of bill of exchange, thus a cheque is similar to a bill of exchange except for the drawee and the tenor. The US Uniform Commercial Code defines a cheque as a "draft, other than a documentary draft, payable on demand and drawn on a bank." Similarly, it also perceives a cheque as a type of bill of exchange drawn on a bank and payable on demand.

The Convention Providing a Uniform Law for Cheques (Geneva, 1930) defines a cheque by stipulating its contents: (1) The term "cheque" inserted in the body of the instrument and expressed in the language employed in drawing up the instrument; (2) An unconditional order to pay a determinate sum of money; (3) The name of the person who is to pay (drawee); (4) A statement of the place where payment is to be made; (5) A statement of the date when and the place where the cheque is drawn; and (6) The signature of the person who draws the cheque (drawer). It further stipulates that a cheque be "drawn on a banker holding funds at the disposal of the drawer and in conformity with an agreement, express or implied, whereby the drawer is entitled to dispose of those funds by cheque." It also stipulates that a cheque be payble at sight.

According to the Negotiable Instrument Law of the People's Republic of China, a cheque is an instrument made by a drawer who orders the drawee bank with which the drawer maintains a cheque deposit account to unconditionally pay at sight a fixed amount of money to the payee or holder.

Similar to a bill of exchange, a cheque is a three-party instrument: the

---

① a bill of exchange drawn on a banker payable on demand: 即期的以银行为付款人的汇票

drawer (the person who writes the cheque), the drawee (the bank on which the cheque is drawn and to which the order to pay is given) and the payee (the person to whom the drawee bank pays). However, cheques are all payable on demand or at sight.

Essential items of a cheque

Based on the different stipulations in different negotiable instrument laws, a cheque usually contains the following items: (1) The word "Cheque" clearly indicated; (2) An unconditional order to pay in writing; (3) The name and address of the drawee bank; (4) The signature of the drawer; (5) Place and date of issue; (6) A sum certain in money; and (8) Name of the payee.

Specimen of a cheque

```
                    ... BANK LIMITED
CH. NO. 123456                                    4 May 1993
Pay David Chan ****************  or bearer   HK$1,000.00
The sum of Hong Kong Dollars one thousand only.
                    Peter Li
A/C No. 834-0-000111-8
```

Types of cheques

Cashier's cheque[①]

The US Uniform Commercial Code defines a cheque drawn by and on the same bank as a "cashier's" cheque.

Teller's cheque[②]

The US Uniform Commercial Code defines a cheque drawn by a bank and on another bank as a "teller's" cheque. In the US, the instrument described by the term "money order" is also a cheque.

---

① cashier's cheque: 出纳支票,《美国统一商法典》把出票人和付款人是同一家银行的支票称为出纳支票

② teller's cheque: 柜员支票,《美国统一商法典》把出票人和付款人是不同银行的支票称为柜员支票

Traveler's cheque[①]

The US Uniform Commercial Code defines a traveler's cheque as an instrument that is payable on demand and drawn on or payable at or through a bank. As a condition to payment, it requires a countersignature by a person whose specimen signature appears on the instrument.

Crossed cheques[②]

According to the UK Bills of Exchange Act 1882, crossed cheques bear two parallel lines on the face. A crossing on a cheque is in effect an instruction by the drawer or holder to the drawee bank to pay a bank only. Thus, a crossed cheque will not be paid over the counter of the drawee bank and must be presented for payment through a collecting bank. The drawee bank also acts as the collecting bank if both the drawer and the payee maintain current accounts with the drawee bank. The cheques bearing no crossing are uncrossed or open cheques. The UK Bills of Exchange Act 1882 stipulates two types of crossed cheques: general and special.

The Convention Providing a Uniform Law for Cheques (Geneva, 1930) also states that a crossing takes the form of two parallel lines drawn on the face of the cheque. The drawer or holder of a cheque may cross it and the crossed cheque generally can be paid by the drawee only to a bank or to a customer of the drawee. The law also mentions two types of crossing: general and special[③].

The following discussion on general and special crossed cheques is based on the UK Bills of Exchange Act 1882.

General crossing A general crossing on a cheque specifies no name of the collecting bank and means that the cheque can be collected through any bank. The forms of a generally crossed cheque are as follows:

---

① traveler's cheque：旅行支票,《美国统一商法典》把见票即付的以另一家银行付款人或者通过另一家银行获得付款的支票称为旅行支票

② crossed cheque：划线支票,支票的票面上有两条平行的线,划线支票不得取现,只能通过银行转账

③ general crossing：普通划线;special crossing：特殊划线

a.

The effect is to make a cheque payable only through another bank, i.e., the money of the cheque must be deposited into a bank account for clearing. Since no name of the bank is indicated here, any bank can do.

b.

The effect is also to make a cheque payable only through another bank. The words 'and Coy.' between the two lines are a relic of early banking days and today are quite unnecessary.

c.

When the term "Not negotiable" are added to a crossed cheque, it has the effect that, if transferred, the transferee gets no better title than the transferor.

d.

"A/C payee" is an instruction to the collecting bank to collect only for the payee's account.

e.

A cheque bearing such a crossing is not negotiable and must be paid through the payee's account.

Special crossing A special crossing usually contains the name of a bank and means that the funds can only be collected through the named bank. In practice, only one name of a bank is allowed, but the named bank can collect the funds through another bank by making another special crossing. But a cheque only can bear no more than two special crossings. The forms of special crossings are as follows:

a.

The effect of such a crossing is that the cheque can only be collected through the Midland Bank Ltd.

b.

Such a special crossing means that the cheque can only be collected through the Midland Bank Ltd. and the funds should be paid to the payee's account.

c.

This special crossing means that the cheque can only be collected through the Midland Bank Ltd. and not negotiable.

d.

The effect of such a crossing is that the cheque can only be collected through the Midland Bank Ltd., not negotiable and must be paid to the payee's account.

According to the UK Bills of Exchange Act 1882, the name of a bank across the cheque without two parallel lines also constitutes a special crossing.

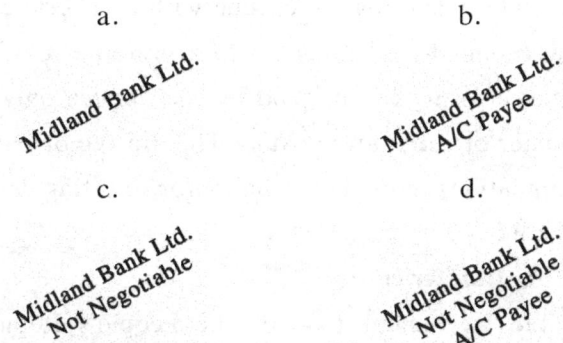

The UK Bills of Exchange Act 1882 states that the crossing may be made by the drawer, the payee or the holder. In making out a cheque, the drawer may cross it generally or specially. Where a cheque is not crossed by the drawer, the payee may cross it generally or specially. Where a cheque is crossed generally by the drawer or the indorser, the holder may cross it specially. Where a cheque is crossed generally or specially, the holder may add words "not negotiable" in the crossing. Where a cheque is crossed specially, the bank to which it is crossed may make a special crossing to another banker for collection. Where a cheque is not crossed or generally crossed and the cheque is sent to a bank for collection, the bank may make a special crossing to itself.

According to the UK Bills of Exchange Act 1882, where a cheque is crossed generally, the drawee bank must pay it to a bank. If it fails to pay a bank but pays someone who is not the true owner, or even though it pays the holder, it will be liable to repay the true owner for his loss. However, if it fails to pay a bank and yet pays the true owner, it is perfectly safe. The danger of not paying a crossed cheque to a bank arises only when the drawee bank does not pay the true owner.

The Convention Providing a Uniform Law for Cheques (Geneva, 1930)① also has stipulations on general and special crossing. The general crossing consists of the two lines only or the two lines with the term "banker" or some equivalent word inserted. The special crossing contains the name of a banker between the two lines. Also, a general crossing may be converted into a special crossing, but a special crossing may not be converted into a general crossing. A cheque with a general crossing can be paid by the drawee only to a banker or to a customer of the drawee. A cheque with special crossing can be paid by the drawee only to the named banker or a customer of the drawee bank. The drawee or banker who fails to observe the stipulations in the law is liable for resulting damage up to the amount of the cheque.

Cash cheque vs. transfer cheque

The Negotiable Instrument Law of the People's Republic of China stipulates that a cheque may be used to withdraw cash or to transfer funds through accounts, i.e., it has two types: cash and transfer. A cash cheque can only be used for cashing while a transfer cheque only in account transfer. The latter is somewhat similar to a generally crossed cheque.

Certified cheques

The US Uniform Commercial Code defines a certified cheque as a cheque "accepted by the bank on which it is drawn."② "Acceptance" is made by the drawee bank by writing on the cheque indicating that the cheque is certified. Of course, the drawee bank has no obligation to certify the cheque and may refuse to certify the cheque, which is not considered as dishonour.

Once a cheque is certified, the bank which has certified it must pay the cheque and all the other parties including the drawer are released of the liability on the cheque. Even if the certified bank refuses to pay, the holder

---

① cash cheque vs. transfer cheque: 现金支票和转账支票

② The Convention Providing a Uniform Law for Cheques (Geneva, 1930) stipulates that a cheque cannot be accepted. The UK Bills of Exchange Act 1882 also thinks that a cheque cannot be accepted

may not enforce his right of recourse against its prior parties and the drawer. The US Uniform Commercial Code and the Negotiable Instrument Law of Japan have such stipulations on certified cheques. However, neither the UK Bills of Exchange Act 1882 nor the Convention Providing a Uniform Law for Cheques(Geneva, 1930) has mentioned certified cheques.

Differences between cheques and bills of exchange

Since the UK Bills of Exchange Act 1882 and the US Uniform Commercial Code both describe a cheque as a bill of exchange drawn on a bank and payable on demand. Thus all the acts relating to bills of exchange are suitable to cheques except for those related to acceptance. The differences between bills and cheques are illustrated in Table 2.2.

Table 2.2 Differences between cheques and bills of exchange

Cheque	Bill of exchange
(1) The drawer maintains a cheque-writing account with the drawee bank.	(1) No specific requirement. The drawer may be a trader or a bank.
(2) The drawee is the bank with which the drawer maintains a cheque-writing account.	(2) No specific requirement. The drawee may be a trader or a bank.
(3) A payment instrument.	(3) Both payment and credit instrument.
(4) According to the US Uniform Commercial Code and the Negotiable Instrument Law of Japan, the drawer, indorsers and the drawee bank are all secondarily liable on the cheque. Once a cheque is certified, the drawee bank that has certified the cheque becomes the principal obligor and all other parties to the cheque are not liable on the cheque.	(4) The drawer of a sight bill or a usance bill before acceptance is the principal obligor. The acceptor of an accepted bill is the principal obligor.
(5) A cheque can be certified or guaranteed. The US Uniform Commercial Code considers "certified" as "acceptance".	(5) A bill can be accepted, guaranteed or accepted for honour supra protest.
(6) A cheque can be cancelled before payment.	(6) After acceptance, the payment is irrevocable.
(7) A cheque is payable on demand.	(7) A bill may be payable on demand or at a determinable future time.

3 Remittance

3.1 Definition

Remittance, a frequently used payment method in international trade, refers to the transfer of funds from one party to another among different countries. In this chapter, remittance particularly means that a bank at the request of its customer transfers a certain sum of money to its overseas branch or correspondent bank and instructs it to pay a named person domiciled in that country. The procedures of remittance are: (1) The remitter submits the funds to the remitting bank; (2) The remitting bank remits the funds to the paying bank; (3) The paying bank makes the payment to the payee or beneficiary.① Remittance can be used for both trade and non-trade payments. According to the directions of the funds transfer and payment instrument, remittance can be divided into remittance and reverse remittance②. Remittance means that the direction of the funds transfer is the same as that of the payment instrument, while reverse remittance means that funds transfer is in the opposite direction to the payment instrument. Moreover, a remittance is perceived as an outward remittance③ by the remitting but inward remittance④ by the paying bank.

---

① remitter: 汇款人; remitting bank: 汇出行; paying bank: 汇入行,解付行; payee or beneficiary: 收款人,受益人
② remittance and reverse remittance: 顺汇和逆汇
③ outward remittance: 汇出汇款
④ inward remittance: 汇入汇款

3.2 Parties to a remittance

Remitter

A remitter, also called the payer, is the person who requests his bank to remit funds to the payee or beneficiary in a foreign country. The remitter may be a debtor, importer or principal.① In remitting funds, a remitter first submits a remittance application which, upon acceptance by the remitting bank, evidences a contract between the remitter and the remitting bank. In the application, the remitter specifies the name and address of the payee, the account number of the payee, if possible, the name and address of the payee's bank, the currency and amount of the funds that will be remitted and the type of remittance② selected by the remitter. Besides, the remitter must submit with the application the same amount of funds in cash or other valid payment evidence. The remitter assumes the expenses incurred by the remittance.

Remitting bank

A remitting bank is a bank that transfers funds at the request of a remitter to its correspondent or its branch in another country and instructs the latter to pay a certain amount of money to the payee or beneficiary. The remitting bank is a bank in the place where the debtor or importer resides. Upon acceptance by the remitting bank of the remittance application, the application becomes the contract binding the remitter and the remitting bank. The remitting bank must do as instructed in the application until the whole remittance is finished. If there is any delay or other mistakes, so long as the remitting bank has conducted strictly according to the remitter's

---

① debtor, importer or principal: 债务人,进口商或委托人

② the name and address of the payee: 收款人的名称和地址;the account number of the payee, if possible: 收款人的账号,如果可能的话; the name and address of the payee's bank: 收款人银行的名称和地址; the currency and amount of the funds that will be remitted: 汇款资金的币种和金额;the type of remittance: 汇款的类型

payment order and the paying bank has done according to the remitting bank's payment order, it is the remitter who assumes the losses incurred. Therefore, in order to ensure the safety and efficiency of remittance, a remitting bank need examine the contents of the remittance application carefully.

Paying bank

A paying bank is a bank that is entrusted by the remitting bank in the payment order to pay a certain amount of money to the payee or beneficiary. The paying bank is a bank in the place where the payee or beneficiary resides. The paying bank must act in strict compliance with the payment order sent by the remitting bank; otherwise, it will assume the consequences. Upon receipt of the payment order, the paying bank should authenticate the relevant signature or test key to ensure its genuineness. Usually, the paying bank will not effect payment to the payee until it receives the funds from the remitting bank.

Payee or beneficiary

A payee or beneficiary is a person who is addressed to receive the funds. The payee may be the exporter, the creditor or even the remitter himself.

3.3 Types of remittance

Based on the means of transferring funds, a remittance usually falls into one of the three types: Mail Transfer(M/T), Telegraphic Transfer (T/T) and Demand Draft(D/D).

Mail transfer

Mail transfer means that the remitting bank on the request of the remitter transfers the funds by mailing a payment order or advice to authorize the paying bank to make payment to the payee or beneficiary. Mail transfer is typically used for remittances of small sums or of little urgency.

Since the payment order is sent to the paying bank by mail, M/T is cheap but slow. Whether M/T is used solely depends on the remitter. Figure 3.1 explains the detailed procedures of mail transfer.

(1) The remitter fills in the application form, submits the proceeds to the bank and pays the commission for remittance;

(2) Upon receipt of the application form, the funds and the commission, the remitting bank offers the remitter a receipt;

(3) The remitting bank sends a payment order or advice by mail to the paying bank, instructing the paying bank to make payment to the payee;

(4) Upon receipt of the payment order and after authenticating the signature, the paying bank notifies the payee of the payment order or advice;

(5) Upon the payment, the payee provides the paying bank with a receipt; and

(6) The paying bank sends the debit advice and the payment receipt from the payee to the remitting bank.

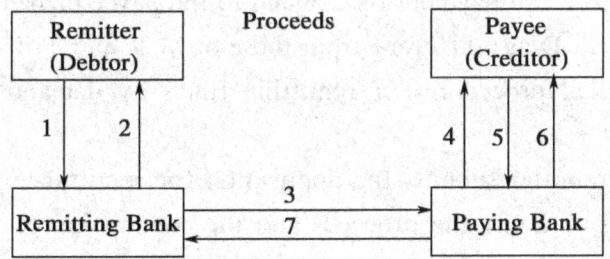

Figure 3.1　Flowchart of the Remittance by M/T

Telegraphic transfer

Telegraphic transfer means that the remitting bank sends the payment order to the paying bank by cable, telex, or SWIFT,① and is referred to as cable transfer or telegraphic transfer.

In a T/T, the remitter submits the remittance application. Based on the instruction of the remitter, the remitting bank sends a payment order or advice by cable, telex or SWIFT to the paying bank, entrusting the paying

---

① cable, telex or SWIFT：电报、电传或 SWIFT；SWIFT：环球同业银行金融电讯协会的通讯系统

bank to make the payment to the payee or beneficiary. Upon receipt of the payment order, the paying bank should authenticate the test keys to make sure its realness.

T/T is safe and fast because the time when funds are kept with the bank is very limited. The payment order sent by the remitting bank can reach the paying bank within one or two days. If the payment order is sent by cable, the fees are based on the number of words and, if by telex the fees are based on the time consumed. Thus, the cost of T/T is more expensive than that of M/T. Even so, it is still a desirable way of remitting funds of large sums or emergency.

Demand draft[①]

In selecting demand draft, a remitter instructs the remitting bank to draw a demand draft on its affiliate or branch bank and to further instruct the drawee bank to make payment on demand to the payee or beneficiary. The procedures of D/D are different from those of M/T and T/T.

The detailed procedures of remitting funds by demand draft are as follows:

(1) The remitter submits the application for remittance that specifies that D/D will be used, the proceeds and the commission to the remitting bank;

(2) Upon receipt of them, the remitting bank draws a demand draft and gives it back to the remitter;

(3) The remitter sends the demand draft directly to the payee, instructing the payee to present the draft for payment to the paying bank in its local place specified in the draft; and

(4) Upon presentation of the demand draft by the beneficiary, the paying bank checks the authenticity of the draft and makes the payment.

The payee or beneficiary of the remittance, as the payee of the demand draft, can transfer the draft before it is presented to the paying bank for payment, if the draft is payable to the payer or order. T/T and

---

① demand draft：即期汇票，这里是银行即期汇票

M/T do not possess the same property of D/D.

Specimen of a banker's demand draft

```
                         ... BANK
        This draft is valid within one year from the date of issue
   No. _____                              AMOUNT _____
   TO:_____                               DATE:_____
   PAY TO THE ORDER OF _____
   THE SUM OF _____
                                                      ... BANK
```

3.4 Reimbursement of remittance cover

When sending a payment order to the paying bank, the remitting bank should specify the way of reimbursing the remittance cover to the paying bank. There are several ways of reimbursement.

If there is a vostro or nostro account[①] between the remitting bank and the paying bank, it will be convenient for the paying bank to obtain the reimbursement. For instance, if the paying bank maintains a current account with the remitting bank, a vostro account from the perspective of the remitting bank, the reimbursement in the payment order should be written as:

"In cover, we have credited the sum to your account with us."

If the remitting bank maintains a current account with the paying bank, a nostro account from the perspective of the remitting bank, the reimbursement in the payment order should be expressed as:

"In cover, please debit the sum to our account with you."

"In reimbursement, you are authorized to debit the face amount to our A/C held with you."

"In cover, you are authorized to debit the sum to our account

---

① vostro account：来账，一家国外银行在一家国内银行开有往来账户，从这家国内银行的角度该账户就是来账；nostro account：往账，一家国内银行在一家国外银行开有往来账户，从这家国内银行的角度就是往账

with you."

If there is no vostro or nostro account between the remitting bank and the paying bank, the remitting bank can find a third bank, say Bank A, with which both the paying bank and the remitting bank maintain current accounts. The reimbursement can be done through the third bank. The instruction in the payment order is written as:

"In cover, we have authorized Bank A to debit our account and credit your account with the above sum."

If the remitting bank maintains a current account with another bank, say Bank A, and the paying bank maintain a current account with a different bank, say Bank B, then the reimbursement instruction will be:

"In cover, we have instructed Bank A to pay the proceeds to your account with Bank B."

If there is a payment agreement between two countries where the remitting bank and the paying reside respectively, the reimbursement instructions must comply with the terms of the agreement. The instruction will be:

"In cover, you are authorized to debit our Central Bank's clearing account with your Central Bank."

"In cover, we have requested our Central Bank to credit the sum to the clearing account of your Central Bank with them."

Obviously, when the remitting bank and the paying bank have current accounts with each other, the time consumed by remitting the funds is the least and the remittance is the most efficient.

3.5 The cancellation of remittance

Cancellation of remittance means that the remitter may cancel the remittance before the funds are paid to the payee. The procedures of cancelling a remittance are:

(1) The remitter submits the application for cancellation indicating the reasons and in the case of D/D, and returns the demand draft issued by the remitting bank;

(2) The remitting bank examines the application for cancellation and, if necessary, requires the remitter to provide a guarantee to ensure that the remitter will assume all the losses incurred by the cancellation, especially when the demand draft has been lost;

(3) The remitting bank notifies the paying bank to stop payment and requires it to repay the remittance cover which has been paid by the remitting bank;

(4) Upon receipt of the cancellation notification and before the payment, the paying bank will return the payment order and the cancellation notice with the remittance cover to the remitting bank; however, if the paying bank has paid the payee, the cancelation will be impossible;

(5) Upon receipt of the remittance cover from the paying bank, the remitting bank will pay back the funds to the remitter and cancel the draft, if any.

3.6 Application of remittance in international trade

As a frequently used payment method in international trade, remittance has its own advantages as well as disadvantages. Between an importer and an exporter who are creditworthy and reliable trade partners, remittance is definitely an efficient, safe, timely and cost effective method of settlement. Based on the timing of effecting payment and the timing of delivering the goods, remittance can be used in two types of payment techniques: cash in advance and open account.

Cash in advance

Cash in advance is also called payment in advance, under which the exporter requires the buyer to pay for the goods either at the time of the order or prior to the shipment of the goods. In other words, the importer remits the proceeds to the exporter and places the proceeds at the disposal of the exporter prior to the shipment of the goods.

It is obvious that cash in advance is the most advantageous to the exporter but expensive and risky to the importer. Nevertheless, it is commonly used when the manufacturing process or services are specialized and capital intensive. In such circumstances, the parties may agree to fund the operation by partial payments in advance or by progress payments. However, before choosing this payment method, the importer should consider whether the exporter is reliable and whether there is a stable political or economic environment in the exporter's country.

The advantage of using cash in advance by an exporter is the immediate availability of funds. From the viewpoint of the importer, however, by providing a trader credit to the exporter, his capital will be tied up prior to the receipt of the goods. At the same time, he has no assurance that the exporter will supply goods as contracted, that the quality and quantity of the goods will meet the terms of the sales contract and that he will receive the goods in time. This is why in certain cases the importer requires the exporter to provide a written undertaking or a letter of guarantee to ensure that the goods be delivered as contracted.

The most often used payment tools by the importer in cash in advance are: (1) Remitting the funds by T/T; (2) Remitting the funds by M/T; (3) Remitting the funds by D/D; (4) Remitting the funds by a cheque; (5) Remitting the funds by a promissory note; and (6) Remitting the funds by a credit card.

Open account

Open account is an arrangement between an importer and an exporter, by which the goods are manufactured and delivered before the payment is required, i.e., the payment will be made by the importer at a stated future date after his receipt of the goods.

Open account is beneficial to the importer because the importer pays for the goods only after the goods have been received. But it is disadvantageous to the exporter. Since the exporter releases the title to the goods without having assurance of payment and his capital is tied up. Under open account, the importer does not issue any negotiable instrument evidencing his legal commitment. Before using this method, the seller must have absolute confidence that he will be paid by the importer at the agreed date.

The most often used payment tools by the importer in open account are: (1) Remitting the funds by T/T; (2) Remitting the funds by M/T; (3) Remitting the funds by D/D; (4) Remitting the funds by a cheque; (5) Remitting the funds by a promissory note; (6) Remitting the funds by a credit card.

3.7 Trade finance under remittance

Financing under T/T

With the intense competition in trade finance area, Chinese commercial banks have designed various types of financing under remittance. T/T finance is one of them, including import T/T financing and export T/T financing.

Import T/T finance Under an outward remittance, if the importer and the exporter choose open account as the payment technique, say, O/A 120 days, the importer need make payment to the exporter at the 120 days after the invoice date. If the importer has difficulty in paying the exporter at the due date, he may apply for financing from his bank for the amount of money needed to make the payment. That is, the importer's bank makes payment to the exporter on behalf of the importer which will pay back the money to the bank after it sells the goods and obtains the funds.

There are some preconditions for a bank to provide such financing to an importer. First of all, the tenor of the financing will not exceed 120 days. It is a short-term financing by the bank to the importer. Secondly, the financing is confined to the payment of the funds under open account. Thirdly, the importer must have credit lines rated and approved by the bank providing financing. Lastly, the bank even requires the importer to provide a letter of guarantee for such financing. All the measures are to protest the default risk of the importer.

Export T/T finance Under the inward remittance, if the exporter has shipped the goods to the importer on open account, say O/A 120 days, the exporter will only receive the payment from the importer at the due date. If the exporter needs funds immediately, he may apply for funds from his bank. That is, the bank may make payment to the exporter before the importer pays and the exporter will pay back the money when he receives the payment from the importer. Export T/T financing is also called export T/T negotiation or export invoice financing by some banks.

Credit insurance and bank financing

Under open account, an exporter may apply insurance from the export insurance company to cover the credit risk for the goods supplied. After the shipment of the goods, the exporter may apply for financing from his bank by transferring the interest under the insurance policy to the bank.

This kind of bank financing can be used under various terms, such as O/A, D/P(documents against payment) or D/A(documents against acceptance) under documentary collection.① Generally speaking, O/A, D/A and D/P are risky from the perspective of the exporters, thus they must be careful in choosing such terms. In December 2001, the State Council approved the establishment of China Export Insurance Corporation②, aiming to help the export enterprises to avoid the political and commercial risks in international trade. The short-term export credit insurance③ provided to the exporters also provides a chance for the exporter to obtain finance from banks.

3.8　Other methods of remittance

T/T, M/T and D/D are traditional ways of remitting funds overseas. With the development of B2C, the international trade with small amount payment developed rapidly, leading to the diversified payment

---

① D/P(documents against payment)：付款交单；D/A(documents against acceptance)：承兑交单；documentary collection：跟单托收
② State Council：国务院；China Export Insurance Corporation：中国出口信用保险公司
③ short-term export credit insurance：短期出口信用保险

techniques.① In practice, foreign traders often use credit cards, PayPal, or Western Union to make payment.②

Credit card

In general, cash in advance or open account are the preferred payment methods for transactions of moderate amounts, such as amounts for replacements, repairs, re-stocking and parts orders.③ Since the year of 2000, a new alternative to cash in advance or open account has been emerged, that is, the credit card payment. Be it American Express, Visa, or MasterCard④, using credit card for small transaction is simple, quick and cost effective.

To accept payment by a credit card, the exporter must become a credit card merchant. Each card issuer sets its own procedures and fees. On a US $10,000 sale, a 3% fee is US $300. This amount is the total cost, but there is no administration, no files and no follow-up. Though expensive, compared to open account, using a credit card eliminates the cost of credit reports, credit file management, invoicing and account receivable management, simplifies the collection and charge-back process and eliminates losses from non-payment.

In November 2009, VISA Money Transfer⑤ entered China via the Industrial and Commercial Bank of China. VISA has more than a billion holders all over the world and offers safe, easy and reliable fund transfer services through Internet bank, ATM, Self-servicing selling outlets, bank counter or telephone.⑥

---

　① B2C：business to consumer，企业对消费者；王炳焕，"国际小额贸易支付工具的种类与比较分析"，《对外经贸实务》，2011 年第 2 期，第 59—61 页

　② PayPal：贝宝（全球最大的在线支付平台）；Western Union：西部联盟电报公司，西联汇款

　③ replacements：换货；repairs：维修；re-stocking：重新进货；parts orders：配件订单

　④ American Express：美国运通卡；Visa：维萨卡；MasterCard：万事达卡

　⑤ VISA Money Transfer：VISA 全球转账服务

　⑥ internet bank, ATM, Self-servicing selling outlets, bank counter or telephone：网上银行、自动柜员机、自助销售网点、银行柜台或者电话

In June 2010, Master card declared its cooperation with the Bank of China and began to offer personal fund transfer services overseas. Remitters may remit funds via their master cards to overseas payees and vise versa. The time consumed for the funds to arrive is within 24 hours. The currencies can be more than 160 currencies in transferring the funds overseas.

In June 2010, the UnionPay cooperated with the Interac Association, an Australian ATM network and the Scotiabank of Australia and declared in Toronto that more than 2,600 sets of ATM had opened its UnionPay service.① In the same month, UnionPay signed an agreement with the Network International②, the largest bank card third party processing firm in the gulf, Middle East and North Africa and agreed that the business firms in more than 20 countries(including AER) in the Middle East, East Asia and Africa would accept UnionPay services.③

PapPal

PayPal is a service that enables one to pay, send money and accept payments without revealing one's financial information. As an online payment company under eBay, it enables individuals or companies to pay or accept payment through email, with the features of safety, simplicity and ease. Currently, about 90% of the sellers and over 85% of the buyers of the cross-border trade trust and use PayPal as an electronic payment tool. Connected with PayPal's global payment platform, a trader can trade with 190 countries and areas and the currencies used include US dollar, Canadian dollar, euro, pound sterling, Australian dollar, Japaness Yen, altogether 23 currencies.

PayPal is similar to PayPal Beibao but the latter can only be used in payment in RMB to and from Chinese users.

---

① UnionPay：银联；Interac Association：澳大利亚自动柜员机网络；Scotiabank：加拿大丰业银行，这里指在澳大利亚的丰业银行

② Network International：在海湾国家、中东和北非最大的银行卡第三方处理公司

③ 周明，"跨境支付：国际卡组织的主战场"，《中国信用卡（专业）》(China Credit Card)，2010年第8期，第19—22页

Western Union and MoneyGram[①]

Western Union has been operating for over 150 years. It now has over 437,000 agents worldwide in over 200 countries and territories and has become the largest international remitting company and the earliest one that has entered into China.

By September 30, 2011, its agents in China consist of the Postal Bank of China, the Agricultural Bank of China, China Everbright Bank, Zhejiang Chouzhou Commercial Bank, Jilin Bank, Haerbin Bank, Fujian Haixia Bank, Yantai Bank, Longjiang Bank, Whenzhou Bank, Huishang Bank and Shanghai Pudong Development Bank.

The procedures of sending money through Western Union are as follows:[②] (1) Fill in the application form; (2) Pay the funds and service fee; (3) Sign on the application and receive a receipt which contains the Money Transfer Control Number(MTCN) for tracing the fund transfer; (4) Notify the payee of the information of the fund transfer, such as the name of the remitter, the amount remitted, the MTCN and remitting country or area; (5) Trace the fund transfer.

MoneyGram is the second largest international remitting company and has a global reach through its network of 267,000 local agents across 192 countries and territories. Its agents in China consist of the Bank of China, the Industrial and Commercial Bank of China, the Bank of Communications, the China Citic Bank, the Industrial Bank, the Agricultural Bank of Fuzhou, Pingan Bank, Shunde Rural Credit Cooperative, the Citic Bank of Guiyang, Anshan Commercial Bank, etc.

The procedures of sending money include: (1) Find an agent; (2) Visit the agent and take one's personal identification card; (3) Complete a simple "Send" form and hand it to the agent along with the money and the transfer fee; (4) Receive a reference number; (5) Contact the person to whom you're sending the money and give him the reference number, and in

---

① MoneyGram：速汇金汇款，全球第二大国际汇款公司
② "如何汇款，"西联汇款 Western Union, Retrieved 2012/3/12 from http://www.westernunion.cn/sc/how_to_send.php

just 10 minutes, the money will be ready to collect.

The first feature of remitting funds via Western Union or Money Gram is that the remitter need not open an account with the bank and the amount of the proceeds less than RMB 10,000 yuan does not require any approval documents from the foreign exchange authorities. Secondly, it takes about 10 minutes for the money to reach to the payee. Thirdly, with the agents around the world, it is convenient and available to everyone to use. Fourthly, the form for application is quite simple.

Cheque payment

Paying by cheques used to be common payment methods, but with the introduction of electronic payments, only less and less traders use cheques as international payment tools. However, in countries like the United States and the United Kingdom, cheque payments are still common and more frequently used for payments in international trade.

In the United States, cheques can be bank cheques or corporate cheques. If the cheque is a bank cheque, it is similar to a bank draft. The importer first buys the cheque and sends it to the exporter. The exporter collects it through a bank. If the cheque is a corporate cheque, the procedures include: (1) The exporter sends the invoice to the importer upon delivery; (2) The importer sends the cheque to the exporter as payment; (3) The exporter receives payment from its bank, either with a longer deferred value date or in many cases only at the later stage when the cheque has been received by the importer's bank; (4) The cheque is cleared between the banks; (5) The cheque is debited to the importer's account.

The first disadvantage of cheque payment is the delayed value date. In some countries it may take weeks to get a corporate cheque from abroad cleared between the banks. Secondly, more fees are involved in cheque payment. Since the cheque has to be sent to the account holding bank for collection, both banks may charge collection commissions. Another risk is the postal risk. If lost in transit to the exporter or delayed because of strikes or any other reasons, the importer can claim that they have paid by sending the cheque, but the exporter has not received payment.

4 Collection

4.1 Definition

According to the Uniform Rule for Collection, ICC Publication No. 522 (URC 522)①, collection means the handling by banks of documents in accordance with instructions received, in order to obtain payment and/or acceptance, or deliver documents against payment and/or against acceptance, or deliver documents on other terms and conditions.② Documents here refer to financial documents and/or commercial documents③. Financial documents are bills of exchanges, promissory notes, cheques, or other similar instruments used for obtaining the payment of money, while commercial documents refer to invoices, transport documents, documents of title or other similar documents, or any other documents whatsoever, not being financial documents.

First of all, this definition is from the perspective of banks, that is, banks deal with documents according to the instructions from customers or other banks. Secondly, there are three purposes of collection: (1) to

---

① The Uniform Rules for Collection:《托收统一规则》,由国际商会(ICC)于1956年首次出版,分别在1967年和1978年修订,最新的修订版在1995年6月被国际商会委员会采用,成为国际商会的第522号出版物

② collection means the handling by banks of documents in accordance with instructions received, in order to obtain payment and/or acceptance, or deliver documents against payment and/or against acceptance, or deliver documents on other terms and conditions: 托收是指银行根据收到的指示处理单据,目的是为了获得付款及/或承兑,或者凭付款及/或承兑交付单据,或者凭其他条款交付单据

③ financial documents: 金融单据,指汇票、本票、支票以及其他凭之付款的单据; commercial documents: 商业单据,指发票、运输单据、权利凭证或其他类似单据,或其他非金融单据的任何单据

collect money or to obtain acceptance of the bill from the drawee, (2) to release documents upon receiving payment or acceptance and (3) to release documents upon other terms and conditions. In purpose (1), the collection is called clean collection① in which financial documents are not accompanied by commercial documents. In purpose (2), the collection is documentary collection② in which there are documentary bills accompanied by shipping documents. In purpose (3), the collection is also documentary collection in which there are shipping documents but without any documentary bills.

From the perspective of the seller, collection means that the seller first ships the goods, prepares a bill of exchange and/or shipping documents and then submits the bill of exchange and/or documents to its bank for collection of the proceeds. The title to the goods will not pass on to the importer until the bill of exchange is paid or accepted by the importer, depending on the term of releasing documents. Collection provides the seller with an alternative arrangement other than open account or cash in advance.

How is collection different from open account or cash in advance? Under open account, the seller ships the goods and sends the shipping documents directly to the importer, which pays the debts to the seller on a predetermined future date, say 120 days after the invoice date. Before it obtains the purchase price, the seller loses his title to the goods and assumes the risk of the importer's non-payment. By selling goods on open account, the exporter extends trade credit to the importer. Thus, open account is favorable to the importer. On the contrary, under cash in advance the importer pays the seller before the seller delivers the goods, so the importer extends trade credit to the seller and assumes the risk of the seller's non-delivery. Under collection, however, after shipping the goods or rendering services to his customer abroad, the seller draws a bill of exchange on the importer with or without shipping documents attached thereto, submits the bill of exchange to his bank along with his appropriate collection

---

① clean collection: 光票托收
② documentary collection: 跟单托收

instructions and entrusts his bank to collect the purchase price from the importer through its correspondent bank abroad. Therefore, collection serves as a compromise between open account and cash in advance. According to John S. Gordon(2002), about one-half of all US short term trade transactions use this payment method.

Irrespective of its relative advantages over open account and cash in advance, collection is a payment technique that a seller should be cautious to use. He can use this payment method only when he believes he has good and adequate credit information on the importer and is certain that political and economic risks in the importer's country are acceptable. Moreover, the seller should establish alternative procedures for the resale, reshipment or warehousing of the goods in the event of non-payment by the importer when the goods has already arrived at the importing country.

4.2 Basic parties to a collection

Principal

The principal[①] is the party entrusting the handling of a collection to a bank. In international trade, it is the exporter that entrusts its bank to collect proceeds from the importer. The exporter, as principal, submits a collection order to the remitting bank accompanied by the bill of exchange and/or documents. The collection order serves as the contract between the principal and the remitting bank. The remitting bank is only permitted to act upon the collection order.

One point that should be noted is that the principal is also called the drawer. It is the drawer who draws the bill of exchange and/or prepares the shipping documents, submits all of them to the remitting bank and entrusts the remitting bank for collection.

In practice, the principal sometimes appoints a representative to act as the payer in the event of non-acceptance and/or non-payment. It is the same as the

---

① principal：委托人,即出口商,托收项下的出票人

"referee in case of need". Its purpose is to prevent the holder of the bill of exchange from enforcing his right of recourse. Based on URC 522, if the principal nominates a representative to act as case-of-need in the event of non-payment and/or non-acceptance, the collection instruction should clearly and fully indicate the powers of such case-of-need. In the absence of such indication banks will not accept any instructions from the case-of-need.

Remitting bank

The remitting bank[①] is the bank to which the principal has entrusted the handling of a collection. It is the bank located in the exporter's country.

According to URC 522, banks shall have no obligation to handle either a collection or any collection instruction or subsequent related instructions. If a bank elects for any reason not to handle a collection or any related instructions received by it, it must advise the party from whom it received the collection order or instruction by telecommunication or, if that is not possible, by other expeditious means without delay.

Before entering into an agreement for a collection, the remitting bank should examine carefully the collection order or instruction and the accompanied documents given by the principal. Once it agrees to collect the money, the remitting bank is only allowed to act upon the instructions given by the principal and in accordance with the rules stipulated in URC 522. The remitting bank will act in good faith and exercise reasonable care, but need not examine documents submitted.

Collecting bank

The collecting bank[②] is any bank, other than the remitting bank, involved in the collection process. Usually, it is a correspondent bank of the remitting bank located in the importer's place. According to URC 522, the remitting bank will use the bank named by the principal as the collecting

---

① remitting bank：托收行，寄单行，出口商的银行，不同于汇款项下的 Remitting Bank，汇款项下的 Remitting Bank 是汇出行

② collecting bank：代收行，接受托收行的指示向付款人（进口商）收款的银行

bank and in absence of such a named bank the remitting bank will use any of its own or another bank.

Upon receipt of the collection instruction and accompanied documents from the remitting bank, the collecting bank should examine them with reasonable care. When finding any inconsistence among them, it must notify the remitting bank without delay. The collecting bank must collect proceeds strictly on the instruction of the remitting bank. Once it receives the payment or acceptance from the drawee, according to URC 522, the collecting bank must send the advice of payment or acceptance to the remitting bank without delay.

All advices or information from the collecting bank to the remitting bank must bear appropriate details including the remitting bank's reference as stated in the collection instruction. In the absence of clear instructions from the remitting bank, the collecting bank will send the relative advices by the method of its choice at the expense of the remitting bank. Upon payment, the collecting bank must send without delay advice of payment to the remitting bank detailing the amount or amounts collected, charges and/ or disbursements and/or expenses deducted, where appropriate, and method of disposal of the funds. Upon acceptance, the collecting bank must send without delay advice of acceptance to the remitting bank.

Presenting bank

According to URC 522, presentation is the procedure whereby the presenting bank[①] makes the documents available to the drawee as instructed. The presenting bank is the collecting bank that makes presentation to the importer. In practice, the collecting bank and the presenting bank are often the same bank, but there are some situations where, due to proximity, the collecting bank uses one of its branches or correspondent banks located closer to the importer to present the documents to the drawee. One possibility is that the drawee finances the goods through

---

① presenting bank：提示行,将汇票和单据提示给付款人要求其付款或承兑的银行,可能是代收行之外的银行,也可能就是代收行

a local bank rather than the collecting bank. In this case, the local bank functions as the presenting bank in order to file a security interest or take an assignment of the title documents to the goods.

According to URC 522, the presenting bank is responsible for seeing that the form of the acceptance of a bill appears to be complete and correct, but is not responsible for the genuineness of any signature or the authority of any signatory to sign the acceptance. In the event of non-payment or non-acceptance, the presenting bank should try to make sure of the reasons for non-payment and/or non-acceptance and advise accordingly the bank from which it received the collection instruction without delay.

The presenting bank must send without delay advice of non-payment and/or advice of non-acceptance to the bank from which it received the collecting instruction.

On receipt of such advice the remitting bank must give appropriate instruction as to the further handling of the documents. If such instructions are not received by the presenting bank within 60 days after its advice of non-payment and/or non-acceptance, the documents may be returned to the bank from which the collection instruction was received without any further responsibility on the part of the presenting bank.

Drawee

Drawee[①] is the one to whom presentation is to be made in accordance with the collection instruction. It is usually the importer who should pay for the goods supplied by the exporter. The drawee has the right to examine the documents to determine whether it will accept or not and at the same time is obliged to pay or accept the bill of exchange based on the terms of the collection. With fair and just reasons, the drawee may refuse to pay. However, once the drawee pays, or accepts and pays at maturity, the bill of exchange, it has the right to retain the bill of exchange, evidencing the discharge of his liability.

Upon receipt of proceeds from the drawee, the collecting bank remits

---

① drawee：付款人，这里指托收项下的付款人，即进口商

proceeds after deducting charges and commission to the account named by the remitting bank, which will discharge the collecting bank's liability. After that, the remitting bank credits the sum after deducting charges and commission to the principal's account and his liability under the collection comes to an end.

Collection instruction

According to URC 522, all documents sent for collection must be accompanied by a collection instruction indicating that the collection is subject to URC 522 and giving precise instructions. Banks will not examine documents in order to obtain instructions. Unless otherwise authorized in the collection instruction, banks will disregard any instructions from any party/bank other than the party/bank from whom they received the collection.

 URC 522 requires a collection instruction containing the following items:

 (1) Details of the bank(remitting bank) from which the collection was received including full name, postal and SWIFT address, telex, facsimile numbers and reference.

 (2) Details of the principal (exporter) including full name, postal address and, if applicable, telex, telephone and facsimile numbers.

 (3) Details of the drawee (importer) including full name, postal address and, if applicable, telex, telephone and facsimile numbers. If the drawee's address is incomplete or incorrect, the collecting bank may try to make certain the proper address but has no liability on it. The collecting bank will not be liable or responsible for any ensuing delay as a result of an incomplete or incorrect address being provided.

 (4) Details of the presenting bank, if any, including full name, postal address and, if applicable, telex, telephone and facsimile numbers.

 (5) Amount(s) and currency(ies) to be collected.

 (6) List of documents and the numerical count of each type of document.

 (7) The terms and conditions upon which payment and/or acceptance

is to be obtained and the terms of releasing documents[①], such as documents against payment (D/P), document against acceptance (D/A), or other terms and conditions.

(8) Charges to be collected, indicating whether they may be waived or not.

(9) Interest to be collected, if applicable, indicating whether it may be waived or not, including rate of interest, interest period and basis of calculation as applicable.

(10) Method of payment and form of payment advice.

(11) Instructions in case of non-payment, non-acceptance and/or non-compliance with other instructions.

Obviously, it is the responsibility of the party preparing the collection instruction to ensure that the terms for the delivery of documents be clearly and unambiguously stated; otherwise banks will assume no responsibility for any consequences arising from that.

The relationship between the basic parties

The relationship between the principal (exporter) and the drawee (importer) is bound by the sales contract between them. Both the exporter and the importer should do as stipulated in the contract.

The relationship between the principal and the remitting bank is bound by the collection application, based on which the remitting bank only serves as an agent for the principal to collect the proceeds of sale. If the remitting bank fails to obtain the money, the principal assumes the loss. But once it provides financing to the principal under collection, the remitting bank will face the risk of non-payment by the importer and the insolvency of the exporter although it has the right of recourse to the exporter.

The relationship between the remitting bank and the collecting bank is an agent relationship. What binds them is the corresponding banking agreement between the two banks and the specific collection instructions. The collecting bank merely serves as an agent on behalf of the remitting bank to collect the proceeds and assumes no liability if the importer refuses to pay.

---

① terms of releasing documents：交单条件

4.3　Types of collection

Clean collection

According to URC 522, clean collection means collection of financial documents not accompanied by commercial documents. It is an arrangement whereby the seller draws only a bill of exchange on the importer for the value of the goods/services and presents the bill of exchange to his bank for collection. The seller's bank (the remitting bank) sends the bill of exchange along with a collection instruction to a correspondent bank (the collecting bank) usually in the same city as the importer. The collecting bank collects money from the importer according to the collection instruction.

　　Clean collection may represent an underlying merchandise transaction or an underlying financial transaction. The payment instrument may be a bill of exchange, a promissory note, or a cheque. For example: One UK importer pays for goods from a US exporter by a cheque. Upon receipt of the cheque, the US exporter submits it to its local bank for collection. Since the local bank has no knowledge of the collection risk associated with the cheque, before crediting the proceeds to the exporter's account, the bank sends the cheque on a clean collection basis to the importer's bank for collection. When the cheque clears, the importer's bank credits the account of the exporter's bank that will then credit the account of the exporter.

Documentary collection

According to URC 522, documentary collection means collection of (1) financial documents accompanied by commercial documents and (2) commercial documents not accompanied by financial documents.[①] It is an

---

　　① collection of (1) financial documents accompanied by commercial documents and (2) commercial documents not accompanied by financial documents: 附带商业单据的金融单据的托收和不附带金融单据的商业单据的托收

arrangement by which the exporter submits the bill of exchange accompanied by shipping documents or shipping documents without any bill of exchange to his bank for collecting proceeds from the importer. Under documentary collection, the shipping documents will not be released to the importer until the bill of exchange is paid or accepted or other conditions are met.

Be it clean collection or documentary collection, collection can be regarded as import collection or export collection by a bank depending on the bank's role in the process. When the exporter's bank remits the documents to a foreign bank to obtain payment or acceptance, it is called an export, outgoing or outward collection. Conversely, when the importer's bank collects the proceeds from an importer based on the collection instruction from the remitting bank, it is an import, incoming or inward collection.

*Direct collection*① One form of collection that has been increasingly favored by a growing number of exporters is direct collection. It is an arrangement between the exporter and its bank, by which the exporter sends the collection items, collection instructions and shipping documents, if documentary, directly to the importer's bank for collection. Since this kind of collection accelerates the paperwork process, it is more cost effective and quicker. The disadvantage is that the exporter is dependent on a foreign bank that may not provide the same level of service as its own local bank.

Procedures of a documentary collection transaction

The procedures of a documentary collection transaction are illustrated by following flowchart:

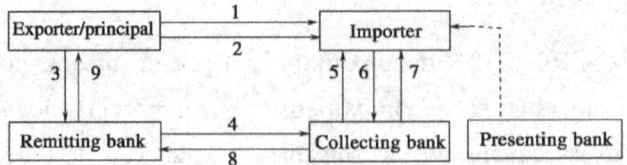

Figure 4.1　Procedures of a documentary collection transaction

---

　①　direct collection：直接托收，托收行根据与出口商的协议直接把出口商的单据直接寄到代收行向进口商收款

(1) The exporter and importer negotiate and sign a sales contract.

(2) The exporter ships the goods and obtains the shipping documents and draws a bill of exchange, either payable at sight or with a tenor, on the importer for the value of the goods.

(3) The exporter submits the bill of exchange and/or documents to his bank and entrusts the bank to act as an agent to collect the proceeds.

(4) The remitting bank sends the bill of exchange and/or documents along with a collection instruction to its correspondent bank, i.e., the collecting bank, which is located in the same city as the importer;

(5) Acting as an agent for the remitting bank, the collecting bank, or the presenting bank, if any, notifies the importer upon receipt of the bill of exchange and/or documents.

(6) The importer pays or accepts the documents based on the terms of the collection instruction.

(7) The commercial documents, especially the bills of lading, are released by the collecting bank to the importer according to the terms of releasing documents described in the collection instructions received from the remitting bank.

(8) Upon receipt of the payment, the collecting bank remits the proceeds to the remitting bank.

(9) The remitting bank credits the amount to the exporter's account.

4.4　Terms of releasing documents

Under a documentary collection, the most frequently used terms of releasing documents are: documents upon payment(D/P), including D/P at sight and D/P after sight and documents upon acceptance(D/A).①

Documents against payment(D/P)

D/P means documents against payment. When it is included in the

---

① documents upon payment(D/P): 付款交单; D/P at sight: 即期付款交单; D/P after sight: 远期付款交单; documents upon acceptance(D/A): 承兑交单

collection instruction, the collecting bank is allowed to release the documents to the drawee only against the drawee's immediate payment of the bill of exchange in the prescribed currency. The bill of exchange drawn under D/P is sight bill. In practice, D/P takes one of the two forms: D/P (or D/P at sight) and D/P at a fixed time after sight.

D/P at sight The bill of exchange drawn under a documentary collection is a sight bill which is immediately payable on presentation. To some extent, D/P at sight is a compromise between open account and payment in advance. It is a kind of cash against documents. To the importer, it is safe to obtain the goods upon making payment; to the exporter, it is safe to obtain the proceeds upon releasing the documents.

D/P at a fixed time after sight The bill of exchange drawn under a documentary collection is payable at a fixed time after sight and the commercial documents will not be released to the drawee against his acceptance of the bill and will be released only against the drawee's payment at maturity. In other words, the collecting bank first presents the bill of exchange to the drawee for acceptance but does not release commercial documents to the drawee upon acceptance. When the accepted bill matures, the collecting bank presents it again to the drawee for payment. Only against payment will the collecting bank release the commercial documents to the drawee.

According to URC 522, if a collection contains a bill of exchange payable at a future date, the collection instruction should state whether the commercial documents are to be released to the drawee against acceptance or against payment. In the absence of such statement, commercial documents will be released only against payment. The collecting bank will not be responsible for any consequences arising out of any delay in the delivery of documents.

Documents against acceptance (D/A)

When D/A is included in the collection instruction, the collecting bank is allowed to release the commercial documents to the drawee against the drawee's acceptance of the bill of exchange. The bill of exchange drawn under D/A is a usance bill. It may be made payable after date or after sight.

Under D/A, the exporter is extending credit to the importer because the importer obtains the documents and picks up the goods before payment. Obviously, D/A is favorable to the importer. What the exporter obtains after releasing the commercial documents is an accepted bill, i. e. , a trader's acceptance. Hence, the exporter is faced with the risk of the importer's non-payment.

From the above discussion, one can see that D/P is safer than D/A and that D/P at sight is safer than D/P at a fixed period after sight. The most frequently used term is D/P at sight, more frequently used D/P at a fixed period after sight, less frequently used D/P after date and the rarely used D/A after sight.

4.5 Liabilities and disclaimers of banks under a collection

Banks have no obligation to handle a collection

According to Article 1(b) of URC 522, banks shall have no obligation to handle either a collection or any collection or subsequent related instructions. This means that a bank has the right to independently decide whether to take up a collection order. If the bank chooses not to handle a collection or any related instructions received by it, it must advise the party from whom it received the collection or the instructions by telecommunication or by other expeditious means without delay.

Even if a bank accepts doing the collection for its customer, the relationship between the bank and its customer is only an agency relationship, i. e. , the bank acts as an agent for its customer to collect the proceeds. If the proceeds cannot be obtained, the principal will assume the loss.

Banks are only permitted to act upon the instructions given. All documents sent for collection must be accompanied by the collection instructions containing complete and precise instructions. Banks are only permitted to act upon the instructions. It is the responsibility of the party preparing the collection instructions to ensure that the terms for delivery of commercial documents are clearly and unambiguously stated; otherwise, banks will not be responsible for any consequences arising from that.

Disclaimer for acts of an instructed party

In utilizing the services of another bank or other banks for the purpose of giving effect to the instructions of the principal, banks do so for the account and at the risk of such principal. Banks assume no liability or responsibility should the instructions they transmit not be carried out, even if they have themselves chosen such other bank. For example, if the collecting bank does not carry out the instructions given by the remitting bank, the remitting bank assumes no responsibility even if the collecting bank was chosen by the remitting bank. However, a party instructing another party to perform services shall be bound by and liable to indemnify the instructed party against all obligations and responsibilities imposed by foreign laws and usages.①

Disclaimer on documents received

Banks must determine that the documents received appear to be as listed in the collection order. If any documents missing or found to be other than listed, banks must advise without delay the party from whom the collection instruction was received. And banks have no further obligation in this respect.

Disclaimer on effectiveness of documents

Banks assume no liability for the form, sufficiency, accuracy, genuineness, falsification or legal effect of any documents, or for the general and/or particular conditions stipulated in the documents, nor do they assume any liability for the description, quantity, weight, quality, condition, packing

---

① a party instructing another party to perform services shall be bound by and liable to indemnify the instructed party against all obligations and responsibilities imposed by foreign laws and usages：一方指示另一方去履行服务，指示方应受到外国法律和惯例施加给被指示方的一切义务和责任的制约，并应就有关义务和责任对受托方承担赔偿责任

delivery, value or existence of the goods represented by any documents, or for the good faith or acts and/or omissions, solvency, performance or standing of the consignors, the carriers, the forwarders, the consignees or the insurers of the goods, or any other person whomsoever.

Disclaimer on delays, loss in transit and translation

Banks assume no liability or responsibility for the consequences arising out of delay and/or loss in transit of any messages, letters or documents, or for delay, mutilation or other errors arising in transmission of any telecommunication or for errors in translation and/or interpretation of technical terms.

Banks do not deal with the goods, services or other acts

Banks have no obligation to take any action in respect of the goods to which a documentary collection relates, including storage and insurance of the goods even when specific instructions are given to do so. Banks will only take such action if, when, and to the extent that they agree to do so in each case. Nevertheless, in the case that banks take action for the protection of the goods, whether instructed or not, they assume no liability or responsibility with regard to the fate and/or condition of the goods and/or for any acts and/or omissions on the party of any third parties entrusted with the custody and/or protection of the goods. However, the collecting bank must advise without delay from which the collection instruction was received of any such action taken.

4.6 Financing provided by banks under a collection

Under collection, banks act only as agents for its customer or correspondent bank and assume no liability on collection. When banks provide financing to its customers, however, their roles are more than merely agents and must assume risks involved with the financing.

Financing provided by the remitting bank to the exporter

Negotiation or export bill purchase under a collection①

Negotiation or export bill purchase under a collection is a short-term finance the remitting bank provides to the exporter. In outward collection, the remitting bank sometimes negotiates(purchases) its customer's bill of exchange drawn on the overseas importer before the importer makes payment. The exporter obtains the proceeds immediately after submitting the bill of exchange and commercial documents. The net proceed the exporter obtains under negotiation or export bill purchase is the face value of the bill minus the interest during the period of collection and some other charges. Negotiation under a collection includes negotiation under D/P and negotiation under D/A.

Such finance is to meet the exporter's need for short-term finance. To the exporter, using such a financing method has the following advantages: (1) speeding up the turnover of funds, i.e., obtaining payment in advance; (2) simplifying the procedures; (3) improving cash flows; (4) saving financial costs; (5) being available to most exporters, even if it has no credit line with the remitting bank.

By purchasing the bill of exchange drawn by the exporter on the importer and commercial documents under an outward collection, the remitting bank will assume the risk of non-payment by the importer. Thus, there are some preconditions for the exporter to satisfy before the remitting bank agrees to such a negotiation.

Let's take the conditions required by the Bank of China as an example. First of all, there are some basic requirements for the qualifications of the exporter. The exporter must prove that it is a qualified legal entity and submit the certification for its business scope. It possesses the loan card②

---

① Negotiation or export bill purchase under a collection: 托收项下的出口押汇或出口汇票买入; negotiation: 议付; 押汇

② 凡需要向各金融机构申请贷款, 办理承兑汇票、信用证、授信、保函和提供担保等信贷业务的法人企业、非法人企业、事业法人单位和其他借款人, 均须向营业执照(或其他有效证件)注册地的中国人民银行各城市中心支行或所属县支行申请领取贷款卡

issued by the People's Bank of China and has the permission of opening an account and opens the account with the remitting bank. And it is qualified to do import and export business. Secondly, if the term of releasing documents is D/P, the exporter should have credit line in the remitting bank. If the bank cannot control the title to the goods, the credit rating of the exporter must be CC or above. If the bank can control the goods, there is no limit on the rating. Thirdly, if the term of releasing documents is D/A, the exporter should have a credit line in the bank and its credit rating must be CCC or above.

The procedures of negotiation under a collection include six steps:

(1) The exporter concludes an agreement with the remitting bank;

(2) The exporter submits the bill of exchange and commercial documents accompanied by the application for negotiation;

(3) The remitting bank examines the documents and credits the proceeds with the exporter's account;

(4) The remitting bank sends the documents to the foreign correspondent bank(collecting bank) to collect the proceeds;

(5) The collecting bank presents the bill of exchange for the drawee for payment or acceptance; and

(6) The collecting bank remits the proceeds to the remitting bank which deducts the negotiation fund from the proceeds.

By negotiating the bill of exchange and the commercial documents, the remitting bank changes its position from an agent to a financing party accompanied with the act is the risk of non-payment by the importer. When the remitting bank negotiates the bill of exchange and if the bill of exchange is payable to the exporter, the exporter must indorse the bill and make it payable to the remitting bank. As the indorser, the exporter guarantees the payment of the importer. If the importer refuses to pay or accept the bill, or accepts the bill but refuses to pay at maturity, the remitting bank as the holder of the bill has the right of recourse to the indorser (the exporter). Just because of this guarantee, the remitting bank would like to purchase the bill of exchange and the commercial documents from the exporter. But in the event of non-payment by the importer and at the same time the exporter becomes insolvent, the bank will assume the loss. This is why few banks are willing to negotiate the bill of exchange and documents under a collection without making sure that the repayment is guaranteed.

Export bill discount under a collection①

Under D/A, after the bill of exchange has been accepted by the importer and if the collecting bank is willing to guarantee the payment of the importer at maturity, the exporter may discount the bill with the remitting bank for finance. This is one of financing ways Chinese banks offer currently. However, the point is that the foreign collecting bank has no obligation to guarantee for the payment by the importer and has right to refuse such request. Without the collecting bank's guarantee, the remitting bank will not provide such finance.

Advance against a collection②

On the request of the exporter, the remitting bank may make a loan to it against the bill of exchange and commercial documents. The amount of the loan is a proportion of the value of the bill of exchange. The guarantee for providing such a loan is the proceeds that the exporter will collect through selling goods to the importer. But the risk of providing advance against collections is just like that of providing a regular loan to a customer.

Financing provided by the collecting bank to the importer

Trust receipt③

Under D/P at a fixed period after sight, when both the goods and commercial documents have arrived at the importer's place, but the bill of exchange is not mature and the importer is eager to obtain the goods, the importer may make a written undertaking to the collecting bank to borrow the commercial documents. The written undertaking is in the form of a

---

① export bill discount under a collection：托收项下出口汇票贴现，在代收行担保进口商付款的前提下托收贴现出口商的汇票

② advance against a collection：托收项下的垫款，托收行以托收项下的汇票和全套单据为抵押向出口商提供的贷款

③ trust receipt：信托收据

Trust Receipt (T/R). Against T/R, the importer may obtain the commercial documents and pick up the goods in advance. When the bill matures, the importer has sold the goods and has obtained the funds to effect payment.

It is risky for the collecting bank to release the commercial documents to the importer against T/R. If the importer is not creditworthy, there is a risk of the importer's non-payment. So, the bank usually requires cash deposits before accepting T/R if the importer has no credit line with the bank. The cash deposits range from a nominal sum to 100 percent.

Under T/R, the real owner of the goods is the collecting bank, but the importer has the right to sell the goods. If the importer has sold the goods to a third party who bought the goods in good faith and paid the value, the collecting bank cannot take the goods back from the third party in case of default by the importer at maturity. The good faith third party is similar to a holder in due course.

Shipping guarantee under a collection[①]

When the goods arrive at the destination before the documents do, the importer may ask the collecting bank to issue a shipping guarantee—an undertaking made by the importer and countersigned by the collecting bank—and pick up the goods against the guarantee from the shipping company. The importer and the collecting bank jointly and severally undertake to submit the bill of lading to the shipping company when the documents arrive.

The procedures are: (1) The importer applies for a shipping guarantee when the goods arrive before the documents under collection; (2) The collecting bank examines the documents and approves to issue the shipping guarantee; (3) The importer picks up the goods against the guarantee; (4) When the documents under a collection arrive, the importer pays the bill, obtains the documents, uses the original bill of lading to exchange for the shipping guarantee and return the shipping guarantee to the collecting bank.

---

① shipping guarantee：托收项下提货担保

It is risky for the collecting bank to issue such a shipping guarantee for the importer. If the importer goes bankrupt, the collecting bank will take the risk of his non-payment and have to surrender the original bills of lading to the shipping company because it has promised to do so under the shipping guarantee.

4.7　Problems frequently arising from a collection

The problems of using D/P at a fixed period after sight

Under D/P after sight, upon receipt of the bill of exchange and the commercial documents, the collecting bank presents the bill of exchange and the commercial documents to the importer (drawee). After the importer accepts the bill of exchange, the collecting bank retains the accepted bill and commercial documents. Only when the bill matures and the importer pays the bill will the collecting bank release the commercial documents to the importer. This term of releasing documents is used because the bill of exchange and the commercial documents arrive at the collecting bank before the goods arrive at the destination. The ideal situation is: the bill becomes due when the goods arrive at the destination and upon payment the importer obtains the commercial documents and picks up the goods. By using this method, the exporter hopes to control the goods before the importer pays.

However, the reality is not always as expected. In practice, the situation that the goods have arrived at the destination while the bill is not mature often occurs. If the importer borrows the documents from the collecting bank to pick up the goods in advance, the risk of non-payment by the importer is transferred to the collecting bank. Not all foreign banks are willing to release documents under T/R. Some banks in European continental countries do not accept D/P at a fixed period after sight. Some banks in Latin American countries simply treat D/P at a fixed period after sight as D/A. Therefore, in choosing D/P at a fixed period after sight as the term of releasing documents, the exporter must know the customs and practice in the importer's country, especially the ways of handling documents by the collecting bank.

Meng Xiaofeng from the Focus Business School and Made-in-China. com investigated several foreign banks for their ways of handling D/P after sight in practice.[①] An American bank named Bank of the Orient replied: "It takes a month or so, or even longer time with transshipment, for a vessel to arrive at the United States from China. D/P after sight is favorable to the drawee. Generally, the drawee with credit line approved by the collecting bank may use Trust Receipt to borrow the documents. Sometimes, the drawee even transfers the documents under D/P at a long period after sight to the collecting bank. In order to protect the drawer, the collecting bank requires the drawee to submit payment undertaking or standby credit as security for such transfer. If the drawee does not want to pay more for this, the drawee may obtain guarantee from the collecting bank to pick up the goods from the carrier. The bank does not think it should release documents against the drawee's acceptance of the bill of exchange. Only when the remitting bank has such instruction will the collecting bank release documents against trust receipt." Thus, the American bank, as a collecting bank under a documentary collection, accepted D/P after sight and would stick to the collection instructions. The drawee(importer) could borrow the documents under a T/R depending on its creditworthiness.

Another reply came from a German bank named Hamburger Sparkasse. In its opinion, D/P after sight was only used in South Asia areas. "It is hard for many drawees to understand. Our importers often make payment when the goods arrive and do not use bill of exchange. We do not think it proper to use D/P 60, 90, 120, or 180 days. German banks do not deal with goods, only release documents upon payment, do not accept trust receipt and release documents against acceptance under D/A."

The reply of the Banque National de Paris was even different from the

---

① 孟晓峰,"部分国家和地区对 D/P 远期的处理方式",爱聘才网,2011 年 7 月 1 日,2014 年 8 月 21 日转引自 http://info.ipincai.com/WaiMaoZhiDao/WTpUKfAKZrhF-1.html

above two. It pointed out that short-term trade could only use D/A, and considered that trust receipt served as "a tool to provide fake guarantee to the creditor, thus it is not supported by law in France". It stated that "trade bill is a payment instrument admitted by the law in France. If the drawee does not pay at maturity, the payee or holder may use protest to enforce payment through the court. Such a security is safer than the trust receipt under the British law."

The Bank of China Hong Kong replied that: "It is common for the affiliate banks in mainland China use D/P after sight as a term of collection. Actually, it is not normal. Because the goods arrive at Hong Kong much earlier than the documents do, the importer often asks the collecting bank to issue a guarantee to pick up the goods in advance. At this moment, our bank does not know whether the terms is D/P or D/A, for the documents have not yet arrived at our bank. When we find that the term is D/P after sight upon receipt of the documents, we ask the importer to pay for the bill but the importer will not be satisfied to pay prior to the maturity, hence making the bank in a disadvantageous status." It further stated that "D/P after sight seems better than D/A, but it is not beneficial to either the exporter or the importer. If the drawee is insolvent, the exporter will face the trouble of warehousing, insurance and disposing the goods. Bank guarantee for picking up goods is not always available to the importer. It depends on the creditworthiness of the importer."

Problems related to insurance

Under FOB and CFR, it is the importer that purchases the insurance cover for the goods. One problem that often occurs is that the importer does not have the whole amount of the goods insured. Then, if the goods meet losses during transportation and at the same time the importer refuses to make payment, the seller will have to take the losses that have not be covered by the insurance company. Under the circumstances that even if the importer has insured the whole amount of the goods, the insurance cover is purchased by the importer and the importer controls the insurance policy, if the importer refuses to pay and the goods happen to be lost, the seller will not be able to claim compensation from the insurance company because it has no insurance policy. Therefore, under collections, it is important to conclude a deal under CIF, that is, the seller purchases the insurance cover for the goods and controls the insurance policy. In this way, the seller can claim compensation from the insurance company.

In some specific transactions, one may find that some countries insist that the insurance on importing goods should be provided by the importer within the importing country, or the importer insists on the terms of FOB or CFR. In order to protect against losses, the exporter may insure "The Seller's Contingent Interest Risk", by which the seller's interest will be well insured by the insurance company.

Negative events that may occur to the exporter

In spite of its merits in that the exporter has the possibility of retaining control of the goods until the drawee either effects payment or accepts a bill of exchange, the handling process is simple and inexpensive and the payment is often quicker than on open account, documentary collection has its own demerits. Under a collection, the exporter is also faced with such risks as political risk, transfer risk, commercial risk, credit risk, uncertain date of payment, etc.

Under D/P, a negative event that may occur to the exporter is that the importer will not pay if he does not want the goods. The reason may be that the importer resists the agreed prices and wants to cut down the prices or that the rules regarding foreign currency payment or import permits in the importing country have changed. In such a negative event, the exporter's goods are already on the dock in the destination country, then what the exporter can do is probably to ship the goods back, resell the good at a lower price, abandon the goods, or seek other channels of distribution in that country. All these will incur great costs for the exporter.

Under D/A, a negative event that may occur to the exporter is that, once the bill of exchange has been accepted and the commercial documents have been released to the importer, the importer refuses to pay the bill at maturity. The reasons might be the importer's bankruptcy, insolvency, fraud or changed rules and regulations in the importing country. The consequences arising from such a negative event are the same as those under D/P when the importer refuses to pay.

Therefore, before using documentary collection as a payment method, the exporter should try to answer the following questions:

(1) Is the importer financially strong?

(2) Is the importer reputable and reliable?

(3) Is the importing country politically and economically stable?

(4) Is there a satisfactory way to settle commercial disputes?

(5) Will the legal system in the importing country protect and facilitate foreign nationals in enforcing their titles to goods?

5 Letters of credit

The formal maturation of documentary credit was in the 1920s, when appeared the first coordinated efforts to establish standards applicable to export credit transactions. Under the auspices of the International Chamber of Commerce, the codified rules were later called the Uniform Customs and Practice for Documentary Credits (UCP), which has experienced the versions of 1933, 1951, 1962, 1974, 1983, 1993 and 2007. Accompanied with the development of letters of credit were air carriage, container shipment and technological advances. The technological advances in the banking industry in turn influenced the terms and conditions of letters of credit. The truly explosive growth of documentary credit occurred from the early 1950s through the early 1980s. Today, letters of credit are still the relatively safe payment method widely used by traders all over the world.

The latest version of UCP is the 2007 Revision of the Uniform Customs and Practice for Documentary Credit, ICC Publication No. 600 (UCP 600), which came into effect on July 1, 2007. Although some complain that the terms and conditions of documentary credit is rigid and inflexible, the payment by documentary credit is much safer than other traditional payment methods, such as T/T, D/P and D/A.

5.1 Definition

According to UCP 600, a documentary credit is defined as "any arrangement, however named or described, that is irrevocable and thereby constitutes a definite undertaking of the issuing bank to honour a complying presentation."① In the definition, three terms—honour, complying presentation, and presentation—need clarification. Honour involves three different possibilities: (1) to pay at sight if the credit is available by sight payment, (2) to incur a deferred payment undertaking and pay at maturity if the credit is available by deferred payment, and (3) to accept a bill of exchange (draft) drawn by the beneficiary and pay at maturity if the credit is available by acceptance.② Complying presentation means a presentation that is in accordance with the terms and conditions of the credit, but also in accordance with the UCP 600 Rules and with the International Standard Banking Practice for the Examination of Documentary Credits.③ Presentation means either the delivery of documents under a credit to the issuing bank or nominated bank or the documents so delivered.④

In brief, a documentary credit is a written undertaking by the bank to the beneficiary, informing the latter that the bank will pay a sum certain in money to him if he provides the bank with the documents stipulated in the

---

① any arrangement, however named or described, that is irrevocable and thereby constitutes a definite undertaking of the issuing bank to honour a complying presentation: 任何协议,不论如何命名或描述,它是不可撤销的并且因此构成了开证行对相符提示兑付的明确保证; irrevocable: 不可撤销的; issuing bank: 开证行; honour: 兑付; complying presentation: 相符提示; presentation: 提示。

② (1) to pay at sight if the credit is available by sight payment: 如果信用证是即期付款信用证,(开证行)则即期付款;(2) to incur a deferred payment undertaking and pay at maturity if the credit is available by deferred payment: 如果信用证是延期付款信用证,(开证行)则承担延期付款责任并在到期日付款;(3) to accept a bill of exchange (draft) drawn by the beneficiary and pay at maturity if the credit is available by acceptance: 如果信用证是承兑信用证,(开证行)则承兑受益人签发的汇票并在到期日付款。

③ Complying presentation means a presentation that is in accordance with the terms and conditions of the credit, but also in accordance with the UCP 600 Rules and with the International Standard Banking Practice for the Examination of Documentary Credits: 相符提示是指提示与信用证条款相符,同时符合 UCP600 和 ISBP 的规则; International Standard Banking Practice for the Examination of Documentary Credits: 用于审核信用证的国际标准银行惯例。

④ Presentation means either the delivery of documents under a credit to the issuing bank or nominated bank or the documents so delivered: 提示是指交付信用证项下的单据给开证行或指定的银行,或者指交付给开证行或指定银行的单据。

credit within a prescribed time frame.

A major difference between UCP 500 and UCP 600 in defining a documentary credit lies in the definition of compliance. UCP 500 emphasizes the conformity of the documents to the terms and conditions of documentary credit, whereas UCP 600 stipulates that the documents must comply with not only the terms and conditions of the credit but also the provisions of both UCP 600 and ISBP.

5.2 Characteristics of a documentary credit

A written undertaking on the part of the issuing bank

UCP 600 expressly states that draft(s) drawn under a documentary credit must be drawn on the issuing bank or any other bank nominated by the issuing bank. The drawee of the draft(s) under a documentary credit must be a bank, be it the issuing bank or the nominated bank. The issuing bank is primarily liable for payment once it issues a documentary credit although the undertaking is subject to a complying presentation.

Under a collection, it is the buyer that promises to pay the seller, whereas under a letter of credit, it is the issuing bank that undertakes to pay the seller. Since a banker is more creditworthy than a trader, a letter of credit is considered more acceptable than a collection. This is why documentary credits are widely perceived to be a relatively safe payment technique by sellers.

Other reasons for a seller to choose a letter of credit include: (1) the seller has no funds to manufacture or acquire the goods to be exported, or (2) the export policy in the seller's country requires all exports be made on a documentary credit or cash in advance. In the first case, a letter of credit can be used as collateral for applying for a loan from a bank other than the issuing bank. The guarantee for repaying the loan is the proceeds from exports which the issuing bank promises to pay.

Moreover, because a letter of credit is an undertaking by the issuing bank, the issuing bank provides a credit to the buyer once it agrees to issue it for the buyer. The ability to obtain a letter of credit not only shows the buyer is creditworthy in the eyes of the issuing bank but also expands the buyer's purchasing power. If the buyer cannot meet the credit rating requirements set by the issuing bank, the buyer will have to deposit enough money with the issuing bank. The amount of cash deposit ranges from a nominal sum to even 100% of the value of the credit, depending on the creditworthiness of the buyer.

Independent of the sales contract

A letter of credit is issued by the issuing bank based on the application of the buyer. The buyer applies for a letter of credit from its bank based on the stipulations in the sales contract. Once the credit is issued, all the parties to the credit are bound by the credit rather than the underlying sales contract.

UCP 600 expressly indicates that "a credit by its nature is a separate transaction from the sales or other contract on which it may be based. Banks are in no way concerned with or bound by such contract, even if any reference whatsoever to it is included in the credit."[①] Thus, whether the issuing bank pays the seller solely depends on the terms and conditions of the credit and the applicable rules of UCP600 and ISBP. The seller cannot use the terms of the sales contract or other contracts between banks or between the applicant and the issuing bank as excuses to ask for payment. Meanwhile, the issuing bank should discourage any attempt by the buyer to include the sales contract or other contracts into the credit.

Exclusively dealing with documents

UCP 600 states that banks deal with documents and not with goods, services or performance to which the documents may relate. Accordingly, a

---

① a credit by its nature is a separate transaction from the sales or other contract on which it may be based. Banks are in no way concerned with or bound by such contract, even if any reference whatsoever to it is included in the credit: 信用证实质上是独立于它开立所基于的销售或其他合同之外的交易。银行绝不受任何这类合同的制约,即便在信用证中提及该合同

negotiating bank[①]only purchases the complying presentation submitted by the seller and pays no attention to the discrepancies[②] between the documents and the goods actually delivered by the seller. When the issuing bank receives the documents forwarded by the negotiating bank, the issuing bank pays so long as it is a complying presentation. The payment by the buyer to the issuing bank is also based on a complying presentation.

5.3　Parties to a letter of credit

Applicant

An applicant[③] is the party on whose request the credit is issued. It is the buyer under the sales contract. Based on the sales contract, the buyer requests its bank to open a documentary credit. The applicant is liable for payment to the issuing bank for a complying presentation; at the same time, the applicant has the right to examine the documents upon receiving them from the issuing bank and may refuse to pay if discrepancies are found in the documents. Thus, the issuing bank is faced with the risk of the applicant's non-payment.

In order to prevent from the non-payment by the buyer, the issuing bank may ask the applicant to submit a written undertaking before opening a letter of credit. In China, such undertaking consists of the terms and conditions on the expenses, the examination of the documents, the rights and liabilities of the applicant, etc.

First of all, in applying for a letter of credit, the applicant must promise to pay the proceeds, commissions, interests and all the other fees incurred under the credit. The credit usually states that "all the banking charges outside the issuing bank is for the account of the beneficiary." UCP

---

① negotiating bank：议付行

② discrepancy：不符点，即受益人提交的汇票和/或单据没有满足信用证条款和UCP600 和 ISBP 的相关条款的要求

③ applicant：开证申请人，信用证开证申请人，即销售合同的买方、进口商

600 (a) stipulates that "a bank utilizing the services of another bank for the purpose of giving effect to the instructions of the applicant does so for the account and at the risk of the applicant." Thus, if the beneficiary refuses to pay the banking charges, the issuing bank will ask the applicant to pay.

Secondly, the applicant must promise to pay or accept within the stipulated period upon receipt of the notice of arrival of the documents. If the applicant decides to dishonour due to the non-complying documents, the applicant must return the documents to the issuing bank and specify the reasons of dishonour. The applicant must promise that, if the issuing bank thinks the reasons of the applicant's dishonour are not proper or if the applicant does not return the whole set of documents or returns the documents after the stipulated time limit, the issuing bank will have the right to honour the documents submitted by the beneficiary and is allowed to debit the money with the applicant's account. If the applicant finds discrepancy in the documents and returns the documents to the issuing bank within the time limit, it is still up to the issuing bank to decide whether to dishonor or not according to the international customs and practice. The applicant must point out all the discrepancies at one time.

The point is that, even if the applicant has the right to refuse to pay, the applicant has given up such right by allowing the issuing bank to pay the beneficiary if the issuing bank thinks the reasons of dishonour given by the applicant are not in accordance with the international customs and practice. From the perspective of the issuing bank, however, asking the applicant to make such promises is a way of protecting itself from the risk of non-payment by the applicant and protecting its fames in the profession.

Thirdly, if the applicant wants to amend the credit, it is up to the issuing bank to decide whether it will be amended and all the amendments of the documentary credit will be valid only after the beneficiary agrees to them.

Other conditions are the disclaimers of the issuing bank. For instance, the missing, delay, mistake or omission are the not responsibility of the issuing bank.

Issuing bank[1]

An issuing bank means the bank that issues a credit at the request of an applicant or on its own behalf. Upon issuing the credit, the issuing bank irrevocably undertakes to honour a complying presentation.

According to UCP 600, provided the documents are presented to the nominated bank or to the issuing bank and constitute a complying presentation, the issuing bank's undertaking to honour has five situations. Firstly, if the credit is available by sight payment, deferred payment or acceptance with the issuing bank, the issuing bank undertakes to pay at sight, incur deferred payment and pay at maturity or accept the drafts and pay at maturity. Secondly, if the credit is available by sight payment with a nominated bank and that nominated bank does not pay, the issuing bank undertakes to pay at sight. Thirdly, if the credit is available by deferred payment with a nominated bank and that nominated bank does not incur its deferred payment undertaking or has incurred its deferred payment undertaking but does not pay at maturity, the issuing bank undertakes to incur the deferred payment and pay at maturity. Fourthly, if the credit is available by acceptance with a nominated bank and the nominated bank does not accept a draft drawn on it or has accepted a draft drawn on it but does not pay at maturity, the issuing bank undertakes to accept such draft and pay at maturity. Fifthly, if the credit is available by negotiation with a nominated bank and the nominated bank does not negotiate, the issuing bank undertakes to negotiate and pay at maturity.

If a credit involves a nominated bank and the nominated bank has honoured or negotiated a complying presentation and forwarded the documents to the issuing bank, the issuing bank undertakes to reimburse the nominated bank. If the credit is available by sight payment, the issuing bank reimburses the nominated bank at sight. If the credit is available by deferred payment or acceptance, the issuing bank will reimburse the nominated bank at maturity no matter whether the nominated bank has

---

[1] Issuing bank：开证行，应申请人要求开立信用证的银行，也称为 opening bank

paid before maturity. The undertaking of reimbursement to the nominated bank is independent of the issuing bank's undertaking to the beneficiary. One thing worth mentioning is complying presentation. Only against a complying presentation will the issuing bank honour or reimburse.

Having discussed, a major difference between a collection and a letter of credit lies in that the former is based on a trader's credit while the latter on a banker's credit. UCP 600 stipulates that a credit must not be issued available by a draft drawn on the applicant. This ensures that a letter of credit is based on a banker's credit rather than a trader's credit.

Beneficiary

A beneficiary[①] is the party in whose favour a credit is issued. It is the seller under the sales contract. Since a documentary credit is independent of the underlying sales contract, whether the beneficiary will be paid or not solely depends on whether the documents he submitted constitute a complying presentation.

Upon receiving a documentary credit, the beneficiary has right to examine the credit and decide whether he will accept it or not. He examines the credit is to see whether the terms and conditions of the credit comply with those in the sales contract. Once he accepts the credit, he will be bound by it, and only when the documents constitute a complying presentation will he be paid under the credit.

The applicant, the issuing bank and the beneficiary are the three basic parties to a documentary credit. Under a documentary credit, there exists a triangular contractual arrangement—a sales contract between the applicant (buyer) and the beneficiary (seller), the "Application and Security Agreement" or the "Reimbursing Agreement" between the applicant and the issuing bank, and the documentary credit between the issuing bank and the beneficiary (seller). Each contract is independent and controls the respective relationship between the parties.

---

① beneficiary: 受益人,信用证的受益人,即卖方、出口商

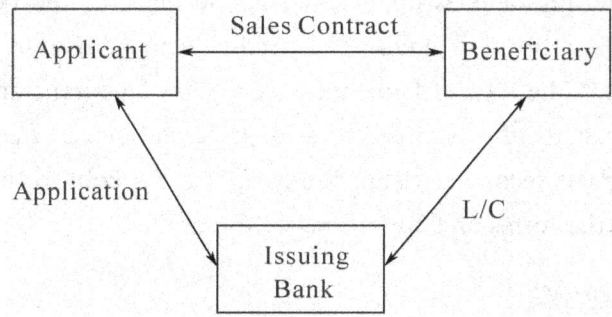

Figure 5.1 The three basic parties to a documentary credit

Advising bank[①]

An advising bank is the bank that advises the credit at the request of the issuing bank. The issuing bank usually asks its branch or correspondent bank to advise the credit or amendment. If a bank chooses to advise the credit or amendment without any undertaking to honour or negotiate the credit, the obligation of the bank is limited to the accurate transmission of the credit and assumes no other liabilities to the beneficiary.

The bank requested or authorized by the issuing bank to advise the credit may choose not to advise the credit. In this case, it must inform the issuing bank without delay. Once a bank chooses to advise a letter of credit, according to UCP 600, it need signify that the credit "has satisfied as to the apparent authenticity of the credit or amendment and that the advice accurately reflects the terms and conditions of the credit or amendment received." This means that the advising bank should take reasonable care to check the apparent authenticity of the credit. If the advising bank cannot establish the apparent authenticity of the credit or amendment, it must inform without delay the bank from which the credit has been received. If the advising bank still decides to advise the credit, it must inform the beneficiary that it has not been able to establish the authenticity of the credit.

---

① Advising bank：通知行，应开证行的要求向受益人通知信用证

If the advising bank is not located in the place of the beneficiary, it may use another bank to advise the credit. The bank is called "second advising bank." The second bank must verify the apparent authenticity of the credit when it advises the credit to the beneficiary. In practice, the advising bank (or second advising bank) is of a big help to the beneficiary in examining the terms and conditions of the credit.

Confirming bank[①]

For various reasons, it is often desirable to have another bank undertake the same obligation assumed by the issuing bank. A confirming bank is a bank that adds its confirmation to a letter of credit based on the issuing bank's authorization or request. A confirming bank is irrevocably bound to honour or negotiate as of the time of it adds its confirmation to the credit. If a bank that has been authorized or requested by the issuing bank to add confirmation to a letter of credit is not prepared to do so, it may refuse to add its confirmation to the credit and must inform the issuing bank without delay and may choose to advise the credit without confirmation.

The undertaking of a confirming bank is the same as that of the issuing bank. The Article 8 of UCP 600 explains the undertaking of the confirming bank. The confirming bank undertakes to honour or negotiate the documents that constitute a complying presentation. The details are as follows:

(1) If the credit is available by sight payment with the confirming bank, the confirming bank will pay at sight.

(2) If the credit is available by deferred payment with the confirming bank, the confirming bank will incur the deferred payment undertaking and pay at maturity.

(3) If the credit is available by acceptance with the confirming bank, the confirming bank will accept the draft drawn on it and pay at maturity.

(4) If the credit is available by sight payment with another nominated

---

① Confirming bank：保兑行，应开证行的要求或授权在信用证上加注保兑条款，保证与开证行一样兑付受益人的相符提示

bank and that nominated bank does not pay, the confirming bank pays at sight.

(5) If the credit is available by deferred payment with another nominated bank and that nominated bank does not incur its deferred payment undertaking, the confirming bank will incur the deferred payment undertaking and pay at maturity.

(6) If the credit is available by deferred payment with another nominated bank and that nominated bank has incurred its deferred payment undertaking but refuses to pay at maturity, the confirming bank will pay at maturity.

(7) If the credit is available by acceptance with another nominated bank and that nominated bank does not accept a draft drawn on it, the confirming bank will accept the draft and pay at maturity.

(8) If the credit is available by acceptance with another nominated bank and that nominated bank has accepted the draft drawn on it but refuses to pay at maturity, the confirming bank will pay at maturity.

(9) If the credit is available by negotiation with the confirming bank, the confirming bank will negotiate the complying documents without recourse.

(10) If the credit is available by negotiation with another nominated bank and that nominated bank does not negotiate, the confirming bank will negotiate the complying documents.

(11) If the credit is available by payment with another nominated bank and that bank has paid a complying presentation and forwarded the documents to the confirming bank, the confirming bank reimburses that nominated bank on demand.

(12) If the credit is available by acceptance with another nominated bank and that nominated bank has accepted the draft drawn on it and has paid at maturity, the confirming bank will reimburse that nominated bank at maturity.

(13) If the credit is available by deferred payment with another nominated bank and that nominated bank has incurred the deferred payment undertaking and paid at maturity, the confirming bank will

reimburse that nominated bank at maturity.

(14) If the credit is available by negotiation with another nominated bank and that nominated bank has negotiated a complying presentation, the confirming bank will reimburse that nominated bank at maturity.

*Paying bank/accepting bank*①

The paying bank is a bank nominated by the issuing bank to pay the beneficiary based on a complying presentation. The issuing bank sometimes makes a letter of credit available with another nominated bank or with any bank. If a letter of credit is available by payment with a nominated bank, the nominated bank will be the paying bank that undertakes to pay a complying presentation at sight. If the credit is available by deferred payment with a nominated bank, the nominated bank will be the paying bank that incurs the deferred payment undertaking and pays at maturity. If the credit is available by acceptance with a nominated bank, the nominated bank will be first the accepting bank that accepts the bills of exchange and then the paying bank that pays at maturity.

The bank nominated bank by the issuing bank to pay or accept may elect not to be the paying bank or accepting bank if there is no correspondent banking relationship or if there is no such arrangement in the correspondent agreement between the issuing bank and the paying bank. Since the bills of exchange are drawn on the paying bank, the paying bank has no right of recourse to the beneficiary after it pays the beneficiary, yet it is entitled to request the reimbursement from the issuing bank or the confirming bank, if any.

*Negotiating bank*②

A negotiating bank is a bank nominated by the issuing bank to negotiate the

---

① Paying bank/accepting bank：付款行/承兑行，是开证行指定的作为信用证项下汇票的付款人或承兑人的银行，作为汇票的付款人/承兑人，其付款是终结性的，对受益人没有追索权

② negotiating bank：议付行，是开证行授权对信用证项下的汇票和/或单据付出对价的银行，根据开证行的授权，议付行可以是指定的银行，也以是任意银行

documents that constitutes a complying presentation. UCP600 specifies the conditions that negotiation should meet. First of all, the nominated bank purchases the drafts drawn on a bank other than the nominated bank. The drawee bank may be the issuing bank, another nominated bank or the confirming bank, if any. Secondly, the documents submitted by the beneficiary must be a complying presentation. Thirdly, the nominated bank advances or agrees to advance funds to the beneficiary on or before the banking day on which reimbursement is due to the nominated bank.

Once it purchases the documents, the nominated bank becomes the negotiating bank. After negotiation, the negotiating bank forwards the complying presentation to the issuing bank or the bank nominated by the issuing bank for reimbursement. If the issuing bank or the nominated bank refuses to pay, the negotiating bank has the right of recourse to the beneficiary. In practice, an extreme risky situation is that: after the negotiating bank has purchased a complying presentation, the issuing bank finds a discrepancy or discrepancies and refuses to pay; and meanwhile, the beneficiary goes bankrupt. In this situation, the negotiating bank will assume the losses.

Claiming bank[①]

A claiming bank is the bank that has paid or negotiated a complying presentation and claims reimbursement from the issuing bank, the nominated bank or the confirming bank, if any. For example, if the credit is available by payment with a nominated bank and the nominated bank has paid the beneficiary, the nominated bank becomes the paying bank. When it claims reimbursement from the issuing bank, another nominated bank or confirming bank, if any, the paying bank becomes the claiming bank.

According to UCP600, a bank in claiming for reimbursement need notprove the compliance of the documents. If it cannot obtain reimbursement from the nominated bank, the claiming bank is entitled to

---

① claiming bank：索付行，经开证行授权对信用证项下汇票和/或单据付款或议付后向开证行或偿付行要求偿付的银行

claim reimbursement from the issuing bank. If there is any loss of interest, it should be assumed by the issuing bank.

*Reimbursing bank*①

A reimbursing bank is the bank that reimburses the claiming bank. It may be the issuing bank, a bank nominated by the issuing bank or the confirming bank, if any. The claiming bank may request cover from the reimbursing bank after paying or negotiating a complying presentation. It is usually a bank with which both the issuing bank and the claiming bank maintain current accounts.

According to UCP 600, if a letter of credit states that the claiming bank may claim reimbursement on the reimbursing bank, the credit must state if the reimbursement is subject to the ICC rules for bank-to-bank reimbursements②. If not stated so, the following rules apply:

(1) The issuing bank must provide the reimbursing bank with a reimbursement authorization and indicate the availability of reimbursement in the credit, and such authorization should not be subject to an expiry date.

(2) The claiming bank need not prove a complying presentation.

(3) If the reimbursement is not provided by the reimbursing bank on first demand and reimburses later, the issuing bank will be responsible for any loss of interest and expenses incurred.

(4) The banking charges of the reimbursing bank are for the account of the issuing bank. If the charges are for the beneficiary's account, the issuing bank should expressly state it in the credit and in the reimbursement authorization, and the charges will be deducted from the amount the reimbursing bank makes to the claiming bank. If no reimbursement is made, the reimbursing bank's charges remain the obligation of the issuing

---

① reimbursing bank：偿付行，开证行指定的对索付行偿付的银行

② the ICC rules for bank-to-bank reimbursements：全称是 The Uniform Rules for Bank-to-Bank Reimbursement under Documentary Credits, ICC Publication No. 525，跟单信用证项下银行间偿付统一规则，国际商会第 525 号出版物

bank.

(5) If the reimbursing bank refuses to reimburse, the issuing bank is obliged to provide reimbursement.

5.4 Stages to a documentary credit operation

Stage 1: The importer applies to its bank for a documentary credit

After signing the sales contract, the importer applies to its bank to issue a documentary credit in favor of the exporter. If the sales contract requires a documentary credit available by sight payment, the importer instructs a prime local bank to issue such a credit within the time limit specified in the sales contract. The issuing bank may be elected either by the importer or nominated by the exporter.

If the importer is creditworthy and has credit lines approved by the issuing bank, the issuing bank will not require any security for the issue; otherwise, the issuing bank will require a certain percentage of cash deposits and the percentage varies depending on the credit status of the importer.

In instructing the issuing bank to open a credit, the importer, as the applicant for the credit, must fill in the application for a documentary credit. Typically, the application for a documentary credit includes, among other details, the following items:

(1) the full (and correct) name and address of the beneficiary (exporter);

(2) the amount of the documentary credit and its ISO currency code;

(3) the type of the credit, whether irrevocable or confirmed irrevocable;

(4) how the documentary credit is to be available, by payment, deferred payment, acceptance, or negotiation;

(5) the party on whom draft(s), if any, are to be drawn and the tenor of such draft(s);

(6) a brief description of the goods, including details of quantity and unit price, if any;

(7) details of the documents required;

(8) the place where the goods are to be dispatched, taken in charge or loaded on board, as the case may be, and the place of final destination or the port of discharge;

(9) whether freight is to be prepaid or not;

(10) whether transshipment is prohibited or not;

(11) the last date for shipment (if applicable);

(12) the period of time after the date of shipment within which the documents must be presented for payment, acceptance or negotiation;

(13) the date and place of expiry of the documentary credit;

(14) whether or not the documentary credit is to be a transferable credit;and

(15) how the documentary credit is to be advised, i.e. by mail or by teletransmission.

Although a particular documentary credit may have its own terms and conditions, the items listed above are mostly included, and the correct contents should be based on the sales contract between the importer and the exporter.

Stage 2: *The issuing bank reviews the importer's application for credit and issues a documentary credit*

Upon receipt of the application, the issuing bank should carefully:

(1) review the terms and conditions of the credit to ensure that they are in compliance with both the policies of the bank and the legal requirements or regulations of the issuing bank's country.

(2) review the way of notifying the beneficiary instructed by the applicant to see if it is acceptable to the issuing bank, and whether the issuing bank is authorized to select its own correspondent bank to advise the credit.

(3) discourage the applicant to contain excessive details in the application. Sometimes, the application contains excessive details for the beneficiary to comply with under the documentary credit. A concern about this is that with excessive details the applicant has an intention that the beneficiary may overlook certain conditions or cannot make a complying

presentation, so that the applicant would be able to refuse to pay as desired. It is desirable if the issuing bank can discourage the applicant to contain excessive details in the application.

(4) review the application to make sure if the intended credit requires the beneficiary to submit a document, the performance or production of which totally depends on a third party and will not be controlled by the beneficiary (other than a transport document, an insurance document or an inspection certificate, etc).

(5) review the application to determine that there are no "non-documentary conditions[①]". If there are such conditions, it is the responsibility of the issuing bank to inform the applicant that these conditions must be transformed into specific documentary requirements.

If the contents of the application are acceptable to the issuing bank, the issuing bank will issue a documentary credit in favor of the beneficiary (the exporter). The terms and conditions of the credit are based on the documentary credit application. After issuing the documentary credit, the issuing bank forwards it to the advising bank by letter, fax or SWIFT message.

Stage 3: The advising bank advises the credit to the seller

As discussed above, the advising bank is not obliged to advise the credit, but if it chooses not to advise the credit, it must inform the issuing bank without delay. Upon its receipt of a documentary credit from the issuing bank, the advising bank should authenticate the realness of the credit. Once it elects to notify a credit, the advising bank must do so according to the instructions of the issuing bank. If it cannot establish the authenticity of the credit, it must inform the issuing bank without delay.

In China, before advising a letter of credit, some banks even help examine the credit to make sure that the terms and conditions of the credit are acceptable to the beneficiary. By doing this, the advising bank serves as

---

① non-documentary conditions：非单据条款，即对出单人和单据内容未做出规定的条款。非单据条款会造成受益人无法履约，从而造成不符点，因此受益人应该避免信用证中出现非单据条款，即使 UCP 600 规定银行可以忽视此类条款

a protection for the beneficiary. But the degree of examining the credit is up to the relationship between the advising bank and the beneficiary.

Stage 4: The exporter examines the credit, prepares for the required documents and submits the documents to the nominated bank

Upon its receipt of the credit advised by the advising bank, the exporter, as the beneficiary of the credit, should check the credit against the underlying sales contract and ensure the credit requirements are acceptable to him. The beneficiary should confirm:

(1) The credit appears to be a valid documentary credit.

(2) The type of credit and its terms and conditions are in accordance with the sales contract.

(3) The credit does not contain any terms and conditions which are unacceptable or impossible to comply with.

(4) The documents required are obtainable and presentable under the documentary credit.

(5) The description of goods or the unit price, if any, are as stated in the sales contract.

(6) There are no conditions indicated in the credit requiring payment of interest, charges or expenses that were not contracted for in the sales contract.

(7) The shipping date and the expiry date indicated in the credit and the period for presentation of documents are sufficient to enable the beneficiary to comply with in order to obtain the payment.

(8) The port of loading or taking in charge, the place of dispatch and the port of discharge or delivery are consistent with those in the sales contract.

(9) The insurance requirement, i.e. whether it is to be covered by the beneficiary or the applicant, is declared in the credit.

(10) The bank's obligation under the credit is conditioned on a complying presentation and the credit is subject to UCP 600.

If there are any terms and conditions not acceptable or impossible to comply with, the exporter should request the applicant and the issuing bank to make necessary changes. If the exporter accepts the terms and conditions of the credit, he should prepare and dispatch the goods and submit the documents as required in the credit. Non-compliance with the terms and conditions stipulated in the credit or irregularities in the documents will oblige the issuing bank to refuse to honour.

After shipping the goods, the exporter receives the transport documents and prepares other documents. Then, which bank should the exporter present the required documents to? It depends on the stipulations in the credit. The following situations may exist.

(1) If the credit is available by sight payment with the issuing bank, the exporter presents the stipulated documents to the advising bank or another transmitting bank which forwards the documents to the issuing bank for payment. If the credit is available by payment with a nominated bank, the exporter presents the documents to the nominated bank for payment.

(2) If the credit is available by deferred payment with the issuing bank, the exporter presents the required documents to the advising bank or another transmitting bank which forwards the documents to the issuing bank and obtains the payment from the issuing bank at maturity. If the credit is available by deferred payment with a nominated bank, the exporter presents the documents to the nominated bank which incurs the deferred payment obligation and pays at maturity.

(3) If the credit is available by acceptance with the issuing bank, the exporter presents the documents to the advising bank or another transmitting bank which forwards the documents to the issuing bank for acceptance and obtains payment at maturity. If the credit is available by acceptance with a nominated bank, the exporter presents the documents to the nominated bank for acceptance and obtains payment at maturity.

(4) If the credit is available by negotiation with any bank, the exporter presents the documents to any bank for negotiation. Then the negotiating bank forwards the documents to the issuing bank for payment. If the credit is available by negotiation restricted with a specified bank, the exporter presents the documents to the specified bank for negotiation.

The advising bank may only serves as an advising bank without any other obligations. In practice it often turns into a paying bank, an accepting bank, a negotiating bank or even a confirming bank, depending on the nature of the credit.

According Article 14a of UCP 600, "the nominated bank, confirming bank, if any, and the issuing bank must examine a presentation to determine, on the basis of the documents alone, whether they appear on their face to constitute a complying presentation." Therefore, be it a paying bank, an accepting bank, a negotiating bank or a confirming bank, if any, the principle for the bank to observe is the documents submitted by the exporter must constitute a complying presentation.

It is noted that the payment by the paying bank or the confirming bank, if any, discharges the debt while the payment by the negotiating bank has not yet discharged the debt. In other words, the issuing bank nominates or authorizes the paying bank to pay, so the paying bank has no right of recourse to the exporter after payment. The negotiation means the purchase of the documents by the negotiating bank before the issuing bank pays. Thus, the negotiating bank is just a transferee of the documents and need forward the documents to the issuing bank for payment or reimbursement. If dishonoured by the issuing bank, the negotiating bank has the right of recourse against the exporter.

Stage 5: The issuing bank examines the documents and pays or reimburses the negotiating bank

Upon its receipt of the documents forwarded by the negotiating bank, the issuing bank examines the documents to determine whether they constitute a complying presentation. Only against a complying presentation will the issuing bank pay. A problem may emerge when the negotiating bank thinks the documents constitute a complying presentation while the issuing bank does not. Thus, the negotiating bank must be careful in examining the documents to avoid such a negative event happening.

If the issuing bank finds discrepancies with the documents, it may refuse to pay. In doing so, according to UCP 600, the issuing bank must give notice to the bank from which the documents were received or the beneficiary without delay and not later than the close of the 7th banking day following the day of receipt of the documents.

Stage 6: *The importer redeems the documents from the issuing bank and picks up the goods against the bills of lading from the shipping company*

Upon its receipt of the documents, the issuing bank notifies the importer of the arrival of the documents. The importer examines the documents to ensure they constitute a complying presentation before agreeing to make payment. Its only excuse to dishonour is that the documents do not constitute a complying presentation. Because of the possibility of dishonor by the importer, it is wise for the issuing bank to make sure that the applicant is reliable and creditworthy before issuing the credit.

After payment, the importer obtains the shipping documents from the issuing bank and arranges for picking up the goods. Till now, the documentary credit operation comes to an end.

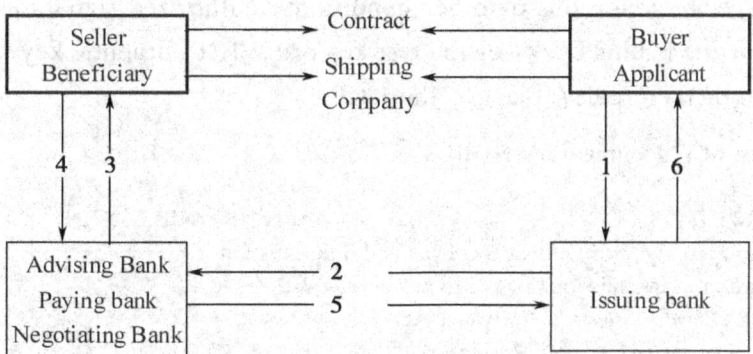

Figure 5.2　Operation of a documentary credit

5.5　Contents of a documentary credit

Items on the credit itself

Items on the credit itself includes the issuing bank, the form of credit, the L/C Number, the issuing date, the beneficiary, the applicant, the expiry date and place and the L/C amount and currency.

Items on draft

It is the drawn clause of the draft(s) and mainly concerns the drawer, the drawee and the payee. If the credit does not require draft(s), there will be no drawn clause in the credit.

Items on goods, shipping documents and transport

Items on goods include the goods' name, description, packing, unit price, price term, quantity, mark, etc. Items on shipping documents are invoices, bills of lading, insurance policy, etc. Items on the tramsport cover the port of loading/shipment, the port of discharge or destination, the latest date of shipment, etc. and whether partial shipment or transshipment permitted or not.

Other items

Other items include the instructions, the undertaking clause of the issuing bank, special conditions or other conditions, authorized signatures of the agent for the issuing bank, or the test key or SWIFT authentic key, and the notation of the credit subject to the UCP 600.

Specimen of a documentary credit

```
11/07/12-18:23:01                              PrinterNJB-3XXX-000005
------------------ Instance Type and Transmission ------------------
Notification (Transmission) of Original sent to SWIFT (ACK)
Network Delivery Status  : Network Ack
Priority/Delivery        : Normal
Message Input Reference  : 1819 120711XXBCCNBJANJB2637XXXXX
------------------------- Message Header ---------------------------
Swift Input    : FIN 700 Issue of a Documentary Credit
Sender         : XXBCCNBJNJB
                 BANK XXX OF CHINA, THE
                 (JIANGSU BRANCH)
                 NANJING CN
Receiver       : GEBABEBBXXX
                 BNP PARIBAS FORTIS (FORTIS BANK SA/NV)
                 (ALL BELGIAN OFFICES)
                 BRUSSELS BE
-------------------------- Message Text ----------------------------
```

27:	Sequence of Total
	1/1
40A:	Form of Documentary Credit
	IRREVOCABLE
20:	Documentary Credit Number
	NJB2012LC00211
31C:	Date of Issue
	120711
40E:	Applicable Rules
	UCP LATEST VERSION
31D:	Date and Place of Expiry
	121021BELGIUM
50:	Applicant
	SUZHOU ABC CO., LTD.
	(ADDRESS AND TEL
	SEE FIELD 47A)
59:	Beneficiary-Name & Address
	XYZ CO. LTD
	1xx 85xx WEVELGEM BELGIUM HR
	KORTRIJK 87452 VAT BE 413.227.xxx
	TEL. 0032. 56.xx.xx.3D
32B:	Currency Code, Amount
	Currency : USD (US DOLLAR)
	Amount : #554,400.#
39A:	Percentage Credit Amt Tolerance
	05/05
41D:	Available with… By… -Name & Addr
	ANY BANK
	BY NEGOTIATION
42C:	Drafts at…
	XXBCCNBJNJB
	BANK XXX OF CHINA, THE
	(JAINGSU BRANCH)
	NANJING CN
43P:	Partial Shipments
	ALLOWED
43T:	Transshipment
	ALLOWED
44E:	Port of Loading/Airport of Dep.
	ANY EUROPEAN PORT
44F:	Port of Discharge/Airport of Dest.
	ZHANGJIAGANG, CHINA
44C:	Latest Date of Shipment
	120930
45A:	Description of Goods &/or Services

288.000 KGS SCUTCHED TOW T2:2 DRUMS AT 0.95 USD/KG
208.000 KGS SCUTCHED TOW T6:6 DRUMS AT 1.35 USD/KG
SHIPMENT: 9 CONTAINERS IN JULY
          11 CONTAINERS IN AUGUST/SEPTEMBER
TOTAL AMOUNT: USD554,400.00
PRICE TERM: CIF ZHANGJIAGANG PORT, CHINA

46A: Documents Required
+ SIGNED COMMERCIAL INVOICE IN 3 COPIES INDIATING L/C NO. AND CONTRACT NO. 2012/1327.
+ FULL SET OF CLEAN ON BOARD OCEAN BILLS OF LADING MADE OUT TO ORDER AND BLANK ENDORSED, MAKRED 'FREIGHT PREPAID' NOTIFYING THE APPLICANT.
+ INSURANCE POLICY/CERTIFICATE IN 2 COPIES FOR 110 PERCENT OF THE INVOICE VALUE ENDORSED, COVERING OCEAN MARINE TRANSPORTATION ALL RISKS, WAR RISKS.
+ CERTIFICATE OF ORIGN IN 1 COPY ISSUED BY BELGIUM COMPETENT AUTHORITY.
+ PACKING LIST/WEIGHT MEMO IN 3 COPIES INDICATING QUANTITY/GROSS AND NET WEIGHTS AND PACKING CONDITIONS AS CALLED FOR BY THE BENEFICIARY.
+ CERTIFICIATE OF QUANTITY/WEIGHT IN 3 COPIES ISSUED BY THE BENEFICIARY.
+ CERTIFICATE OF QUALITY IN 1 COPY ISSUED BY THE BENENFCIARY.
+ PHYTOSANITARY CERTIFICATE IN 1 ORIGINAL ISSUED BY BELGIUM COMPENTENT AUTHORITY.
+ NON-WOOD PACKING CERTIFICATE IN 3 COPIES ISSUED BY THE BENEFICIARY.

47A: Additional Conditions
+ APPLICANT'S TEL: 0086-512-5220××××, FAX: 0086-512 5220××××.
+ BENEFICIARY'S FAX. 0032.56.41.××.××
+ BOTH CREDIT AMOUNT AND SHIPMENT QUANTITY 5 PERCENT MORE OR LESS ARE ALLOWED.
+ THIRD PARTY AS SHIPPER IS NOT ACCEPTABLE. SHORT FORM/BLANK BACK B/L IS NOT ACCEPTABLE.
+ ALL DRAFTS AND DOCUMENTS MUST BE ISSUED IN ENGLISH OR IN OTHER LANGUAGES CONTAINING ENGLISH ANNOTATION (S).
+ A DISCREPANCY FEE OF USD75.00 OR EQUIVALENT AND THE RELATIVE CABLE CHARGES, IF ANY, WILL DEDUCTED FROM THE PROCEEDS FOR EACH PRESENTATION OF DISCREPANT DOCUMENTS UNDER THIS CREDIT.
+ ONE EXTRA COPY OF INVOICE AND BILLS OF LADING ARE REQUESTED TO BE PRESENTED FOR ISSUING BANK'S REFERENCE ONLY

71B: Charges
ALL BANKING CHARGES OUTSIDE THE
ISSUING BANK INCLUDING REIMBURSING
CHARGES ARE FOR ACCOUNT OF BENEFICIARY.

48: Period for Presentation
DOCUMENTS TO BE PRESENTED WITHIN
21 DAYS AFTER SHIPMENT DATE BUT
WITHIN THE VALIDITY OF THIS CREDIT

49: Confirmation Instructions
WITHOUT

78: Instr to Payg/Accptg/Negotg Bank
+ALL DRAFTS AND DOCUMENTS TO BE FORWARDED IN ONE LOT BY COURIER TO THE BANK XXX OF CHINA, JIANGSU BRANCH, INTERMEDIARY BUSINESS DEPARTMENT, xx FLOOR, xx PLAZA, NO. xx ZHONGSHAN SOUTH ROAD, NANJING, JIANGSU PROVINCE, P.R. CHINA 210005.
+THE AMOUNT OF EACH DRAWING MUST BE ENDORSED ON THE REVERSE OF THIS CREDIT AND THE NEGOTIATING BANK'S COVERING SCHEDULE TO CERTIFY THE SAME.
+UPON RECEIPT OF DRAFTS AND DOCUMENTS AT OUR COUNTERS CONSTITUTING A COMPLYING PRESENTATION, WE SHALL REIMBURSE THE NEGOTIATING BANK AS PER THEIR INSTRUCTION AT MATURITY.

72: Sender to Receiver Information
THIS IS AN OPERATIVE INSTRUMENT
AND NO MAIL CONFIRMATION WILL
FOLLOW. PLEASE ACKNOWLEDGE RECEIPT
OF THIS CREDIT THROUGH OUR SWIFT
ADDRESS EIBCCNBJNJB.

5.6 The examination of a documentary credit

The examination of a documentary credit in this subsection will be discussed from the perspectives of the advising bank and its customer (the exporter) respectively.

The examination by the advising bank

Establishing the authenticity of the authorized signatures or the test key
Upon receipt of a documentary credit from a foreign bank, the

advising bank should first establish the authenticity of the credit. If the authorized signature (of the letter) or the test key or authentic key (of the cable, telex or SWIFT) is in compliance with those kept by the advising bank, the advising bank makes a notation on the credit certifying its authenticity. If the signature or the test key is not correct, the advising bank need notify the issuing bank to add the signature or test key again to prove its realness. In addition, the advising bank should check the authority of the authorized signatures. If it is not the person who has the authority to sign, the credit is invalid.

Investigating the creditworthiness of the issuing bank

When a bank receives a documentary credit from a foreign bank, the two banks are usually correspondent banks. In establishing a correspondent banking relationship, a bank usually selects creditworthy banks. If the issuing bank is one of the correspondent banks of the advising bank, the advising bank will accept it as agreed. However, if the credit is from a bank rather than a correspondent bank, the advising bank usually only advises the credit to the beneficiary and, in order to avoid risks, will not accept to be the paying bank, negotiating bank or confirming bank. In this case, the advising bank will not investigate the creditworthiness of the issuing bank. If the advising bank intends to pay, negotiate or confirm the credit, it must investigate the issuing bank's creditworthiness.

Investigating the credit standings of the issuing bank and the country where the issuing bank resides

In China, the head offices of different banks are responsible for rating the credit standings of different countries. If the issuing bank and its country is below the standard requirements set by its head office, the bank will refuse to pay, negotiate or confirm the credit. It only advises the credit to the beneficiary and reminds the beneficiary of the bad credit rating of the issuing bank and its country.

Checking the liability clause of the transmitting bank, if any

If the issuing bank has no correspondent banking relationship with the advising bank, the issuing may require another bank to transmit the credit to the advising bank. Then, the bank, serving as a transmitting bank, will first establish the credit's authenticity and then transmit it to the advising bank. The advising bank should examine the liability clause of the transmitting bank. If the credit requires the advising bank to negotiate, pay or confirm the credit, the advising bank must investigate the transmitting bank's creditworthiness. If there is no correspondent banking relationship between the issuing bank and the transmitting bank, what the advising bank should do is only to advise the credit.

Checking the credit rating of the transferring bank

If the credit is a transferable credit and has been transferred by another bank (the transferring bank), the advising bank should check the liability of the transferring bank and investigate the creditworthiness of the transferring bank.

Checking the credit itself

The form of the credit The form here means whether the credit is revocable or irrevocable. According to UCP 600, a credit is irrevocable even if there is no indication to that effect.

The date of issue The date of issue must be clearly indicated. In absence of such a date, the date of the letter of credit or the date of receiving the cable will be deemed to be the date of issue. The date of issue may be used to determine whether the buyer asks the issuing bank to issue the credit in accordance with the stipulations in the sales contract. It is also used to see whether the date of presentation of documents is after the date of issue.

The expiry date and place The expiry date is the last date allowing the beneficiary to submit the documents to the issuing bank, another nominated bank or the confirming bank, if any. The beneficiary must present the documents to the issuing bank or the nominated bank on or before the expiry date.

The expiry place is the place where the beneficiary must present the documents to the issuing bank, another nominated bank or the confirming bank, if any. If the expiry place is in a foreign country, say the issuing bank's place, the beneficiary (the exporter) must submit the documents earlier to make sure that the documents arrive at the foreign bank within the specified time. In most cases, the advising bank suggests the beneficiary to ask the importer and the issuing bank to amend it and change it to be the beneficiary's place. Then it will be convenient for the beneficiary to submit the documents before the expiry date. If the credit does not indicate the expiry place, the advising bank should confirm it with the issuing bank immediately.

The applicant of the credit The applicant of the credit is the importer under the sales contract. The credit must indicate expressly the full name and address of the applicant correctly.

The beneficiary The beneficiary of the credit is the exporter under the sales contract and the credit is issued in favor of the exporter. The credit must indicate clearly the full name and address of the beneficiary. In the event of missing or error, the advising bank must contact the issuing bank without delay or notifies the beneficiary of it. Then the beneficiary contacts the applicant to amend the credit.

The L/C number The L/C number is the issuing bank's reference number. When contacting the issuing bank on this L/C transaction, the advising bank must quote the number. It should be clearly indicated in the credit. If the number appears in the credit more than once, they must be consistent with one another. If they are not consistent with one another, the advising bank needs to contact the beneficiary to ask for an amendment.

The currency code and amount The currency used in the credit must be freely convertible. If the currency is not internationally convertible, the advising bank should remind the beneficiary of it. The currency code must be the ISO currency code. The description of the amount must be in the internationally acceptable form, such as USD1,000,000.00. If the amount is written both in words and figure, the two should be consistent.

The type of credit According to UCP 600, a letter of credit may be made available by sight payment, deferred payment, acceptance or negotiation. Thus, there are four basic types of credit: sight payment credit, deferred payment credit, acceptance credit and negotiation credit[①]. Any credit falls into one of the four types.

If a credit is available by payment with the advising bank, the credit must contain a clause by which the paying bank may claim reimbursement from the issuing bank or the reimbursing bank, if any. Since the paying bank has no recourse to the beneficiary after payment, if there is no such clause in the credit, the paying bank will not be properly reimbursed. One reason for the advising bank to refuse to be the paying bank is that there is no reimbursement clause included in the credit. If the advising bank refuses to be the paying bank, the advising bank must notify the issuing bank without delay. The cases for deferred payment credit, acceptance credit and negotiation credit are the same. Other reasons for the advising bank to refuse to be the paying bank are as follows:

(1) The issuing bank is not a correspondent bank of the advising bank.

(2) The issuing bank's country has no foreign exchange or adopts strict controls on it.

(3) The issuing bank country is troubled with civil disturbance, war or political instability.

(4) The issuing bank once refused to pay the advising bank in the past without any reasons.

A credit may be made available by negotiation with a nominated bank or any bank. If the credit is available by negotiation with the advising bank, the credit should contain a reimbursement clause. It will be easier for the negotiating bank to get reimbursed after negotiation.

A credit may require or authorize the advising bank to be the confirming bank. In this case, the advising bank must carefully examine the creditworthiness of the issuing bank and determines whether to accept it or not.

Other types of credit include transferable, revolving, back-to-back, red clause and standby.

---

① Sight payment credif：即期付款信用证；deferred payment credif：延期付款信用证；acceptance credit：承兑信用证；negotiation credit：议付信用证

Drawn clause This clause authorizes the beneficiary to draw draft(s) under the credit on the issuing bank or on a nominated bank. In a credit that requires draft(s), the drawer is the beneficiary (the exporter), the payee is the beneficiary himself or the negotiating bank and the drawee may be the issuing bank, the paying bank, the accepting bank or the confirming bank.

The drawn clause may be expressed as:"Draft (s) drawn on us bearing 'drawn under L/C NO. 12345 issued by National Australian Bank Melbourne DD October 10, 1994.'" Here, "us" means the issuing bank. The expression of "drawn on us" means the drawee is the issuing bank. UCP 600 prescribes that a credit "must not be issued available by a draft drawn on the applicant." In other words, the draft under a credit must be drawn on a bank, i.e. the issuing bank or a nominated bank.

The description of the goods[①] The description of the goods must be complete and precise. Too detailed description will bring about trouble to both the beneficiary and the advising bank in preparing and examining documents. The description of the goods includes the name, quantity, size or specifications, etc.

The documents required A credit usually lists the documents that the beneficiary must surrender. The requirements for the same item in different documents must be consistent with one another. For example, if the clause on the bills of lading requires "Freight Prepaid", then the price term in the commercial invoice must be CIF or CFR. If it requires "Freight Collect", the price term is usually FOB. The key point is that a credit must require the beneficiary to surrender 3/3 original clean on board bills of lading. And no other clauses contain any indication that the beneficiary may send an original bill of lading directly to the importer. Moreover, the clauses on various documents must be acceptable.

The price term The most often used price terms are FOB, CIF, CFR, such as "FOB Shanghai" or "CIF Liverpool". Incoterms 2010 have detailed description of different trade terms. Details on it can be found in Chapter 1.

The date of shipment It is the latest date for the beneficiary to ship the

---

① description of the goods：货物描述，品描

goods. The beneficiary must ship the goods on or before the date. The date should contain the year, month and day.

The period of presentation of documents[①] A credit usually stipulates a period of presentation of documents. For example: "Documents to be presented within ten days after the date of transport documents but within the validity date of this documentary credit." It means the beneficiary must submit the documents to the issuing bank or the nominated bank within 10 days after the bills of lading date and no later than the expiry date of the credit. If there is no such a stipulation in the credit, the period of presenting documents, according to UCP 600, is within 21 days after the date of shipment and within the validity of the credit. The frequently used period of presenting documents is 10, 15 or 21 days after the date of transport documents. If the credit requires a period of more than 21 days, it is also acceptable so long as it is within the validity of the credit.

The reimbursing bank It is the bank designated by the issuing bank to reimburse the paying bank or negotiating bank. It may be the issuing bank's branch or a third bank. Usually both the issuing bank and the advising bank maintain accounts with the reimbursing bank. The reimbursing bank's payment is against the authorization of the issuing bank and the reimbursement claim from the paying bank. However, its payment does not discharge the draft(s) because the issuing bank may dishonour when it finds discrepancies with the documents. If the documents do not constitute a complying presentation, the issuing bank may claim the negotiating bank to return the money paid to it by the reimbursing bank.

The reimbursement clause This reimbursement clause must be correct and reasonable. If the reimbursement route is too complex and the advising bank is requested to be the paying bank, the negotiating bank or the confirming bank, the advising bank should notify the beneficiary to contact the issuing bank to amend it. If the clause stipulates that the advising bank may debit the issuing bank's account with the advising bank, the advising bank should check whether the account has enough money and whether the

---

① period of presentation of documents: 交单期

currency of the account and the currency of the credit are the same.

The confirmation clause It is the clause in which the issuing bank authorizes another bank (usually the advising bank) to add confirmation to the credit. Such a clause is stated as: "Please advise this documentary credit adding your confirmation". The advising bank must check the issuing bank's creditworthiness and the contents of the credit. Based on the amount of the credit and other related stipulations, the advising bank decides whether it agrees to it or not. Reasons for the advising bank to refuse to add confirmation include:

(1) The issuing bank is not the bank's correspondent bank.

(2) The issuing bank's country has no foreign exchange or adopts strict control on it.

(3) The issuing bank's country is confronted with riots, war or other political instability.

(4) The issuing bank once dishonored the documents negotiated by the advising bank without any reasons.

Banking charges The issuing bank's charges are for the applicant's account while the advising bank and negotiating bank's charges are for the beneficiary's account. For example, a credit may state: "All banking charges outside the opening bank are for the beneficiary's account." If so, the advising bank should notify the beneficiary of it to reduce unreasonable charges. If there is no such stipulation, all charges of the bank is for the account of the applicant. But if the applicant refuses to pay any banking charges to the negotiating bank, the negotiating bank has the right to collect them from the beneficiary.

The validity of the credit Some letters of credit may contain a special condition on the validity of the credit. If the advising bank finds any statement or condition that makes the credit invalid, the advising bank should notify the beneficiary that the credit is not valid for the moment and suggest that the beneficiary prepare and dispatch the goods when receiving the validity notification.

Special conditions Some letters of credit may contain special conditions concerning the beneficiary, the advising bank, the paying bank, the accepting bank, the confirming bank or the negotiating bank. The advising bank should examine the conditions carefully to see if they are acceptable. If the credit is in the form of letter, the bank should check all the contents in the letter including the printed words, typed words, words in the margins and on the back because all of them constitute the text of the credit.

The engagement clause Different credits have different engagement clauses. If a credit is issued via SWIFT MT700, there will be no engagement clause and may not be required to add such a clause.

Subject to UCP 600 A letter of credit must indicate it is subject to UCP 600. It may be stated as: "Subject to Uniform Customs and Practice for Documentary Credits (2007 Revision), International Chamber of Commerce Publication No. 600."

The examination by the exporter

The above has discussed how the advising bank examines a documentary credit upon receiving it from the issuing bank. The following are the questions the exporter should ask upon receiving the credit from the advising bank[1].

(1) Is the L/C irrevocable? Although UCP 600 prescribes that a credit is irrevocable even if it does not state so, there might be some wordings in the credit which makes the credit invalid. The exporter must be careful about such hidden wordings.

(2) Are the name and address of the beneficiary as per those of the exporter? If not, the exporter should ask the applicant to amend the credit; otherwise, the documents submitted by the exporter containing the name and address of the beneficiary must be consistent with those written in the credit.

(3) Are the name and address of the applicant as per those of the importer? If not, the exporter should ask the applicant to amend it; otherwise, the documents submitted by the seller containing the name and

---

[1] John S. Gordon. *Export/Import Letters of Credit and Payment Methods: Making Payments in International Trade.* Global Training Center, Inc.. 2002: 3-35

address of the applicant must be consistent with those written in the credit.

(4) Is the issuing bank creditworthy and acceptable? In other words, which bank issued the credit? Can the exporter reply on this bank for payment? If the issuing bank is not creditworthy, the credit is not acceptable to the exporter.

(5) Is the credit confirmed? If the issuing bank is not creditworthy, the exporter may ask the credit to be confirmed by another prime bank in the exporter's place.

(6) Is the confirming bank creditworthy and acceptable? If the confirming bank is not creditworthy, the credit is not acceptable to the exporter.

(7) Is the latest shipping date acceptable and reasonable? If the latest shipping date is too early, the exporter will not have enough time to prepare and ship the goods. For example, if the credit calls for port to port shipment to a foreign country, suppose the exporter is in Chongqing, China, this means the goods has to be loaded on to an ocean vessel on or before the latest date rather than shipping directly from Chongqing on or before the latest shipping date. If there is no latest shipping date, the shipment must occur and the complying presentation must be submitted on or before the expiry date of the credit.

(8) Is the goods described correctly? If the description of the goods is not correct, the exporter should consider whether he can comply with the incorrect description in every document containing the description of the goods. If not, the exporter should ask the applicant to amend it.

(9) Are weights, measures and the unit price as agreed in the sales contract? If not, the exporter should ask the applicant to amend it; or, he will comply with such stipulations.

(10) Are the place of dispatch and the destination as per those in the sales contract? If not, the exporter should ask the applicant to amend it. Otherwise, the documents submitted by him will not constitute a complying presentation.

(11) Is the amount of the credit sufficient to cover the value of drawing? If not, the exporter should ask the applicant to amend it. If he

accepts it, he will not be paid the full value of the invoice.

(12) Is the insurance as agreed? It is customary for marine insurance coverage to be 110% of the transaction value. It is stated as 110% of invoice value, 110% of CIF or 110% of FOB, etc.

(13) Are the amount and currency of the credit as per the quote? If not, the exporter should ask the applicant to amend the credit.

(14) Is the amount in numbers the same as that in words? If not, the amendment is also needed.

(15) Does the credit allow free negotiation? If not, the exporter can only negotiate the complying documents with the nominated bank; otherwise, the negotiating bank will not be reimbursed by the issuing bank or the reimbursing bank, if any.

(16) Is the nominated bank acceptable? If the credit requires a nominated bank to be the accepting bank, the paying bank or the negotiating bank, the exporter should determine whether the bank is acceptable to him. Otherwise, the exporter should ask the applicant to amend the credit.

(17) Are there more than 21 days from latest shipping date to the credit expiry date? UCP 600 states that the complying presentation must be done within 21 day after the latest date. If there is no 21 days from the latest shipping date to the expiry date of the credit, the exporter should make sure that he presents the complying documents on or before the expiry date of the credit. Even if there is no latest shipping date, the exporter should ensure that the documents be submitted on or before the expiry date of the credit.

(18) Is the credit transferable? If yes, the exporter should determine whether the transferring bank is acceptable to him; otherwise, it should ask the applicant to amend the credit.

(19) Are banking charges payable as agreed? If the credit does not mention it, all banking charges are for account of the importer (other than the charge by the reimbursing bank). If the credit states "all banking charges outside the issuing bank is for beneficiary's account, the beneficiary (the exporter) will be responsible for the banking charges of the advising

bank, paying bank, negotiating bank or confirming bank, if any.

(20) Are there other unacceptable clauses? A credit may contain boycott language or requirements or other clauses or conditions that may be unacceptable to the exporter. If so, the exporter must ask the applicant to amend the credit.

(21) Are partial shipments allowed? If not, the exporter should know whether the goods can be shipped once from the seller's place to the destination. If it is impossible, the exporter should ask the applicant to amend the credit.

(22) Is transshipment allowed? If not, the exporter should make sure the goods will be directly shipped to the destination.

(23) Will be is the price term of shipping term as agreed? This is also important to the exporter because changing the terms incurs extra costs or even difficulty in shipping the goods.

(24) Are port to port carriers available? If not, the credit should allow the transshipment.

(25) Where does the credit expire? The expiry place is usually in the issuing bank's place, but it is favorable to the exporter if the expiry place is in the exporter's place.

(26) Is the draft(s) clause as required? If not, the exporter should determine whether it accepts it or not.

(27) Are there any non-documental clauses? UCP 600 states that if a credit contains a condition without stipulating the document to indicate the compliance with the condition, banks will deem such a condition as not stated and will regard it. From the perspective of the exporter, if the credit contains a non-documentary clause, he had better ask the applicant to amend it.

(28) Is the credit subject to UCP 600? If not, the exporter should know which laws will be used to determine the compliance of the documents and how the exporter will be treated under the related laws. The wise way is to ask the applicant to contain such a clause in the credit.

5.7 Types of credit

Irrevocable credit[①]

An irrevocable credit is a definite undertaking by the issuing bank to pay, accept and pay or negotiate the beneficiary's complying documents. It cannot be amended or canceled without the consents of all the parties to the credit. Although an irrevocable credit provides the beneficiary with greater assurance of payment, whether it will be paid solely depends on the undertaking of the foreign issuing bank and the precondition for payment is a complying presentation.

An irrevocable credit usually has an "irrevocable" notation in it. Although UCP 600 states that a credit is irrevocable even if there is no indication of "irrevocable," the beneficiary should be aware that some conditions incorporated in the credit can make it invalid. For instance, if a credit may contain such condition as "subject to cancellation or amendment at any time without prior notice to the beneficiary" or "the advice is for your guidance only in preparing drafts and documents and conveys no engagement or obligation on our part or on the part of our above-mentioned correspondent," such conditions will change the credit into a revocable credit.

Confirmed irrevocable credit[②]

When a bank is authorized or nominated by the issuing bank to add confirmation to an irrevocable credit and the authorized bank does add confirmation to the credit, the credit becomes a confirmed irrevocable credit. The nominated bank that has added confirmation to the credit is the

---

① irrevocable credit：不可撤销信用证，即一经开出，在有效期内未经受益人或议付行等有关当事人同意，开证行不得随意修改或撤销的信用证；revocable credit：可撤销信用证，即不需要经过受益人等有关当事人的同意，开证行可以随时撤销的信用证

② confirmed irrevocable credit：保兑、不可撤销信用证

confirming bank. According to UCP 600, confirmation means "a definite undertaking of the confirming bank, in addition to that of the issuing bank, to honour or negotiate a complying presentation." Under a confirmed irrevocable credit, both the issuing bank and the confirming bank undertake to pay the beneficiary against a complying presentation. Hence, a confirmed irrevocable credit gives the beneficiary a double assurance of payment.

UCP 600 prescribes that the confirming bank is a bank that adds its confirmation to a credit upon the issuing bank's authorization or request. If a bank adds its "confirmation" to a credit without the authorization or request of the issuing bank, the bank is not a confirming bank. In practice, such an action is called "silent confirmation[①]," which is an agreement between the beneficiary and the "so-called confirming bank". Since the bank has not been authorized to add its confirmation, the bank has no right to claim reimbursement from the issuing bank.

Usually, there is a special instruction in a confirmed irrevocable credit, requiring the advising bank to add confirmation. If a credit issued by mail, for example, the request is like this: "The advising bank is requested to add its confirmation." If the advising bank agrees to it, the advising bank will write in the advising bank's instruction: "We have been requested to add our confirmation to this credit and we therefore undertake that any draft drawn by you in accordance with the terms of this credit will be only paid by us." If a credit is issued by SWIFT, it is indicated in the confirmation instruction whether it is confirmed or not.

Sight payment credit

A sight payment credit is a credit that provides for drawing by the beneficiary at sight, i. e. the issuing bank, the nominated bank or confirming bank, if any, undertakes to pay the beneficiary at sight against

---

① silent confirmation：沉默保兑，即在没有开证行授权或要求下的保兑，是加沉默保兑的银行与受益人之间的协议，加沉默保兑的银行不是真正意义上的保兑行，没有权利要求开证行偿付

a complying presentation.

A sight payment credit is marked as "available by payment with … bank". "Available by payment" indicates that beneficiary will get payment at sight while "with… bank" indicates which bank will pay the beneficiary. The beneficiary can specify the paying bank from the name of the bank. In practice, the paying bank may be the issuing bank or a nominated bank. If the credit is a confirmed credit, the bank after the word "with" is usually the confirming bank. Some sight payment credits require the beneficiary to submit draft(s) while others do not. If a sight payment credit requires draft(s), the credit is marked as "available with … Bank by payment at sight draft"; if the credit does not requires draft(s), the wording is expressed as: "available with … bank by payment at sight against the documents detailed herein."

Under a sight payment credit, it is wise for the beneficiary to ensure that the place of payment is at the beneficiary's place and the paying bank is the beneficiary's bank. If the place of payment is at the issuing bank, the beneficiary must take the time of sending the documents to the issuing bank into account and make sure that the required documents arrive at the place of payment before the stipulated time of payment. Some unexpected events might occur before the documents safely arrive at the issuing bank. If the paying bank is the advising bank in the beneficiary's country, it is easy for the beneficiary to submit the documents. So long as the documents constitute a complying presentation, the paying bank will pay the beneficiary without recourse. The beneficiary can obtain payment immediately after submitting documents, ensuring his immediate use of funds and avoiding the exchange rate fluctuation risk and the importer's non-payment risk. A sight payment credit is advantageous to the exporter.

Acceptance credit

An acceptance credit is a credit that is available by acceptance with the issuing bank or a nominated bank. The procedures to an acceptance credit are:

(1) The beneficiary prepares and ships the goods and obtains the

transport documents.

(2) The beneficiary prepares all the documents required by the credit and draws the time draft(s) on the issuing bank or the nominated bank.

(3) The beneficiary presents the draft(s) and the stipulated documents that constitute a complying presentation to the advising bank.

(4) If the advising bank is the nominated paying bank, it accepts the time draft(s) and keeps the documents and returns the accepted drafts to the beneficiary.

(5) If the issuing bank is the paying bank, the advising bank will forward the draft(s) and documents to the issuing bank for acceptance. After acceptance, the issuing bank keeps the documents and returns the accepted draft(s) to the beneficiary.

(6) In either case, the beneficiary holds the accepted draft(s) as security. By accepting the draft(s), the paying bank promises to pay at the maturity date. The beneficiary can only obtain payment from the paying bank at the maturity date.

(7) If he does not want to wait till the due date, the beneficiary can discount the draft(s) with a discounting house or a bank and obtain the proceeds in advance.

Upon acceptance, the issuing bank or the nominated paying bank obtains the documents, but it will not release them to the applicant until the applicant redeems the documents at maturity. There may be a situation that the documents are in the issuing bank and the goods have arrived at destination, but the applicant (the importer) cannot obtain the documents to pick up the goods. Only against payment at maturity will the applicant get the documents. Under this situation, the applicant may submit a Trust Receipt (T/R) to the issuing bank to borrow the documents from the issuing bank, but it is up to the issuing bank's approval. The Trust Receipt is not accepted by banks in some countries, though.

An acceptance credit requires the time draft(s) because acceptance only occurs in the case of the time draft(s). An acceptance credit is marked as: "available with… bank by acceptance of draft(s) at… days after sight against the documents detailed herein and beneficiary's draft(s) drawn on us."And there is usually an undertaking by the issuing bank:"We hereby engage that draft(s) drawn in conformity with the terms of this credit will be duly accepted on presentation and duly honored at maturity."

Acceptance credit with usance drafts payable at sight①

The beneficiary of an acceptance credit may either hold the accepted draft(s) till maturity or discount it with a bank to obtain the funds immediately. If the beneficiary chooses to hold the draft(s) and presents the draft(s) to the paying bank for payment, it is an ordinary acceptance credit. If the beneficiary chooses to discount the draft(s) in advance, the beneficiary will obtain payment by paying the discounting charges. The transferee or the ultimate holder will present the draft(s) to the paying bank for payment at maturity. This is also an ordinary acceptance credit.

One possibility is that under an acceptance credit it is the applicant that pays the accepting and discounting charges and the beneficiary obtains payment immediately. In order to achieve this result, the acceptance credit must contain a clause:"The usance drafts are payable on a sight basis, discount charges and acceptance commission are for the buyer's account." This clause in effect changes the acceptance credit into a sight payment credit, although the source of the funds used for payment comes from the transferee of the drafts and the credit itself is still a usance credit. This is why people call such credits "fake usance credit" in Chinese banks.

Deferred payment credit

A deferred payment credit is a credit that is available by deferred payment with the issuing bank or another nominated bank at a fixed time after the date of the bills of lading or after the presentation of documents. It is similar to an acceptance credit, except for that no draft is required and the maturity date is determined based on the bills of lading date or the presentation of the documents.

The deferred payment credit was first introduced in Japan in the early

---

① acceptance credit with usance drafts payable at sight：远期汇票即期付款的承兑信用证，即假远期信用证

1950s when Japanese banks refused to issue any credits with time drafts and only issued credits with sight drafts in order to discourage Japanese imports from abroad. Under this circumstance, Japanese buyers developed a kind of "deferred sight credit". Such a credit was made available by payment against a sight draft, but contained a provision that the sight draft could only be presented for payment at a fixed time after the documents was submitted and before the expiry date of the credit. Seemingly, the credit is a sight payment credit but in effect a deferred payment credit.

To the beneficiary, a deferred payment credit is not as good as an acceptance credit. Under acceptance credit, the beneficiary obtains an accepted draft after presenting the documents and the accepted draft can be negotiated or discounted. Under a deferred payment credit, however, the beneficiary has no negotiable instrument to hold after presenting the documents and has to wait till the maturity.

A deferred payment credit is usually marked as:"available with… bank by deferred payment at 60 days after sight against the documents detailed herein."

Negotiation credit

A negotiation credit is a credit that permits the nominated bank or any bank to negotiate or purchase the drafts and/or documents. Negotiation credit can be divided into two types: restricted negotiation credit and free negotiation credit.

Restricted negotiation credit[①]

Under a restricted negotiation credit, the beneficiary can only negotiate the draft(s) and/or documents with the bank nominated by the issuing bank. The negotiating bank is usually the issuing bank's branch or correspondent bank. A restricted negotiation credit is marked as:

(1) "Negotiation restricted to… Bank";

(2) "Restricted Negotiation";

---

① restricted negotiation credit:限制议付信用证,受益人只能到指定的银行议付汇票及/或单据

(3) "Negotiation under this Credit is restricted to Advising Bank";

(4) "Draft(s) drawn under this Credit are negotiable through… Bank at…";

(5) "We (Issuing bank) hereby issue in your favor this Irrevocable Documentary Restricted Negotiation Credit which is available by negotiation of your draft(s)";

(6) "Draft(s) drawn under Irrevocable Documentary Restricted Negotiation Credit No. … of … Bank";

(7) "Draft(s) so drawn must be inscribed with the number and date of this Restricted Negotiation Credit".

A credit that is available by restricted negotiation with a nominated bank usually contains the engagement clause of the issuing bank, such as: "We hereby engage with you that all draft(s) drawn in conformity with the terms of this Restricted Negotiation Credit will be duly honored on presentation."

Free negotiation credit[①]

In a free negotiation credit, the issuing bank invites any bank to negotiate the drafts and/or documents and implies its promise to honor drafts properly drawn and negotiated by any bank. This kind of credit is marked as:

(1) "available with any bank by negotiation";

(2) "credit available with the advising bank by negotiation against the documents detailed and beneficiary's draft at 90 days after sight drawn on issuing bank";

and accompanied by engagement clauses such as:

(1) "We (Issuing bank) hereby engage with drawers, indorsers and bona fide holders of draft(s) drawn under and in compliance with the terms of the credit that such draft(s) shall be duly honored on due presentation and delivery of documents as specified";

(2) "Provided such drafts are drawn and presented in accordance with

---

① free negotiation credit：自由议付信用证，开证行邀请任何银行议付受益人提交的汇票及/或单据

the terms of this credit, we hereby engage with the drawers, indorsers and bona fide holders that the said drafts shall be duly honored on presentation";

(3) "We hereby agree with the drawers, indorsers and bona fide holders of drafts drawn under and in compliance with the terms of this credit that the same shall be duly honored on due presentation, and negotiated at the Negotiating Bank on or before…";

(4) "We hereby agree with the drawers, indorsers and bona fide holders of drafts drawn in compliance with the terms of the credit that such drafts shall be duly honored on presentation and paid at maturity".

Straight credit

Under a straight credit[①], the obligation of the issuing bank is extended only to the beneficiary in honoring the complying presentation and the credit expires at the counter of the issuing bank. This kind of documentary credit conveys no commitment or obligation on the part of the issuing bank to the parties other than the named beneficiary. Thus, the beneficiary is the only party entitled to demand payment and cannot negotiate the complying documents with any other bank. Straight credit is usually advised to the beneficiary by the issuing bank directly.

Other Banks may choose to purchase the beneficiary's complying documents under a straight credit, but the purchaser acquires no rights against the issuing bank and just presents the documents to the issuing bank on behalf of the beneficiary.

The engagement of the issuing bank in a straight credit may be expressed as: "We hereby agree with the Beneficiary that all Drafts drawn under and/or documents presented hereunder will be duly honored by us provided the terms and conditions of the Credit are complied with and that presentation is made at this office on or before (the expiry date)".

---

① straight credit: 直接信用证，开证行仅对受益人提交的相符单据兑付

Anticipatory credit[①]

An anticipatory credit is also known as a red clause credit or a packing credit. A red clause credit is so called because it traditionally contains a special condition printed in red that authorizes the nominated bank or the confirming bank, if any, to make advances to the beneficiary before its presentation of the documents. The red clause is incorporated into the credit by the issuing bank at the specific request of the applicant. Printing the clause in red is to draw attention to the unique nature of this credit.

If the applicant allows the beneficiary to draw all or part of the credit amount prior to the shipment, the applicant may request the issuing bank to insert a special clause in the credit, authorizing the advising bank or the confirming bank, if any, to make advances to the beneficiary. An anticipatory credit may be used as a way to provide the exporter with the funds needed to acquire and pack the goods prior to the shipment. Such a credit is favorable to the beneficiary but risky to the bank making advances to the beneficiary. In order to protect the bank making advances, two conditions are included in the special clause. First, the clause requires the beneficiary submit the drafts and/or documents to the bank making advances for negotiation. In order to receive the advances, the beneficiary must submit a receipt for the funds and an undertaking that he will negotiate the draft(s) and/or documents with the bank making advances. By negotiation, the bank making advances will deduct the funds advanced and give the remaining funds to the beneficiary. Second, the clause contains the issuing bank's undertaking to pay the funds back to the bank making advances if the beneficiary does not negotiate the drafts and/or documents with the bank making advances.

---

① anticipatory credit：预支信用证，即信用证中包含一个条款，要求指定的银行或保兑行预支一笔款项给受益人用于采购货物。因该条款最初用红色打印，故而此类信用证被称为红条款信用证(red clause credit)，又因预支款项专门用于采购和打包货物，所以也被称为打包信用证

A typical special clause is expressed as:

"The negotiating bank is hereby authorized to make advances to you to the extent of $5,600 or the unused balance of this credit, whichever is less, against your receipt for the amount advanced which must state the advance is to be used to pay for the purchase and shipment of the merchandise for which this credit is issued and be accompanied by your written undertaking to deliver documents in conformity with the credit terms to the negotiating bank on or before the latest date for negotiation. The advance with interest is to be deducted from the proceeds of the drafts drawn under this credit. We hereby undertake the payment of such advances, with interest, should they not be repaid to the negotiating bank by you on or before the latest date for negotiation."

"You are authorized to draw clean sight drafts on us to the extent of $5,600 accompanied by your signed statement that the amount drawn is to be used for purchase and shipment of the merchandise for which this credit is opened and your written undertaking to deliver documents in conformity with the credit terms to the negotiating bank on or before the latest date for negotiation."

Green clause credit[①]

A green clause credit is also a type of anticipatory credit, which permits the advising bank or the confirming bank, if any, to make advances to the beneficiary before the beneficiary presents the required documents. But the difference is that a green clause credit requires the storage of the goods be in the name of the bank making advances. In addition to the two special conditions in an ordinary anticipatory credit, there is one more protection, i.e. storing the goods in the name of the bank making advances. This condition implies the bank making advances can control the goods if it cannot take back the funds advanced. This is why the clause is called green rather than red.

---

① green clause credit：绿条款信用证，要求信用证项下的货物以预支行的名义采购、包装和装运，预支行控制货权

Transferable credit[①]

First of all, let us distinguish the two terms: assignment and transfer[②]. According to UCP 600, assignment means the beneficiary assigns the proceeds to which it may be or may become entitled under a credit in accordance with the provisions of applicable law. In other words, the beneficiary of a credit may assign the proceeds to a third party so long as he does it according to applicable laws. Transfer means that the beneficiary transfers his right to perform under a credit to a third party. UCP 600 has specific stipulations on the transferable credit in Article No. 38.

A transferable credit is marked "transferable" and may be made available in whole or in part to another beneficiary ("second beneficiary") at the request of the beneficiary ("first beneficiary"). In other words, the first beneficiary may request the transferring bank to make the credit available in whole or in part to one or more second beneficiaries. The basic parties involved in a transferable credit are the applicant, the issuing bank, the first beneficiary, the transferring bank and one or more second beneficiaries.

The applicant

The applicant under a transferable credit is the importer that has signed a sales contract with the exporter. He applies to his bank to issue a transferable credit in favor of the exporter based on the conditions of the sales contract.

The issuing bank

The issuing bank is the importer's bank which issues a transferable credit at the request of the importer and in favor of the exporter. The issuing bank transmits the credit to the advising bank which advises the credit to the exporter (the first beneficiary). The issuing bank may

---

① transferable credit：可转让信用证。可转让信用证的受益人(第一受益人)可以要求指定的转让行将全部或部分信用证的金额转让给一个或多个第二受益人

② assignment and transfer：让渡和转让。让渡是指信用证的受益人将自己可以使用的信用证的资金转让给第三方；转让则是受益人将自己履行信用证条款的权利转让给第三方

authorize or request the advising bank to be the transferring bank.

The first beneficiary

The first beneficiary is the exporter who has signed the sales contract with the importer, the applicant of the transferable credit. Although it signed the sales contract with the importer as the exporter, it is a middleman who does not manufacture the goods. He has to find the real supplier to supply the goods to the importer. A transferable credit just meets the need of the middleman. Unless otherwise agreed at the time of transfer, all charges including commissions, fees, costs or expenses in transferring the credit must be paid by the first beneficiary.

The transferring bank

The bank nominated by the issuing bank to transfer a credit has no obligation to do so. But if it has transferred the bank as authorized by the issuing bank, it becomes the transferring bank. The issuing bank itself may be a transferring bank.

The transferred credit

A transferable credit takes two forms in the process: transferable credit and transferred credit. Before the transferable credit is transferred, it is a transferable credit. Once the transferring bank transfers the credit and makes it available to one or more second beneficiaries, the credit that has been transferred is called the transferred credit.

When the first beneficiary asks the transferring bank to transfer the credit, he must indicate how amendments to the credit would be advised to the second beneficiary. Such conditions must be contained in the transferred credit. Moreover, the first beneficiary may indicate that payment or negotiation will be made to the second beneficiary at the place of transferring on or before the expiry date of the credit.

UCP 600 stipulates that the transferred credit should accurately reflect the terms and conditions of the transferable credit, including confirmation, if any, "with the exception of the amount of the credit, any unit price stated therein, the expiry date, the period for presentation, or the latest shipment date or given period for shipment①."Any or all of these may be reduced or curtailed. Meanwhile, since the unit price or the amount of the credit has been reduced, the percentage of insurance cover may be accordingly increased to comply with the amount of cover stipulated in the credit.

If the transferable credit requires the name of the applicant to appear in any document other than the invoice, such requirement must be reflected in the transferred credit.

The second beneficiary

The second beneficiary is the real supplier who manufactures the goods. A transferable credit can only be transferred once. But it can be transferred to one or more second beneficiaries so long as partial drawings or shipment are allowed. Any second beneficiary is not allowed to request to transfer it further. If one second beneficiary rejects an amendment, it does not affect other second beneficiaries to accept the amendment. For the second beneficiary that rejected the amendment, the transferred credit remains not amended. For the second beneficiary that has accepted the amendment, the transferred credit is amended.

The presentation of documents by or on behalf of a second beneficiary must be made to the transferring bank. After the second beneficiary submits the drafts and/or documents stipulated by the transferred credit to the transferring bank, the first beneficiary has the right to substitute its own invoices and drafts for those of a second beneficiary for an amount not in excess of the amount of the transferable credit. Upon such substitution the first beneficiary can draw under the credit for the difference, if any, between its invoices and the invoices of the second beneficiary. If the first beneficiary fails to substitute its drafts and invoices for those of the second beneficiary when the transferring bank demands it to do so, the

---

① with the exception of the amount of the credit, any unit price stated therein, the expiry date, the period for presentation, or the latest shipment date or given period for shipment: 信用证金额、任何表明的单价、有效期、交单期限,或者最迟装运期或给定的装运期限等是例外

transferring bank has the right to present the documents received from the second beneficiary to the issuing bank and has no responsibility for the first beneficiary. Meanwhile, if the invoices presented by the first beneficiary create discrepancies but fails to correct it on first demand by the transferring bank, and at the same time the documents presented by the second beneficiary constitute a complying presentation, the transferring bank has the right to present the complying presentation made by the second beneficiary to the issuing bank.

Back-to-back credit[①]

A back-to-back credit is a new credit backed by an original credit. One reason for the use of a back-to-back credit is the exporter is not the real supplier and cannot obtain a transferable credit. The exporter, as the beneficiary of the original credit, may apply to its bank for a new credit in favor of the real supplier.

Different from a transferable credit which involves only one credit which has two stages—the transferable and the transferred, a back-to-back credit involves two separate credits in which one (the new credit) is backed by the other (the original credit). Similar to a transferred credit, the terms and conditions of a back-to-back credit must be consistent with those in the original credit so that the exporter (the beneficiary of the original credit and the applicant of the back-to-back credit) can make a complying presentation to the issuing bank of the original credit. Moreover, the amount of the original credit, any unit price stated, the expiry date, the period for presentation or the latest shipment date or given period for shipment may be reduced or curtailed. And the percentage of insurance cover in the new credit may be increased to provide the amount of cover stipulated in the original credit.

Since it is a separate credit from the original credit, a back-to-back credit permits the exporter (the middleman) to hide the name of the real

---

① Back-to-back credit：背对背信用证，是指一个信用证的受益人以该信用证为保证要求一家银行开立一个以原受益人为申请人的新的信用证

supplier from the importer. However, the exporter must ensure that the documents submitted by the real supplier constitute a complying presentation to both the back-to-back credit and the original credit. Since the security for issuing the back-to-back credit is the original credit, the issuing bank of a back-to-back credit should examine the documents submitted by the real supplier (the beneficiary of the new credit) carefully to ensure them to be a complying presentation so as to constitute a complying presentation under the original credit. Generally, banks do not like to issue a back-to-back credit because the protection of payment depends on the foreign issuing bank of the original credit as well as the creditworthiness of the exporter (the beneficiary of the original credit and the applicant of the new back-to-back credit).

Revolving credit[①]

A revolving credit is one the amount of which can be renewed or reinstated without any amendment to the credit.

Revolving as to time

A revolving credit may revolve as to time. For example, if a credit is available for up to $15,000 per month during six months, the credit becomes automatically available for $15,000 each month no matter how much has been drawn during the previous month.

A credit revolving to time can be cumulative or non-cumulative[②]. "Cumulative" means that any sum not used during a period may carry over and add to the amount in the subsequent period. "Non-cumulative" means that any sum not used in a period ceases to be available in the subsequent period. In the above example, be it cumulative or non-cumulative, the obligation of the issuing bank would be limited to $90,000, i.e. $15,000 multiplied by six.

---

① revolving credit：循环信用证，是指信用证金额被全部或部分使用后，其金额恢复到原金额可以再次使用

② cumulative or non-cumulative：累积或非累积；cumulative revolving credit：可累积的循环信用证，即前一期没有使用的金额可以累积到下一期使用；non-cumulative revolving credit：非累积的循环信用证，前一期没有使用的金额不可以累积到下一期使用

A cumulative revolving credit may be stated as: "This credit is revolving at USD20,000.00 covering shipment of goods per month cumulative operation from May 1994 to September 1994 inclusive up to a total amount of USD100,000.00".

A non-cumulative revolving credit is usually stated as: "This credit is revolving for amount drawn there under up to a maximum amount of USD200,000.00 per month non-cumulative from October 1994 to December 1994".

Revolving as to amount

A revolving credit may revolve as to amount; that is, the amount of the credit can be renewed or reinstated upon utilization within a given period of time. There are three types of reinstatement: automatic, semi-automatic and non-automatic. ①

An automatic revolving credit is stated as: "This amount paid under this credit are again available to you automatically until the total of the payment reaches USD200,000.00."

A semi-automatic revolving credit is stated as: "Thirty days after a draft has been negotiated under this credit, the credit reverts to its original amount of USD100,000.00 unless otherwise notified".

A non-automatic revolving credit is stated as: "Upon receipt by the beneficiary of notice from the issuing bank that a draft has been paid under this credit, a sum equal to the amount of such draft again become available under the credit."

Reciprocal credit

A reciprocal credit② may be used in barter trade, the processing of incoming materials, counter trade or compensation trade. The reason of using a reciprocal credit is that the importer is afraid that the exporter does

---

① automatic, semi-automatic and non-automatic: 自动、半自动和非自动,按金额循环的信用证分为自动、半自动和非自动循环三种

② reciprocal credit: 对开信用证,即一个信用证的开证申请人要求在该信用证的受益人申请开立一张以该证申请人为受益人的另一个信用证时该信用证才能生效。该证受益人申请开出来另一个新的信用证则为对开信用证

not want to buy back the products or the manufactured products by using the materials the exporter provided. For example, in a trade concerning the processing of incoming materials, there are two transactions from the perspective of the party receiving the materials, i.e. the importing of the incoming materials and the exporting of the products manufactured by using the incoming materials.

Suppose that A provides the materials to B for processing, A is the exporter of the first deal and B the importer of the first deal. When B the importer finishes the products, B will export the products to A, then B becomes the exporter and A the importer in the second deal. Suppose A and B agree to use documentary credit as the settlement method. In the first deal, B as the importer asks its bank to issue a credit in favour of A the exporter; in the second deal, A as the importer asks its bank to issue another credit in favour of B the exporter.

The two credits may be effective separately or together. If the two credits become effective separately, there will be two independent credit transactions. In the first deal, if A, the beneficiary of the first credit, presents the required documents that constitute a complying presentation, the issuing bank must pay A. The potential risk B is faced with is that the incoming materials do not meet the requirements of the sales contract or A does not want to buy back the finished products. In either case, B the applicant of the first credit will assume the losses.

In order to prevent from such an unfavorable situation, B may ask the two credits become effective together. That is, the second credit is a reciprocal credit. Without the reciprocal credit will the first credit not be valid. In order to make the two credits effective together, the first credit must contain a condition specifying that it will be effective only when its beneficiary as the applicant to asks its bank to issue a credit within the specified time in favour of the applicant of the first credit. The first credit is available by acceptance or deferred payment while the second credit is available by sight payment. B, the party receiving the incoming materials, is the applicant of the first credit and the beneficiary of the second credit. A, the party providing the materials, is the beneficiary of the first credit and the applicant of the second credit. The advising bank of the first credit is usually the issuing bank of the second credit. In settlement, A, the party providing the materials, only needs to pay the processing fees.

A reciprocal credit is usually stated as:

(1) "This credit is available by draft(s) drawn on us at 180 days after bill of lading date. Payment will be effected by us on maturity of the draft against the above-mentioned documents and our receipt of the credit opener's advice stating that a reciprocal credit in their favor issued by … Bank on your account available by sight draft has been received by and found acceptable to them."

(2) "This documentary credit shall not be available unless and until the reciprocal credit is established by ABC Bank in favor of American National Import and Export Company for amount of USD100,000.00 covering shipment from New York to Xingang. The availability shall be telex advised to the beneficiary through UBS Bank… This is reciprocal credit against ABC Bank credit No. 12345 favoring ABS Corporation covering shipment of…"

5.8 Trade finance provided by banks

Finance provided to the exporter

Negotiation or export bill purchase[①]

Negotiation under a documentary credit is called export bill purchase in China. By purchasing the draft(s) and/or documents submitted by the beneficiary before the issuing bank pays, the exporter's bank provides a short-term finance to its customer (the exporter). Even if the issuing bank refuses to pay after the examination of the documents, the negotiating bank has the right of recourse to the exporter.

A negotiation credit has two types: restricted negotiation and free negotiation. If the credit is available by negotiation restricted to a nominated bank, the exporter's bank cannot negotiate the credit unless it is

---

① negotiation or export bill purchase: 信用证项下出口押汇或汇票买入

the nominated bank. If the credit is available by negotiation with any bank, the exporter's bank can negotiate the credit. After negotiation, the negotiating bank forwards the documents that constitute a complying presentation to the issuing bank and claims reimbursement from the issuing bank or the reimbursing bank, if any.

In order to obtain such a short-term finance from its bank, the exporter needs to meet certain requirements of the bank. Let us take the Bank of China as an example. Firstly, the exporter must meet the basic requirements: (1) it is a legally registered entity and has passed the annual examination;(2) it has a loan card;(3) it has the license of opening account and has opened the account with the Bank of China; and (4) it is qualified to do import and export businesses. Secondly, if the exporter applies for negotiation of the draft(s) and/or documents that do not constitute a complying presentation, the bank requires the exporter to have a credit line approved by the bank. Thirdly, if the bank cannot control the title to the goods, the bank may require the exporter to have a credit rating of CC or above;if the bank can control the title to the goods, there is no requirement for the credit rating of the exporter.

The procedures of export bill purchase are as follows:

(1) The beneficiary (the exporter) and its bank conclude a finance agreement.

(2) The beneficiary submits the draft(s) and/or documents and the negotiation application.

(3) After examining the documents, the bank negotiates the draft(s) and/or documents that constitute a complying presentation and credits the proceeds to the exporter's account.

(4) The negotiating bank forwards the draft(s) and/or documents to the issuing bank and claims reimbursement.

(5) Upon receipt of the draft(s) and/or documents, the issuing bank presents them to the applicant for examination.

(6) If the draft(s) and/or documents constitute a complying presentation, the applicant (the importer) will agree to pay and the issuing bank will honour the credit as stipulated and remits the proceeds to the

negotiating bank.

(7) The negotiating bank takes back the proceeds negotiated to the exporter and pays the remaining to the exporter.

Before reimbursement, the issuing bank will examine the draft(s) and/or documents. Should be any discrepancies found, the issuing bank would dishonour. If dishonored by the issuing bank, the negotiating bank will have to go back to the exporter to enforce its right of recourse for refunds. But if at the same time the exporter goes bankrupt, the negotiating bank will assume the losses. In order to protect against such risks, banks are suggested not to negotiate the draft(s) and/or documents under the following circumstances:

(1) When the advising bank, the paying/accepting bank and the negotiating bank are different banks.

(2) When a credit has been used as a collateral for a packing loan.

(3) When the period of negotiation exceeds 90 days.

(4) When the credit is available by payment.

(5) When the bank finds discrepancies with the documents and credit.

(6) When the valid place of the credit is in a foreign country.

(7) When the period of presentation of documents is very close to the expiry date of the credit.

(8) When the documents have been dishonored under an acceptance credit.

(9) When the issuing bank is not of a good fame.

(10) When the issuing bank's country has political instability, low creditworthiness, civil war, etc.

Packing loan[①]

Packing loan is a short-term loan provided by the exporter's bank to the exporter (the beneficiary of a credit). Since the loan will be used to purchase, manufacture, pack and ship the goods described in the credit, it is called packing loan. Upon receipt of a documentary credit and if the

---

① packing loan：信用证项下的打包放款，信用证的受益人以信用证作为抵押向一家银行申请到的贷款，专门用于采购或生产、打包和装运信用证项下的货物

exporter is short of money to purchase or manufacture the goods under the credit, he may use the credit as a collateral to apply to his bank for such a loan. Thus, packing loan is a way of financing for short-term fund need of the beneficiary.

The bank providing a packing loan uses the proceeds that will be paid by the issuing bank as security for taking back the loan. In a sense, providing packing loans is in a way promoting a country's exports. However, the bank providing such financing is faced with some risks. If the credit is not genuine, some clauses of the credit are not acceptable or the documents submitted by the beneficiary do not constitute a complying presentation, the payment by the issuing bank will not be guaranteed.

With the rapid growth of international trade, international frauds tend to be active. Although all the terms and conditions of the credit are right, the importer and the exporter will probably collude to cheat the bank. One possibility is that the importer does not want to buy the goods and tries to find one or more discrepancies on purpose. All this will lead to the non-payment by the issuing bank.

Considering the risks inherent in packing loans, banks are very cautious in providing them. In China, for example, there are strict requirements for a firm to apply for a packing loan: (1) It must be a legally registered entity;(2) It possesses the loan card;(3) It has the license for opening an account and has opened the account with the bank to which it applied for a packing loan;(4) It has the qualification of doing export and import businesses;(5) It has a credit line approved by the bank to which it applies for a packing loan. If the exporter meets all the requirements, it must submit a written application for the loan, the original sales contract, the description of the transaction and the original copy of the letter of credit.

The procedures of providing a packing loan are as follows:

(1) The exporter and the bank conclude a financing agreement, and the exporter submits the application for the loan, sales contract, original copy of the credit and other relevant documents.

(2) After approving the application, the bank offers the loan to the

exporter's account.

(3) The exporter uses the money to purchase, manufacture and ship the goods described in the credit and submits the draft(s) and/or documents required by the credit to the bank providing the loan.

(4) If the bank providing the loan is the negotiating bank, it takes back the loan in negotiating the draft(s) and/or documents and forwards them to the issuing bank or the nominated bank for reimbursement. If the bank providing the loan is not the negotiating bank, it just forwards the draft(s) and/or documents to the issuing bank or the nominated bank.

(5) The issuing bank or the nominated bank examines the draft(s) and/or documents to ensure they constitute a complying presentation and reimburses the negotiating bank. The negotiating bank credits the proceeds with the exporter's account after deducting the expenses and fees. If the bank providing the loan is the bank forwarding the draft(s) and/or documents to the issuing bank, the bank will take back the loan from the money paid by the issuing bank and credit the remaining to the exporter's account.

In order to prevent against risks, the following should be given more attention:

(1) The bank providing the loan asks the exporter to sign a formal agreement with the bank.

(2) There must not be any "soft clauses" in the credit which will render the credit invalid or be not easy to comply with.

(3) The original copy of the credit must be kept in the bank providing the loan.

(4) The draft(s) and/or documents under the credit must be surrendered to the bank providing the loan.

(5) If the exporter cannot meet the credit rating stipulated by the bank, the bank had better ask the exporter to find a guarantor.

(6) The importing country must be politically stable.

(7) If the credit is a restrictive negotiation credit, the negotiation must be restricted to the bank providing the loan. If the credit is available by negotiation with any bank, the bank providing the loan must be cautious to

confine the exporter to negotiate the documents with it.

(8) The tenor of the draft drawn under the credit should not exceed 90 days.

(9) The amount of packing loan is not in excess of 80% of the value of the credit, the period of the packing loan should not exceed 15 days after the expiry date of the credit and is from 3 months to half a year.

Finance provided to the importer

Issuing a letter of credit based on the importer's creditworthiness

Issuing a letter of credit based on the importer's creditworthiness means the issuing bank issues a credit for its customer without asking for cash deposit.

When a customer applies to its bank for a credit, the bank first investigates the creditworthiness of the applicant and determines whether a credit line can be approved to the applicant. The result of such an investigation may be the approval or the disapproval of a credit line. If the amount of the proposed credit is within the approved credit line, the bank will issue a credit without asking for any deposit from the applicant. If the amount of the credit is more than the approved credit line, the bank will ask a percentage of the credit amount as deposit for security. If the bank does not approve any credit line for the customer, the customer must submit a deposit of 100% of the credit amount in order to obtain the issuing of the credit. Thus, when the issuing bank issues a letter of credit as requested by the importer based on the creditworthiness of the applicant, the issuing bank is providing finance to the importer.

Import bill advance[①]

Inward bill advance means that the issuing bank makes advances to the beneficiary upon a complying presentation before the applicant pays.

In order to obtain such finance, the applicant of the credit must first apply to the issuing bank for a credit line. If the amount is within the credit line approved by the issuing bank, the issuing bank will pay the beneficiary

---

① import bill advance：信用证项下进口押汇，开证行在进口商付款之前对受益人的相符提示先行兑付

and the applicant will repay the advance to the issuing bank when the credit is due.

A major risk involved is that the applicant refuses to pay at maturity by finding some discrepancies with the documents intentionally. But this risk can be prevented by clarifying in the formal financing agreement between the applicant and the issuing bank.

Trust receipt

Under an acceptance credit, one possibility is: the goods have arrived at the destination and the drafts and documents have arrived at the issuing bank, but the drafts are not mature and only against payment at maturity will the applicant obtain the shipping documents to pick up the goods from the carrier. In this situation, the applicant might use a trust receipt to borrow the shipping documents. The trust receipt is a written undertaking by the applicant by which the applicant assigns the ownership of the goods to the issuing bank. Under the trust receipt, the applicant borrows the goods from the issuing bank and promises to pay the proceeds after he has sold the goods.

A risk inherent in trust receipt is that the applicant will not pay the proceeds to the issuing bank at maturity and meanwhile the issuing bank has no right to take back the goods that have been sold to a bona-fide third party.

Delivery against bank guarantee[①]

When the goods have arrived at the destination but the shipping documents are still on the way and the importer is eager to obtain to the goods for sale, the importer (the applicant of the credit) may apply to the issuing bank for a guarantee and uses it to ask the shipping company to release the goods. By issuing the guarantee, the issuing bank and the applicant are jointly and severally liable to the shipping company, undertaking to submit the transport documents to the shipping company

---

① delivery against bank guarantee：担保提货，是指在货物先于货运单据到达的情况下，开证行应申请人的要求出具书面担保给承运人，申请人凭此担保提货，开证行承诺日后在单据到达时补交正本提单给承运人换回担保书

when they arrive.

A risk is that when the documents arrive at the issuing bank but the applicant will not come to redeem them, the issuing bank must submit the transport documents to the shipping company and assume the losses incurred. In order to prevent against the risk, the issuing bank usually asks the applicant to have credit line approved by the bank and a cash deposit ranging from 0 to 100% depending on the creditworthiness of the applicant.

Import bill advance by overseas banks[①]

This financing is similar to import bill advance, but the difference is that the advance is made by an overseas bank. The overseas bank and the issuing bank may be the branches of the same parent bank or of different banks. In either case, there must be an agreement between the overseas bank and the issuing bank by which the overseas bank will make the advance to the beneficiary before the applicant pays. In China, this financing method can be used to take advantage of the low costs of funds in the overseas markets.

The procedures of such financing are as follows:

(1) The overseas bank and the domestic bank (the issuing bank) sign an agreement of import bill advance.

(2) The domestic bank (the issuing bank) applies to the overseas bank for advance for the import bill according to the agreement by sending the copy of credit to the overseas bank.

(3) Upon receipt of the bills and documents that constitute a complying presentation, the domestic bank (the issuing bank) agrees to provide the financing to the applicant and then notifies the overseas bank by telex to ask for the advance.

(4) The overseas bank pays according to the instructions of the domestic bank.

---

① import bill advance by overseas banks：信用证项下的海外代付业务,海外代付业务指银行根据进口的资信由开证行指示海外银行代替进口商先行对受益人付款。除信用证外,进口托收和电汇结算方式项下银行均可以为客户提供海外代付业务

(5) When the applicant pays at maturity, the domestic bank will reimburse the overseas bank.

5.9 Letters of credit vs. other payment methods

In order to sell the goods into a certain overseas market, the exporterssometimes have to adopt more flexible payment methods to meet the various needs of different buyers. Thus, different payment methods can be combined to meet the requirements of a buyer in a particular market.

In exporting the goods, the relatively safe payment method chosen by the exporter is a sight payment credit. In order to promote the sales, however, the exporter may be willing to provide other payment methods more favorable to the importer, such as an acceptance credit or the D/P term under a documentary credit. When the export goods are abundant in stock or not so popular, the exporter may even agree to the D/A term. Sometimes, a documentary credit can even be combined with T/T. For example, part of the proceeds will be paid by a documentary credit while the rest by telegraphic transfer.

In practice, a documentary credit may be combined with a documentary collection, i.e. part of the proceeds are paid by a documentary credit while the rest by a documentary collection. For example,"50% of the value of goods by irrevocable documentary credit and remaining 50% on collection basis at sight, the full set of shipping documents are to accompany the collection item. All the documents are not to be delivered to buyer until full payment of the invoice value". The merits of using both a documentary credit and a documentary collection are obvious. First, the importer will need less cash deposit to counter guarantee the opening of the documentary credit and meanwhile, the exporter will face less risk with the documentary collection since part of the proceeds are backed by the documentary credit. Moreover, it is wise to expressly stipulate in the credit that the delivery of documents is only against the payment. The expression used in the credit may be that:"We hereby issue this credit stipulating that 50% of the invoice value is available against clean draft at sight while the remaining 50% of documents will be held against payment at sight under this credit. The full set of the shipping documents of 100% invoice value shall accompany the collection item and shall only be released after full payment of the invoice value. If the buyer fails to pay full invoice value, the shipping documents shall be held by the issuing bank (or paying bank) at the seller's disposal".

Sometimes, a standby documentary credit can be combined with a documentary collection. The purpose is to protect the exporter against the importer's default under collection. The statement in the standby credit is usually written as:"Payment available by D/P at sight with a standby L/C in favour of seller for the amount of … as undertaking. The standby L/C should bear the clause: In case the drawee of the documentary collection under the credit No. … fails to honour the payment upon due date, the Beneficiary has the right to draw under this L/C by their draft with a statement stating the payment on the credit No. … was not honored." Thus, with a standby credit, the exporter may claim the compensation from the guarantor (the issuing bank of the standby credit) in case of the dishonour by non-payment.

Another practice is to combine a documentary collection with cash in advance. Under a collection, for example, the importer is required to pay cash in advance as a deposit, and the rest will be collected through banks after the shipment of the contracted goods. In the event that the importer refuses to pay, the exporter will have to reship or resell the goods and all the expenses will be deducted from the cash advanced. In such a case, words that should be included in the sales contract or the collection order are:"Shipment to be made subject to an advanced payment or payment amounting … to be remitted in favour of seller by T/T or M/T with indication of S/C No. … and the remaining part on collection basis, documents will be released against payment at sight."

6 Standby letters of credit

6.1 Definition

Origin

Standby letters of credit originated in the 1920s in the United States when commercial banks were forbidden to issue bank guarantees. A standby letter of credit is in the form of a letter of credit but has a nature of a bank guarantee. According to the Banking Regulatory Commission of the U.S. Federal Reserve in 1977, a standby credit is "a documentary credit or similar arrangement, however, named or described, which represents an obligation to the beneficiary on the party of the issuing bank to: (1) repay money borrowed by the applicant or advanced to or for the account of the applicant;(2) make payment on account of any indebtedness undertaken by the applicant; or (3) make payment on account of any default by the applicant in the performance of an obligation." In this definition, a standby letter of credit is also referred to as a documentary credit or similar arrangement and there are three basic parties (the applicant, the issuing bank and the beneficiary), but the obligations of the issuing bank of a standby letter of credit are quite different those of the issuing bank in a commercial documentary credit. By issuing a standby credit, the issuing bank undertakes to make payment to the beneficiary on demand if the applicant defaults in its repaying advances or indebtedness or in the performance of an obligation. Therefore, a standby letter of credit has the nature of a bank guarantee. It is now widely used by both U.S. banks and Non-U.S. banks.

UCP 600 vs. ISP 98

UCP 600 is the Uniform Customs and Practice for Documentary Credits, ICC publication No. 600 whereas ISP 98 is the International Standby Practice 98 which came into effect since January 1, 1999. ① UCP 600 states that its rules apply to any documentary credit, including any standby letter of credit if the standby letter of credit is made subject to the rules. However, ISP98 provides a separate set of rules for standby letters of credit. The formulation of ISP98 reflects the maturity and importance of standby letters of credit.

Definition by ISP 98

ISP98 refers to a standby letter of credit as "standby" for short and defined it as "an irrevocable, independent, documentary and binding undertaking when issued and need not so state②." "Irrevocable" means the issuer's obligation under a standby cannot be amended or cancelled once it is issued. "Independent" means that the enforceability of a standby is independent from other situations. Such situations include: (1) the issuer has no right or ability to obtain the reimbursement from the applicant after payment; (2) the beneficiary has no right or ability to obtain payment from the applicant; (3) there is a reference in the standby to any reimbursement agreement or underlying transaction; or (4) the issuer is not in a position to get to know whether the applicant has actually breached the underlying transaction. "Documentary" means that the beneficiary must present the required documents that constitute a complying presentation. "Binding" means that a standby is enforceable against the issuer once issued no matter whether the applicant authorized its issuance, the issuer received a fee or the beneficiary received or relied on the standby or the amendment.

---

① UCP600 既适用于跟单信用证又适用于备用信用证，ISP98 仅适用于备用信用证
② an irrevocable, independent, documentary and binding undertaking when issued and need not so state: 一经签发无需说明,（备用信用证）是（开证行）不可撤销的、独立的、跟单的以及具有约束力的保证

The relationship between the issuer and the beneficiary is independent of any agreement between the issuer and the applicant. One thing worth mentioning is that the issuer's obligation is only under the standby. The issuer is not responsible for the performance or breach of any underlying transaction, the accuracy, genuineness or effect of any document presented under the standby, any action or omission of others even if the other person is chosen by the issuer or nominated person, or observance of law or practice other than that chosen in the standby or applicable at the place of issuance.

Examples of scenarios under which a standby letter of credit may be used include the following:

(1) If A the exporter is providing the contractual goods or services to B the importer. B has paid the down payment for the goods and thus is faced with the risk of non-delivery by A. B may require A to ask its bank to issue a standby letter of credit in favour of B to ensure that the issuing bank will pay if B defaults. That is, as the beneficiary of the standby credit, B may claim payment from the issuing bank in case of non-delivery or non-performance by A.

(2) If A the exporter is selling goods or services to B the importer on open account, A is faced with the risk of non-payment by B. A may require B to ask its bank to issue a standby letter of credit in favour of A to ensure that the issuing bank will pay if B fails to pay at maturity. That is, as the beneficiary of the standby letter of credit, A may claim payment from the issuing bank in case of non-payment by B.

In either case, the beneficiary transfers the risk to the issuing bank. Therefore, a standby letter of credit may be used to support a trade credit.

6.2 Characteristics of a standby letter of credit

Clean credit[①]

Although a standby letter of credit is "documentary," the documents

---

① clean credit：光票信用证，即信用证中要求的汇票不附带货运单据。备用信用证虽然具有单据性，但要求的单据较简单，如汇票、受益人关于申请人的违约申明和发票副本等，其中的汇票是光票

stipulated in the standby are much simpler than those in a commercial documentary credit. The bills of exchange drawn by the beneficiary under a standby letter of credit are clean bills. Other documents usually include a written statement stating that the applicant has defaulted and a copy of invoice. As a result, a standby credit is referred to as clean credit.

Financial obligation

A standby letter of credit can be used to protect the beneficiary against the losses due to the applicant's failure to meet its financial obligations. For instance, a standby letter of credit may be used by the borrower to borrow a certain amount of money from a bank (the lender). Under this standby letter of credit, the borrower is the applicant and the lender is the beneficiary. If the borrower does not pay back the money borrowed, the bank may claim payment from the issuing bank of the standby letter of credit. In this case, the standby credit is used to guarantee a financial obligation. Such a standby letter of credit is a repayment standby[①].

Non-financial obligation

A standby letter of credit can be used to protect the beneficiary against the losses due to the applicant's failure to meet its non-financial contractual or performance obligations. For instance, a standby letter of credit can be used by the exporter to obtain the advance payment from the importer. Under this standby letter of credit, the exporter is the applicant and the importer is the beneficiary. If the exporter fails to deliver the goods as contracted to the importer, the importer can claim payment from the issuing bank. Such a standby credit is a performance standby[②].

Irrevocable form

A standby letter of credit is irrevocable once issued. It provides a guarantee

---

① a repayment standby：还款备用信用证，用于保证申请人（借款人）偿还受益人（贷款人）的贷款的义务

② a performance standby：履约备用信用证，用于保证申请人（供货商、投标人）对受益人（进货商、招标人）履约的义务

for the payment or performance to the beneficiary. A revocable will be useless to the beneficiary because it can be amended or cancelled at any time without the consent of the beneficiary.

Duration and amount

According to ISP98, a standby letter of credit must contain an expiry date or permit the issuer to terminate the standby upon reasonable prior notice payment. In other words, ISP98 allows the issuer to terminate the standby letter of credit so long as it has given the reasonable notice of payment. If there is no expiry date stated in a standby letter of credit, the expiry date will be on the day when the business is closed at the place of presentation.

The duration of a standby letter of credit varies depending on the intended uses. In some countries, however, there is no requirement for the expiry date in a standby letter of credit. It is risky for the issuing bank to issue a standby letter of credit without an expiry date. A standby letter of credit with no expiry date means that the obligation of the issuing bank to pay the beneficiary remains forever. In this situation, a bank guarantee should be considered to replace a standby letter of credit.

Payment procedures

A standby letter of credit is payable on simple demand by the beneficiary. Most standby letters of credit have relatively simple conditions for drawing by the beneficiary. And the issuing bank cannot be placed in the position of interpreting whether the applicant has actually defaulted under the underlying sales contract with the beneficiary. This leaves the applicant at risk should the beneficiary draw the credit for unreasonable or illegitimate reasons.

6.3 Parties to a standby letter of credit

Applicant

ISP98 defines "applicant" as "a person who applies for issuance of a standby or for whose account it is issued, and include (ⅰ) a person applying in its own name but for the account of another person or (ⅱ) an issue acting for its own account." In other words, the applicant is a person who applies for a standby and the standby is issued for its own account or a person who applies a standby and the standby is issued for the account of another person.

In international trade, the applicant of a standby may be the importer or the exporter depending on the specific cases. If the exporter sells goods on open account to the importer, the exporter will face the credit risk of the importer and may ask the importer to apply for a standby credit in favor of the exporter. Under this standby, the importer is the applicant and the exporter is the beneficiary. On the contrary, if the importer has paid the proceeds in advance before the exporter ships the goods, the importer will face the credit risk of the exporter and may ask the exporter to apply for a standby credit in favor of the importer. Under this standby, the exporter becomes the applicant and the importer the beneficiary.

There are some obligations for an applicant of a standby to fulfill. Firstly, ISP98 stipulates that an applicant must "timely object to an issuer's honour of a non-complying presentation by giving timely notice by prompt means." In other words, if the applicant finds discrepancies in the documents presented by the beneficiary and does not want to accept the discrepancies, it must promptly notice the issuing bank within a time after it receives the documents from the issuing bank. ISP98 also mentions the concept of complying presentation, which means a presentation that "appears on its face to comply with the terms and conditions of the standby in accordance with these rules supplemented by the standard standby practice." Secondly, ISP98 states that the applicant must indemnify the issuing bank against all claims, obligations and responsibilities (including attorney's fees) arising out of (ⅰ) the imposition of law or practice other than that chosen in the standby or applicable at the place of issuance; (ⅱ) the fraud, forgery, or illegal action of others; or (ⅲ) the issuer's performance of the obligations of a confirmer that wrongfully dishonours a confirmation. The applicant must pay the issuing bank's charges and reimburse the issuing bank for any charges that the issuer is obligated to pay to persons nominated with the applicant's consent to advise, confirm, honour, negotiate, transfer or to issue a separate undertaking.

Issuer

An issuer is the party who issues a standby letter of credit on the request of the applicant or for its own account and in favor of the beneficiary. If another person has been authorized to add confirmation by the issuer, the confirmer who has confirmed the standby is also considered as the issuer. The confirmation is considered as a separate standby issued by the confirmer for the account of the issuer.

The issuer has the right to examine the documents (although the documents are simple), and if the documents do not constitute a complying presentation, the issuer may dishonor the presentation. If a nominated person obtains reimbursement before the issuer timely dishonours the presentation, the nominated person must refund the reimbursement with interest to the issuer.

According to ISP98, the issuer's undertaking based on a complying presentation is summarized as follows:

(1) If the standby is available by sight payment, the issuer pays the beneficiary the amount demanded at sight.

(2) If the standby credit is available by acceptance of a draft drawn by the beneficiary on the issuer, the issuer timely accepts the draft and pays the holder on presentation of the accepted draft on or after maturity.

(3) If the standby credit is available by deferred payment of a demand made by the beneficiary, the issuer timely incurs a deferred payment obligation and pays at maturity.

(4) If the standby credit is available by negotiation, the issuer pays the amount demanded by the beneficiary at sight without recourse.

(5) Whether the issuer honours or dishonours a presentation, it must acts in a timely manner within the time permitted for examining the presentation and giving notice of dishonor.

(6) An issuer is obligated to pay the charges of other persons. Such

charges may be those payable in accordance with the terms of the standby. If the issuer requests another person to advice, honour, negotiate, transfer a standby credit, or to issue a separate standby credit, but the fees and expenses are not paid by the beneficiary, the issuer is obligated to pay the reasonable and customary fees and expenses incurred.

Beneficiary

A beneficiary is a named person who is entitled to draw under a standby. If the standby has been transferred, the beneficiary may be the transferee beneficiary[①]. The beneficiary may be an importer, an exporter, the bank which has lent money to its customers or the project owner who invites bidders to submit their tenders, depending on the underlying transaction based on which a standby credit is issued.

The beneficiary has the right to draw a standby so long as the applicant fails to fulfill its obligations listed in the standby, but must make sure the drafts and documents constitute a complying presentation.

Transferree beneficiary

According to ISP 98, a standby letter of credit is "not transferable unless it so states." In other words, if a standby letter of credit states it is transferable, a beneficiary may "request that an issuer or a nominated person honour a drawing from another person as if that person were the beneficiary." Here, "another person" is the transferee beneficiary. A transferable standby letter of credit cannot be partially transferred but can only be transferred entirely to a transferee beneficiary. The transferee beneficiary may transfer the standby letter of credit further to another transferee beneficiary.

According to the ISP98, in order to transfer a standby letter of credit, the beneficiary must submit the following materials: (1) a request in a form acceptable to the issuer or nominated person including the effective date of the transfer and the name and address of the transferee, (2) the original

---

① transferee beneficiary：受让受益人，类似可转让信用证中的第二受益人

standby, (3) verification of the signature of the person signing for the beneficiary, (4) verification of the authority of the person signing for the beneficiary, (5) payment of the transfer fee, and (6) any other reasonable requirement.

If a standby letter of credit has been transferred to a transferee beneficiary, the transferee beneficiary may draw a draft under the standby and the name of the transferee beneficiary may be used in any other required documents. If the nominated bank which has transferred the standby pays the transferee beneficiary under a transferrable standby credit, it is entitled to get reimbursement from the issuer as if it had made payment to the beneficiary.

Confirmer

A confirmer is the party which has added its confirmation to a standby letter of credit. The undertaking by the confirmer can be summarized as follows:

(1) If the standby is available by sight payment, the confirmer pays the amount demanded at sight.

(2) If the confirmation permits presentation to the issuer and the issuer wrongfully dishonors the presentation, the confirmer will honour the presentation.

(3) If the standby permits presentation to the confirmer, and the confirmer wrongfully dishonours the presentation, the issuer will honour the presentation.

According to ISP98, an issuer's branch, agency or other office acting or undertaking to act under a standby in a capacity other than as issuer is obligated in that capacity only and shall be treated as a different person. So, a confirmer is a separate bank.

6.4　Types of documents required in a standby letter of credit

The structure of a standby letter of credit is similar to that of a commercial documentary credit, but the documents required in standby are much simpler. However, simple document requirement does not necessarily mean the documents are not important. To ensure a complying presentation, an issuer or a nominated person will examine the documents for consistency with each other and compliance with the terms and conditions of the standby and applicable rules.

The documents required in a standby include a demand for payment, a statement of default or other drawing event, negotiable documents, legal or judicial documents and other documents.

Demand for payment

According to ISP98, a standby letter of credit usually does not require a separate demand for payment and often incorporated into the beneficiary's statement or other document. But if a standby letter of credit does require a separate demand for payment, the beneficiary must submit such a separate demand for payment to the issuer or the nominated person.

The contents of a demand for payment include a date, the amount demanded and the beneficiary's signature. A demand for payment may be in the form of a draft or other instruction, order or request to pay. If a standby letter of credit requires presentation of a draft, the draft need not be in a negotiable form unless the standby so states.

Statement of default or other drawing event

The statement of default or other drawing event refers to the beneficiary's statement of the applicant's default or the beneficiary's statement of other event that entitles the beneficiary to draw under a standby letter of credit.

A standby letter of credit usually states that the beneficiary submits a statement of default to claim for payment from the issuer if the applicant defaults (fails to fulfill its obligation) or a drawing event described in the standby letter of credit occurs. Such a document contains a date and the beneficiary's signature.

Negotiable documents

The most often used negotiable instruments in a standby letter of credit are drafts drawn by the beneficiary on the issuing bank. Such drafts are clean drafts, to which no shipping documents are attached.

According to ISP98, if a standby letter of credit requires the beneficiary to present a negotiable instrument that is transferable by indorsement and delivery "without stating whether, how, or to whom indorsement must be made, then the document may be presented without indorsement, or, if indorsed, the indorsement may be in blank and in any event the document may be issued or negotiated with or without recourse." In other words, if a standby letter of credit requires a negotiable instrument that can be transferred, but does not state whether it can be indorsed, how it should be indorsed or to whom it should be indorsed to, then the beneficiary can either hold the instrument or transfer it to a transferee. To transfer the instrument, the beneficiary may make an indorsement in blank. In any case, the indorsement may be made with or without recourse to the indorser.

Legal or judicial documents[①]

A standby letter of credit sometimes requires the beneficiary submit a government-issued document, a court order, an arbitration award or the like. Such a document submitted must be an original one that appears to be issued by a government agency, court, tribunal or the like, and it must be suitably titled or named, signed and dated.

Other documents

A standby letter of credit may require a copy invoice or bill of lading in addition to the demand for payment and the statement of the applicant's default.

Documents issued, signed or countersigned by the applicant

A standby letter of credit should not require a document be issued, signed or countersigned by the applicant. If a standby so states and the beneficiary does not object it, the issuing bank will examine the documents strictly based on the requirement. If the applicant refuses to issue, sign or

---

① legal or judicial document：法律或司法文件

countersign such a document, the beneficiary shall face the difficulty in obtaining the document. The beneficiary should ask the applicant to revise the standby.

Non-Documentary Terms or Conditions

If a standby letter of credit does not specify a document in a term or condition, the term or condition is non-documentary. According to ISP98, such a term or condition will be disregarded. The beneficiary should ask the applicant and the issuer to amend it, though.

Examination of the documents

Compliance[①]

Both UCP600 and ISP98 emphasize a complying presentation. No matter whether a standby letter of credit is subject to UCP600 or ISP98, the documents presented by the beneficiary must constitute a complying presentation. The issuer will examine the documents carefully to determine whether the demand for payment and other required documents comply with the terms and conditions of the standby letter of credit and applicable rules. The compliance or non-compliance is solely determined by examining the presentation on its face against the terms and conditions of the standby credit and the rules to which the standby is made subject to.

Inconsistency[②]

In addition to the compliance with the terms and conditions of a standby and the applicable rules, the issuer will also examine the documents to make sure the consistency of documents, that is, all the documents are consistent with one another.

---

① compliance：相符，是指受益人提交的单据与备用信用证的条款和适用的规则或惯例的条款相符。

② inconsistency：不一致，是指受益人提交的单据之间有相互不一致的地方。备用信用证项下提交的单据要做到相符提示，必须保证单据与备用信用证条款和适用的规则或惯例的条款相符，同时还要做到单据之间的一致性，也就是所谓的"单单一致"。

6.5 Types of standby credit

A standby letter of credit can be divided into different types based on its function or usage in the underlying transaction.

Performance standby

A performance standby is used to support the applicant's obligation to perform other than to pay money, to cover the potential losses arising from the applicant's failure to complete the underlying transactions. The performance may be to provide the goods or services or to perform a specific project the applicant has contracted with the beneficiary. If the applicant fails to provide the goods or services or fails to perform its contractual obligation, the beneficiary may claim payment from the issuer.

Advance payment standby

An advance payment standby[①] is used to support the obligation of the applicant (the seller, the supplier or the exporter) to deliver the goods or services and return the advance payment in his failure to provide the goods or services. If the applicant fails to provide the goods or services and at the same time fails to return the money advanced, the beneficiary (the buyer or the importer) of the standby may claim payment from the issuer.

Bid bond/tender bond standby

A bid bond/tender bond standby[②] is used to support the applicant's obligation to execute a contract if the applicant is awarded a bid. If the applicant (the bidder/tenderer) fails to sign the contract after the project

---

① advance payment standby：预付款还款备用信用证。开证行应申请人(卖方,供货方)的要求保证在收到受益人(买方)预付款后履行已订立的合约义务,如果申请人不履约,开证行保证退还给受益人预付款和利息

② bid bond/tender bond standby：招标/投标备用信用证。开证行应申请人(投标人)的要求开立的保证投标人在开标前不中途撤标或片面修改标书内容,并保证投标人中标后签约和履约

has been awarded to him or fails to provide a performance standby in signing the contract, the beneficiary (the inviter or owner of the project) may claim payment from the issuer.

Counter standby

A counter standby① is used to support the issuance of a separate standby or other undertaking by the beneficiary of the counter standby. When an applicant asks a bank to issue a standby letter of credit in favour of a foreign beneficiary, but the bank is not allowed to or not willing to issue a standby letter of credit directly in favour of a foreign beneficiary, the bank may issue a counter standby credit in favour of a foreign bank and asks the foreign bank to issue a separate standby in favour of the foreign beneficiary. Once the beneficiary claims payment from the foreign issuing bank, the foreign issuing bank, as a beneficiary of the counter standby may claim payment from the issuer of the counter standby.

*Financial standby*②

A financial standby is used to support an obligation to pay money, including any instrument evidencing an obligation to repay borrowed money. If an applicant (borrower) borrows money from a beneficiary (lender) and the applicant fails to repay the money borrowed, the beneficiary may claim payment from the issuer of the standby credit.

*Direct payment standby*③

A direct payment standby is used to support the payment when due of an underlying payment obligation, typically in connection with a financial standby without regard to a default. It is different from the nature of

---

① counter standby: 反担保备用信用证
② financial standby: 融资备用信用证。开证行应申请人(借款人)要求开立的保证申请人在到期日对受益人(贷款人)还款,如果申请人违约,开证行保证偿还受益人贷款
③ direct payment standby: 直接付款备用信用证,用于担保到期付款,尤其是指到期没有任何违约时支付本金和利息。例如,直接付款备用信用证可用于担保企业发行债券时到期支付本息的义务

"standby" because the issuing bank undertakes to pay the beneficiary when the debt is due. For instance, a direct payment standby can be used to support the issuance of bonds by a corporation, by which the issuing bank undertakes to pay the bondholders when the bonds mature.

Insurance standby[①]

An insurance standby is used to support an insurance or re-insurance obligation of the applicant. If the applicant (the insurer) cannot compensate the beneficiary (the insured) the money owed under the insurance contract, the insured may claim payment from the issuer.

Commercial standby[②]

A commercial standby is used to support the obligations of an applicant (the buyer) to pay for goods or services to the beneficiary (the seller) under O/A or D/A terms. If the beneficiary provides the good or services on open account and the applicant fails to pay the goods or services at maturity, the beneficiary may claim payment from the issuer.

6.6　The problems arising by making a standby subject to UCP

When a copy bill of lading is required

In 2005, a seller provided the goods to a buyer on open account and the payment date was at 120 days after the invoice date. The buyer, as the applicant, applied for a standby letter of credit in favour of the seller (beneficiary) and made it subject to UCP500 (UCP600 became effective in July 1, 2007). The standby required the beneficiary to submit a statement

---

① insurance standby：保险备用信用证，是开证行应申请人（保险人）的要求开立的，保证在受益人（被保险人）索赔时付款

② commercial standby：商业备用信用证，用于保证申请人对货物或服务的付款义务，通常用于赊销、承兑交单等支付方式以加强商业信用

of default, a copy of commercial invoice and a copy bill of lading indicating the date of shipment in claiming payment from the issuer. The applicant did fail to pay at 121 days after the invoice date, so the beneficiary submitted the required documents to the issuer for payment at the same day. The issuer examined the documents and refused to pay by pointing out a discrepancy—the beneficiary submitted the documents late.

The issuer used Article 43 of UCP500 as a support for the discrepancy. This article states that documents may not be submitted at later than 21 days after the date of shipment. In this case, the date of presentation was far more than 21 days after the bill of lading date. This is one problem arising by making a standby subject to UCP. Thus, if a standby credit is subject to UCP500, the Article 43 should be excluded. If it is subject to UCP600, Article 14 c should be excluded.

When partial payment is used

In 2004, a debtor made four promissory notes to the creditor and the notes would be mature on January 1, 1999, February 1, 1999, March 1, 1999 and April 1, 1999 respectively. The debtor was the maker and the creditor was the payee of the four promissory notes. The maker, as the applicant, applies to a bank to issue a standby letter of credit in favour of the payee and made it subject to UCP500. If the applicant failed to pay the payee at one of the four maturities, the beneficiary may claim payment from the issuer of the standby. The applicant paid on January 1, 1999, February 1, 1999 and March 1, 1999 respectively, but failed to pay on April 1, 1999. Thus, the beneficiary submitted the requirement documents to the issuer for payment. The issuer examined the documents and refused to pay by identifying a discrepancy.

The issuer cited Article 41 of UCP500 as a support. It stipulates that if a credit allows for partial drawing and if any of them is not used, the following drawings are void. The issuer argued that the beneficiary did not claim payment at the first three maturities, so the fourth became void. In order to prevent against this problem, the wise way is to exclude Article 41 of UCP500 or Article 32 of UCP600 when the standby is made subject to UCP and containing partial drawings.

7 Letters of guarantee

7.1 Definition

The two important rules for guarantees are the Uniform Rules for Demand Guarantees (URDG, the ICC Publication No. 758) applicable to demand guarantees and *the Uniform Rules for Contract Guarantees* (URCG, the ICC Publication No. 325) applicable to contract guarantees. The URDG has been widely used by banks and businesses all over the world and proved to be a set of reliable and successful rules. The previous version of URDG was URDG 458 which had been used in practice from 1992 to 2009. The revised URDG 758 came into force on July 1, 2010. The fact that URDG 458 has been revised to URDG 758 implies the wider usage of demand guarantees than that of contract guarantees. To aim for clarity, URDG 758 adopts the drafting style of UCP 600 by bringing together the terms into Article 2 "Definitions" and the clarifications into Article 3 "Interpretation".

Demand guarantee

According to URDG 758, demand guarantee means "any signed undertaking, however named or described, providing for payment on presentation of a complying demand." In other words, it is a letter of undertaking issued by a guarantor on the request of an applicant to pay the beneficiary on demand provided that the beneficiary presents a complying demand. Similar to a complying presentation under documentary credits, a complying demand under a guarantee means the presentation made by the beneficiary is in accordance with "the terms and conditions of the guarantee, applicable rules in URDG 758 and the international standard demand guarantee practice."

Contract guarantee

URCG 325 lists three types of contract guarantees—tender guarantee, performance guarantee and repayment guarantee.

Under a tender guarantee, the applicant is the tenderer, the beneficiary is the party inviting tenders, and the guarantor undertakes to make payment to the beneficiary if the tenderer fails to fulfill the obligations under the submission of the tender. Under a performance guarantee, the applicant is the supplier of goods or services or the contractor, the beneficiary is the buyer or the employer, and the guarantor undertakes to make the payment to the beneficiary a stated sum of money if the applicant fails to fulfill its obligations. If it is stipulated in the guarantee, the guarantor will arrange for the performance of the contract. Under a repayment guarantee, the applicant is the supplier or the contractor who has received the down payment from the buyer or the employer, the beneficiary is the buyer or the employer who has paid the down payment, and the guarantor undertakes to repay the beneficiary if the applicant fails to repay the money.

According to URCG 325, in the event of default by the applicant, the guarantor of a contract guarantee may "rely on the defenses which are based on the terms and conditions specified in the guarantee" or are allowed under the rules of URCG. It means that, if there is a claim under a contract guarantee, the guarantor may refuse to pay until they see an arbitration award or at least conduct an inquiry into the facts supporting the claim before paying. This is why contract guarantees are not as acceptable as demand guarantees in trade transactions. Although URCG aims to achieve a fair balance between the legitimate interests of all the parties concerned and to encourage the users' greater confidence in such guarantees, it is not successful as URDG in practice.

However, the name of a guarantee does not necessarily mean whether it is a demand guarantee or a contract guarantee. A guarantee named as tender guarantee or performance guarantee may be in fact a demand guarantee so long as it states that the guarantor will waive all rights of objections and defenses arising from the guarantee and irrevocably undertakes to pay the beneficiary the specified amount on the first demand upon receiving the request for payment in the event of default of the applicant.

7.2　Characteristics of a demand guarantee

First of all, according to URDG 758, a demand guarantee is "irrevocable on issue even if it does not state so." It means the undertaking by the guarantor is irrevocable. Once it leaves the control of the guarantor, the guarantee is issued. So long as the beneficiary presents a complying demand, the guarantor must pay.

Secondly, a demand guarantee is independent of the underlying relationships between the applicant and the beneficiary and between the guarantor and the applicant. The guarantor is only bound by the guarantee itself. Even if there is reference to the underlying relationship in the guarantee, it cannot change the nature of independence of the guarantee. Moreover, the guarantor's undertaking to pay under a demand guarantee is not subject to any claims or defenses arising from any relationship other than a relationship between the guarantor and the beneficiary. And a demand guarantee is payable on demand.

Thirdly, the guarantor of a demand guarantee deals with documents and not with goods, services or performance to which the documents may relate. Whether a guarantor will pay or not solely depends on the documents presented by the beneficiary. Only when the documents constitute a complying demand will the guarantor pay.

7.3　Basic parties to a demand guarantee

Four basic parties are involved in a demand guarantee: an applicant, a guarantor, a beneficiary and an advising party.

An applicant is the party who requests for the issue of a guarantee. It is the debtor under the underlying contract based on which the guarantee is issued. For instance, the applicant under a tender guarantee is the tenderer, the applicant of an advance payment guarantee is the supplier who has received a certain sum of money as advance payment, and the applicant of a performance guarantee is the supplier who provides the goods or services.

A guarantor is the party who issues a guarantee on the request of the applicant. It may be a bank, an insurance company, a corporation or an individual.

A beneficiary is the party in whose favour a guarantee is issued. It is the creditor under the underlying contract based on which the guarantee is issued. For instance, the beneficiary of a tender guarantee is the party who invites tenders, the beneficiary of an advance payment guarantee is the buyer who has paid a certain sum of money as advance payment, and the beneficiary of a performance guarantee is the buyer or the employer. The beneficiary claims the payment from the guarantor by submitting a complying demand.

An advising party is the party that advises the guarantee to the beneficiary at the request of the guarantor. It is a bank in the beneficiary's place.

Three separate underlying contracts are involved in a guarantee transaction: a commercial contract, a credit agreement and a guarantee.

The commercial contract is the underlying business arrangement between the applicant and the beneficiary of the guarantee. The credit agreement is the documentation between the guarantor and the applicant. Before issuing a guarantee, the guarantor requires the applicant to sign a security agreement (i. e. counter guarantee) obligating him to reimburse the guarantor for the payment made. The amount the guarantor undertakes to pay is based on the applicant's borrowing facilities. The guarantee is the undertaking issued by the guarantor obligating itself to pay the beneficiary under stipulated conditions upon its receipt of a complying demand.

7.4 Direct and indirect guarantees

A direct guarantee is issued by a guarantor directly to the beneficiary. It may be advised through a local bank but bears no responsibility of the local bank. An indirect guarantee is a counter guarantee. For instance, a foreign bank requests a local bank to issue the required guarantee in favour of the beneficiary and the foreign bank issues a counter guarantee in favour of the local bank in which the foreign bank undertakes to irrevocably pay the local bank the amount paid by it under its guarantee.

The indirect guarantee is used when the law prohibits or restricts the issuance of guarantee to a beneficiary that is not a financial institution or when the beneficiary insists on a guarantee issued by a local bank. Some countries only allow banks to issue guarantees in favour of local firms. If a foreign bank wants to support its multinational firm client, it can issue a counter guarantee in favour of a local bank which in turn issues a guarantee in favour of the said client.

In the United States, federally chartered banks are prohibited from issuing guarantees. According to the U.S. courts and regulators, underwriting another party's performance is considered to be outside the definition of normal banking business. However, U.S. banks are allowed to issue standby letters of credit and to deal in negotiable instruments.

A guarantee is issued for a specific amount and tenor although certain government agencies may require a guarantee with no ultimate expiry date. It is payable upon an event of default under the terms of a guarantee. Unlike a standby letter of credit, a guarantee can be structured to require the guarantor to verify the default when it is issued as a contract guarantee.

7.5 Types of guarantee

Guarantees can be divided into different types for different uses. The following are the types often used in practice.

Tender guarantee/bid bond

A tender guarantee, also called bid bond, is used to provide an assurance of the intention of the party submitting the tender to sign the contract if his tender is accepted. A tender guarantee or bid bond is usually issued for 3%—5% of the contract value.

Performance guarantee

When signing the contract which has been awarded to him, the tenderer must submit a performance guarantee to assure its performance. The performance guarantee is usually issued for 20% of the contract value.

Repayment guarantee

Once the tenderer has been awarded and has signed the contract, due to the large sum of the contract value, the employer, at the request of the tenderer, usually makes about 10% of the contract value as down payment to the tenderer. But before such payment, the employer may require the tenderer to submit a repayment guarantee. By a repayment guarantee, the guarantor protects the interest of the employer in respect of the repayment of the money in the event of the applicant's failure to fulfill its obligation under the contract.

Advance payment guarantee

When making payment in advance to the supplier in purchasing the equipment or supplies, the buyer is providing a trade credit to the supplier and is faced with the credit risk of the supplier. In doing so, the buyer may require the supplier to submit an advance payment guarantee to assure that the supplier will return the money to the buyer in the event of non-delivery by the supplier.

Maintenance guarantee

A maintenance guarantee provides for the maintenance and/or repair of the equipment during a specified period after installation. The buyer may require a maintenance guarantee as compensation in case that the equipment does not perform well. If the seller does not correct the performance deficiencies, the buyer may claim from the guarantor.

Retention money guarantee

A retention money guarantee can be used instead of maintenance guarantee. Usually, the buyer need retain a portion of the payment due to the supplier to cover the maintenance and repair costs after the completion of the project. If the buyer does not retain the money, it may ask the supplier to submit a retention money guarantee to protect its interest.

Counter guarantee

A counter guarantee is an indirect guarantee. The counter guarantor on the request of its customer authorizes another party, usually referred to as the guarantor, to issue a guarantee and undertakes to reimburse the guarantor when claimed by the beneficiary in the event of the default of the applicant. Thus, a counter guarantee is a guarantee, bond or other undertaking, however named or described, which is provided to assure the issuance of another guarantee.

A counter guarantee is a separate transaction from the guarantee whose issuance is guaranteed by it and from any underlying contract, despite the inclusion of a reference to such a contract in the counter guarantee.

In certain circumstances, such as the case of guarantee for payment of negotiable instruments, the words "per aval" or "as guarantor" will be annotated on a bill of exchange. In these cases, it is advisable to indicate for whose obligation the guarantee is incurred. "Aval" is a term utilized mainly in Europe to express a third party guarantee of payment on a bill of exchange or promissory note, indorsed by the guarantor and evidenced as such by his signature.

7.6 Contents of a guarantee

Basic contents of a guarantee

The basic contents of bank guarantees are quite similar although the forms vary from one to another. In general, a bank guarantee contains the following items:

(1) The name and address of the beneficiary;
(2) The name and address of the applicant;
(3) The name, nationality and detailed address of the guarantor bank;
(4) The type and purpose of the guarantee;
(5) The relative contract number, agreement number, tender number and/or the name of the project, i.e. the description of background of opening the guarantee and the relative reference number;
(6) The value and currency of the guarantee;
(7) The duration or the expiry date of the guarantee; and
(8) The undertaking clause, i.e. the specific conditions under which the guarantor undertakes to pay.

The forms and contents of guarantees may be different from one country to another, and sometimes a guarantee may only have some of the above items. However, a guarantee usually starts as: "At the request of ⋯, we, ⋯ Bank, located at ⋯, hereby issue a letter of guarantee in favor of ⋯ for the amount of US Dollars ⋯ valid until ⋯". Then, the contents of the relative contract number, tender number or the name of the project are added, say, "In respect of the contract no. ⋯ as a tender/performance/advance payment guarantee ⋯" In the end of a guarantee is the undertaking clause, such as: "We hereby undertake to pay immediately upon our receipt of your written demand accompanied by supporting documents such as ⋯"

Additional clauses of a guarantee

In addition to the basic items, a guarantee contains additional clauses[①] to stipulate the rights and liabilities of the guarantor.

The validity date

It is to define the duration of the guarantee. If there is no validity date, the issuing date will be considered as the date of validity. In order to avoid the risks arising from the beneficiary's claiming, the guarantor usually incorporates a validity clause in the text of the guarantee. For examples:

"This performance bond will come into force only when the seller has received a letter of credit acceptable to him."

"The guarantee shall become effective as from the date when the applicant is in receipt of the first installment of the said advance payment, and the amount available hereunder shall always correspond to the total advanced sum the applicant has actually received…"

The reduction of the value

Under a guarantee, the guarantor's liability will not be always the same, i. e. it may change according to the fulfillment of the underlying contract. For example,

The guaranteed amount of this L/G shall be diminished automatically and proportionally in accordance with the value of each shipment as shown in the relevant invoices.

Authentication

The beneficiary of a guarantee is the only party that has the right to claim from the guarantor. To ensure the genuineness of the claim by the beneficiary, a guarantee often include an authentication clause, for example,

"For authentication purpose, your written demand, if any, shall be sent to us through … Bank after its confirmation of your signature affixed

---

① 张燕玲、王仲和主编,《国际结算业务指南》,中华工商联合出版社,1997 年,第 223—239 页

thereon, or shall be confirmed by… Bank in the way of its tested telex to us".

The applicable law

It is the law applicable to a guarantee. Since different countries have different laws, it is a question which law will be applicable. In order to assure the applicable law or jurisdiction, a guarantee usually contains a clause such as,

"This guarantee is governed by the law of… country, and is subject to the exclusive jurisdiction of the court of…""This bond shall be subject to the law of… country, and the proceedings shall be executed exclusively in the court of…"

Automatic extension of the maturity

Since some guarantees' maturity dates cannot be determined at the time of issuing or the beneficiary may worry about the completion of the project on the maturity of the guarantee, the beneficiary may require the guarantor to add an automatic extension of the maturity, for examples,

"This guarantee shall be automatically extended for another three months if the guarantor shall not have received, by the end of the validity hereof of any extension thereto, any confirmation from the beneficiary that it can be released from its obligation hereunder."

"At the time during the period in which this guarantee is still valid, if the employer agrees to grant a time extension of the contract to the contractor, or if the contractor shall fail to complete the works within the time of completion as stated in the contract, or fail to discharge himself of the liabilities or damages, it is understood that this guarantee will be automatically extended under the same conditions until we receive from you a declaration that it can be null and void and released by you".

In addition to such an automatic extension clause, the beneficiary may require even stricter clause by which the guarantor undertakes to reimburse the beneficiary if not extending the validity of the guarantee. For example,

"This bond is extendable for the period requested by the beneficiary. Should the guarantor not be able or willing to extend the validity hereof, or the applicant not provide the necessities of extension and obtain the concurrence of the guarantor for the extension, then the guarantor undertakes to pay immediately without any need for a second demand the said amount in favor or to the order of the beneficiary".

No change or addition clause

To ensure a guarantee not to be bound by the underlying transaction, the beneficiary may request the guarantor to contain a clause in the guarantee to make sure that all the terms and conditions of the guarantee should not be changed or added. For examples,

"We further agree that no change or addition to or other modification to the terms of the contract or of works to be performed thereunder or of any of the contract documents, which may be made between the contractual parties, shall in any way release us from any liability under this guarantee, and we hereby waive our right to ask for the notice of any of such changes, additions or modifications…";

"The covenants herein contained constitute unconditional and irrevocable direct obligations of the guarantor. No alteration in the terms of the contract and no allowance of time or other forbearance or concession of any other act or omission by the beneficiary, which but for this provision might exonerate or discharge the guarantor, shall in any way release the guarantor from any liability hereunder";

"No waiver, extension of time, or modification of any terms or conditions of the agreement between you and the applicant shall in any manner detract from any of our obligations hereunder, nor in any manner whatsoever shall in any such similar actions between you and the applicant void this L/G".

The joint and several liability

Due to the skeptical fame of the guarantor, the beneficiary sometimes requests the guarantor to add a liability clause in the beginning of the guarantee. For example,

"Know all men by this bond that we (the guarantor) and the applicant are held and firmly bound onto the beneficiary in the sum of USD…, for the payment of which sum well and truly to be made, the applicant and us bind ourselves, our heirs, assigns, executors, administrators and successors jointly and severally by these presents…"

Interest of the guaranteed amount

A guarantee sometimes contains an interest clause. For examples, "We hereby undertake to pay you the guaranteed amount plus interest at the rate of… % per annum calculated from the date falling three days after your claim until our actual payment."

"If due to any reason whatsoever, a refundment is going to be made to you according to our above undertaking, an interest at the rate of… % per annum shall also be paid to you together with the proceeds of your claim, counting from the date on which the applicant has received the said advance payment until the date of its refund".

Expiration

In countries such as Jordan, Pakistan and Thailand, the laws stipulate that when a guarantee is issued to a government or quasi governmental department, even if the guarantee expires, the beneficiary shall have the right of claim within a certain period of from 3, 5, to even 60 years. Faced with such conditions, the guarantor will ask the beneficiary to return the guarantee after its expiration. For example,

"Upon its expiration, this L/G shall be null and void, and shall be immediately returned to us for cancellation. Any action of maintaining the original of this guarantee or any of its amendments shall then give no right to the beneficiary for lodging any more claim hereunder."

Non-negotiable

A guarantee may be used to assure a payment or a credit. Under a payment guarantee, the reimbursement by the guarantor is based on the beneficiary's fulfillment of the terms of the guarantee, so the negotiation or transferability of the guarantee will involve little risks for the applicant or the guarantor. Under a credit guarantee, however, the negotiation of the guarantee means that there is a risk for the third party, i.e. the transferee of the guarantee, to claim for payment without default. This is why some of the guarantees contain clauses such as:

"This surety bond is neither negotiable nor transferable, and the beneficiary nominated hereunder shall be the only one whose claim, if any, will be duly entertained by us."

"Transfer of this guarantee is forbidden to take place no matter whether with or without the knowledge or prior consent of us or of the applicant, and we will only be responsible to the claim lodged by the beneficiary stated herein."

Assignment of proceeds

Due to the risks involved in the negotiation of a guarantee, the applicant is unwilling to see the guarantee's transferring, but the beneficiary likes to see it because by assigning the proceeds of the guarantee the beneficiary can obtain finance from banks or other financial channels. In order to balance the interests of both sides, an assignment clause is usually incorporated into the guarantee. For examples:

"We hereby irrevocably agree that the proceeds resulting from a claim, if any, lodged by the beneficiary shall be assigned to…"

"… shall be entitled to receive the claimed amount from us on the condition that we are in receipt of your written demand in conformity with the terms of this guarantee…"

"In case of any claim hereunder, payment will be effected to the financers of the project in proportion to their financing participation which you shall indicate to us when lodging your claim."

Unconditional undertaking to pay on first demand

Guarantees tend to be payable on demand unconditionally. For examples:

"The beneficiary shall be the sole and final judge for deciding whether or not the applicant has duly performed his obligations of the contract, and we hereby undertake to pay you immediately upon receipt of your written claim notwithstanding any contestation, defence, or objection from the applicant and without it being necessary for you to produce or adduce any proof or any judicial or administrative proceedings whatsoever in support of your claim…"

"The guarantor is engaged to pay to the beneficiary any amount upto and inclusive of the aforementioned full sum upon written order from the beneficiary to indemnify him for any liabilities or damages resulting from the defects or shortcomings of the contractor, or the debts he may have incurred to any parties involved in the works under the contract mentioned above, whether these defects or shortcomings or debts are actual or estimated or expected. The guarantor will deliver the money required by the beneficiary immediately without delay and without the necessity of a previous notice or of judicial or administrative proceedings, and without being proved to the guarantor the defects or shortcomings or debts of the contract."

"We undertake to accept intimation from you as conclusive and sufficient evidence of the existing of a default or non-compliance as aforesaid on the part of the applicant and to make payment accordingly without being necessary for you to prove the correctness of your claim."

"We hereby renounce any claim, defence or other objection, whether in court or otherwise, which we may have against you with respect of this guarantee or any money we may pay thereunder."

No deduction

In a guarantee, one may also find a no deduction clause, such as:

"Any payment hereunder shall be made free and clear of and without deduction, set-off for or on account of any present or future taxes, duties, charges, fees, previous debts, deductions or withholdings of any nature whatsoever and by whomsoever imposed. If such deduction or withholding is inevitable by whatsoever reason, we promise to hold you compensated for the sum thus deducted or withheld so as to keep you always in the position to receive the whole amount of your claim."

Primary obligor

The guarantee is the primary obligor, for examples,

"We hereby agree to stand as a primary obligor, and not merely as a surety..."

"We undertake as a principal and not as an accessory debtor to make payment of any amount due hereunder upon our receipt of written demand from the beneficiary..."

Basic contents of a counter guarantee

The contents of a counter guarantee are not as detailed as those of a guarantee. A counter guarantee mainly contains two clauses: the authorization instruction clause and the reimbursement clause. The authorization instruction may be expressed as: "Please issue under our full responsibility your tender/performance/advance payment guarantee…" and the reimbursement clause as: "In consideration of your issuing the said guarantee on our behalf, we hereby undertake to keep your reimbursed subject to the same conditions as mentioned above upon our receipt of your claim declaring that you have been called upon to make payment under your guarantee, together with a copy of beneficiary's demand on you…"

The value of the counter guarantee is the same as that of the guarantee backed by the counter guarantee, but the expiry date of the counter guarantee is usually 15 to 30 days longer than that of the guarantee to ensure the guarantor to have enough time to claim reimbursement from the counter guarantor in the event that the beneficiary claims compensation.

Specimen of a tender guarantee

Tender Guarantee
No. _____

To: _____ (*Beneficiary's full name and address*)
Issuing date: _____
Dear Sirs,

We have been informed that _____ (hereinafter referred to as the "Applicant"), responding to your invitation to tender No. _____ dated _____ for the supply of _____ (*description of goods and/or services*), has submitted (or will submitted) to you its offer No. _____ dated _____. Furthermore we understand that, according to your conditions, offers must be supported by a tender guarantee.

At the request of the Applicant, we, _____ Bank, hereby irrevocably undertake to pay any amount up to _____ (say _____) (hereinafter referred to as the "Guaranteed Amount") upon receipt by us of your complying demand, indicating that the Applicant is in breach of its obligations under the bid conditions due to occurrence of any of the following events:

1. The Applicant has withdrawn its offer during the period of tender validity specified in the tender documents; or
2. The Applicant, while it was declared the successful bidder by you, during the period of tender validity, failed or refused to:
(a) enter into a contract; or
(b) furnish the performance guarantee, in accordance with the tender documents.

This Guarantee shall expire on…. days after the period of tender validity, or after the date of _____ (*calendar date*), whichever is earlier (hereinafter referred to as the "Expiry Date"). Any demand under this Guarantee must be received by ☐us ☐our _____ Branch, with its office at _____, on or before the Expiry Date. After the Expiry Date, this Guarantee shall automatically become null and void whether it is returned to us or not.

This Guarantee is subject to the Uniform Rules for Demand Guarantees (URDG) 2010 revision, ICC Publication No. 758.

Any dispute or claim arising out of or in relation to this Guarantee shall be submitted to the exclusive jurisdiction of the courts of Beijing, the People's Republic of China.

(Authorized Signature)
For or on Behalf of… Bank

Specimen of a performance guarantee

Performance Guarantee
No. _____

To: _____ (Beneficiary's full name and address)
Issuing date: _____

Dear Sirs,

We have been informed that _____ (hereinafter referred to as the "Applicant"), has entered into a _____ contract No. _____ dated _____ (hereinafter referred to as the "Underlying Contract") with you for the supply of _____ (*description of goods and/or services*).
Furthermore, we understand that, according to the terms of the Underlying Contract, a performance guarantee is required.

At the request of the Applicant, we, _____ Bank, hereby irrevocably undertake to pay any amount up to _____ (say _____) (hereinafter referred to as the "Guaranteed Amount") upon receipt by us of your complying demand, supported by such other documents as may be listed below and in any event by your statement, indicating in what respect the Applicant is in breach of its obligations under the Underlying Contract.

Your demand for payment must also be accompanied by the following document(s):
(specify document(s), if any)

_____
_____
_____

Your demand and accompanying documents shall be forwarded to us through your bank for verification of your authorized signature thereon.

This Guarantee shall become effective upon the effectiveness of the Underlying Contract and ☐receipt by the Applicant of Master Letter of Credit specified in the Underlying Contract ☐ _____.

The Guarantee amount shall be automatically and proportionally reduced according to the progress of the Underlying Contract, which is evidenced by our receipt of the following document(s) from the Applicant:

_____
_____
_____

This Guarantee shall expire after the date of _____ (calendar date) (hereinafter referred to as the "Expiry Date"). Any demand under this Guarantee must be received by ☐us ☐our _____ Branch, with its office at _____, on or before the Expiry Date. After the Expiry Date, this Guarantee shall automatically become null and void and be cancelled whether it is returned to us or not.

This Guarantee is subject to the Uniform Rules for Demand Guarantees (URDG) 2010 revision, ICC Publication No. 758.

Any dispute or claim arising out of or in relation to this Guarantee shall be submitted to the exclusive jurisdiction of the courts of Beijing, the People's Republic of China.

_____
(Authorized Signature)
For or on Behalf of… Bank

Specimen of an advance payment guarantee

Advance Paymetn Guarantee
No. _____

To: _____ (*Beneficiary's full name and address*)
Issuing date: _____

Dear Sirs,

We have been informed that _____ (hereinafter referred to as the "Applicant"), has entered into a _____ contract No. _____ dated _____ (hereinafter referred to as the "Underlying Contract") with you for the supply of _____ (*description of goods and/or services*).

Furthermore, we understand that, according to the terms of the Underlying Contract, an advance payment in the sum of _____ is to be made to the Applicant against an advance payment guarantee.

At the request of the Applicant, we, _____ Bank, hereby irrevocably undertake to pay any amount up to _____ (say _____) (hereinafter referred to as the "Guaranteed Amount") upon receipt by us of your complying demand, supported by such other documents as may be listed below and in any event by your statement, indicating in what respect the Applicant is in breach of its obligations under the Underlying Contract.

Your demand for payment must also be accompanied by the following document (s): (specify document (s), if any)
_____
_____
_____

Your demand and accompanying documents shall be forwarded to us through your bank for verification of your authorized signature thereon.

This Guarantee shall become effective upon the receipt of the advance payment by the Applicant on his account number _____ at our bank. It is a condition for any demand and payment under this Guarantee to be made that the advance payment referred to above has been actually received by the Applicant.

This Guarantee Amount of this Guarantee shall be automatically and proportionally reduced by the total value of each part-shipment/interim work finished against presentation to us by the Applicant of copies of the relevant invoice (s) and transport document (s)/the interim work certificate (or other specific documents).

This Guarantee shall expire upon the time when the Guaranteed Amount has been reduced to zero in the above-mentioned manner, or after the date of _____ (calendar date) whichever is earlier (hereinafter referred to as the "Expiry Date"). Any demand under this Guarantee must be received by ☐us ☐our _____ Branch, with its office at _____, on or before the Expiry Date. After the Expiry Date, this Guarantee shall automatically become null and void and be cancelled whether it is returned to us or not.

This Guarantee is subject to the Uniform Rules for Demand Guarantees (URDG) 2010 revision, ICC Publication No. 758.

Any dispute or claim arising out of or in relation to this Guarantee shall be submitted to the exclusive jurisdiction of the courts of Beijing, the People's Republic of China.

(Authorized Signature)
For or on Behalf of … Bank

Specimen of a counter guarantee

Counter Guarantee
No. _____

To: _____ (*Guarantor's full name and address*)
Issuing Date: _____

Dear Sirs,

Please issue under our responsibility in favor of _____ (*Beneficiary's full name and address*) your guarantee in the following wording:

[Quote
TEXT
Unquote]

In consideration of your issuing the guarantee above, we, _____ bank, hereby accept and confirm the following:

1) As Counter-guarantor, we hereby irrevocably undertake to pay you, any amount up to _____ upon receipt of your complying demand, supported by your statement, indicating that you have received a complying demand under your guarantee, □ together with the copy of the Beneficiary's demand to you.

2) The maximum amount of our Counter-guarantee will be automatically reduced by the total amount of your above guarantee's reduction.

3) Our Counter-guarantee shall become effective from the issuing date and remain valid until 30 (thirty) days after the expiry of your above guarantee, or until the date of _____ (calendar date), whichever is earlier (hereinafter referred to as the "Expiry Date"). Any demand under this Counter-guarantee must be received by □us □our _____ Branch, with its office at _____, on or before the Expiry Date. After the Expiry Date, this Counter-guarantee shall automatically become null and void and be cancelled whether it is returned to us or not.

4) Your commissions and charges will be paid by _____. In case they fail to pay your commissions, we undertake to pay your commissions by telegraphic transfer as demanded by you.

5) After you issuing the guarantee above, please deliver the original guarantee to _____, and airmail us two copies for our records.

6) This Counter-guarantee is subject to the Uniform Rules for Demand Guarantees (URDG) 2010 revision, ICC Publication No. 758.

7) Any dispute or claim arising out of or in relation to this Counter-guarantee shall be submitted to the exclusive jurisdiction of the courts of Beijing, the People's Republic of China.

_____
(Authorized Signature)
For or on Behalf of … Bank

8 International factoring

8.1 Origin and legal framework

Origin

The origin of factoring can be traced far back to the period of industrial revolution when the textile mills in the northern part of England used the agencies in North America to sell their products and then to remit the proceeds back to England. The agencies were the embryos of factors today. The embryo factors more contacted with the customers in America than with their principals in England, thus they had a better understanding of the customers who bought the products. At that time, factoring only involved the agencies' purchases of receivables from the English suppliers.

With the advent and development of the textile industry in America, the factors began to provide services to domestic textile suppliers. Gradually, the textile mills themselves also began to sell products. With the growth of international trade, especially with the development of trade terms, transport means, financing methods and the existence of buyers' markets, factoring finally developed into a package of financial services. By the 1960s, domestic factoring could only be found in North America and several countries in Europe. The idea of international factoring was rare and its growth was restricted due to geographical reasons. Nevertheless, people at that time had already farsighted the need of introducing factoring to the countries that had not adopted it and the need of developing a framework that could be referred to by all the countries that were conducting or would conduct factoring. As a world independent protective organization for international factoring, the Factors Chain International

(FCI) was established in the Netherlands in 1968, with its headquarters in Amsterdam.

The purpose of FCI is to provide its members with standard criteria, procedures, law and technological consulting relating to international factoring. Of course, those who want to join FCI must meet certain criteria concerning the financial and service commitment. In recent years, international factoring has developed significantly. The statistics of FCI indicate that in 1998 the global total volume of factoring had reached more than US $ 500 billion. Based on the 1998 statistical data of the Trade Development Center of the United Nations, the use of letters of credit in international trade settlement had declined to the rate of 16% and it was below 10% in developed countries, while the global total volume of factoring had grown from US $ 266 billion in 1991 to more than US $ 500 billion in 1998. By the end of 2012, the total world factoring turnover via FCI had increased to 2,132,230 millions of Euro. In Europe and America, especially in such countries as Germany, Italy, Belgium, and the Netherlands, international factoring is replacing the letters of credit as an important payment method.

Legal framework

The world's most widely recognized legal framework for international factoring is the FCI General Rules for International Factoring (GRIF)[①], which was developed and is monitored by the FCI Legal Committee. The GRIF, first introduced in July 2002, has become the standard for correspondent factoring relationships and about more than 90% of the world cross-border factoring volume has been governed by those rules. The FCI even offers an Arbitration process to solve the problems between export factors and import factors. The GRIF was revised in November 2007.

---

① General Rules for International Factoring：国际保理通则，国际保理联合会(FCI)编制

8.2 What is factoring?

According to the GRIF, factoring contract refers to a contract pursuant to which a supplier may or will assign accounts receivable to a factor, whether or not for the purpose of finance, for at least one of the following functions: receivables ledgering, collection of receivables, or protection against bad debts.

The supplier, commonly referred to as client[①] or seller, is the party who invoices for the supply of goods or services. If it is a domestic factoring, only one factor is involved; if it is an international factoring, two factors are involved—export factor[②] and import factor[③]. The export factor is the party to which the supplier assigns his accounts receivable in accordance with the factoring contract and the import factor is the party to which the export factor assigns the said accounts receivable. Another party to both domestic and international factoring is the debtor[④], who is commonly referred to as buyer or customer[⑤] and is liable for payment of the accounts receivable.

The accounts receivable are those arising from sales on credit terms of goods or services. In general, the basis for factoring is O/A or D/A. The term O/A means a supplier sells the goods to a customer on open account, i.e. the supplier ships the goods and sends the shipping documents to the buyer first and the buyer pays later after it receives the goods. The due date for the buyer to pay is usually at 30, 60, 90 or 120 days after the invoice date. The supplier may wait until the due date and collect the proceeds from the buyer but is faced with the buyer's credit risk. To secure the payment, one choice is the supplier asks the buyer to apply to its bank for a guarantee or a standby credit in favor of the supplier. Alternatively, the

---

① client：客户,指保理商的客户,即卖方
② export factor：出口保理商
③ import factor：进口保理商
④ debtor：债务人,即买方
⑤ customer：客户,指供货商的客户,即买方

supplier may use the services provided by a factor, i.e. the supplier may sell its accounts receivable to a factor.

Before purchasing the accounts receivable, the factor first investigates the creditworthiness of the buyer and approves a credit line to the buyer. If the invoice value is within the approved credit line, the factor will purchase it from the supplier and assumes the credit risk of the buyer. If the invoice value is above the approved credit line, the factor will only buy the amount within the line. If no credit line is approved, the factor will not purchase the accounts receivable but can still help collect the accounts receivable but assumes no credit risk of the buyer.

D/A is a term of releasing documents by the collecting bank to the buyer under documentary collection. It means the collecting bank will release the shipping documents to the buyer upon its acceptance of the usance bill drawn by the supplier on the buyer. The tenor of the usance bill is usually 30, 60 or 90 days after sight. In this case, the accounts receivable arises and the supplier may use the services offered by factors.

8.3 The procedures of international factoring

The procedures of international factoring are illustrated in the following flowchart.

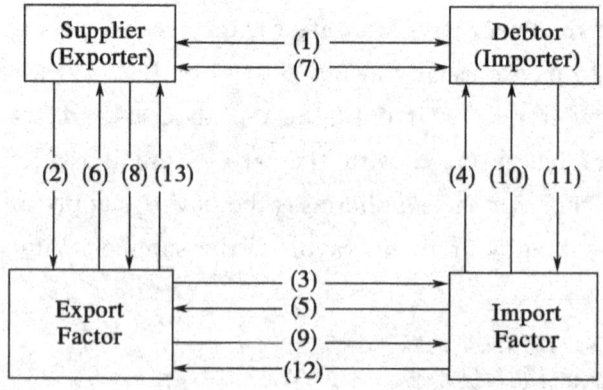

Figure 8.1 Flowchart of international factoring

(1) The importer and the exporter negotiate and propose to use factoring as a way of financing.

(2) The exporter signs a factoring contract with the export factor, entrusting the latter to investigate the importer's creditworthiness.

(3) The export factor entrusts the import factor (its correspondent factor) to investigate the importer's creditworthiness.

(4) The import factor investigates the importer's creditworthiness and approves a credit line.

(5) The import factor notifies the export factor of the creditworthiness of the importer and the approved credit line.

(6) The export factor notifies the exporter of the result of credit investigation.

(7) The exporter goes back to the importer and signs the sales contract and provides the goods/services. The invoice value should be limited within the credit line approved by the import factor.

(8) The exporter submits the copy invoice to the export factor for finance and the advance is about 85% of the invoice value.

(9) The export factor sends the copy invoice to the import factor.

(10) The import factor duns the buyer to make payment periodically.

(11) The buyer makes payments due to the import factor.

(12) The import factor remits the proceeds to the export factor.

(13) The export factor pays the exporter for the rest 15% of the invoice value after deducting relative charges.

8.4　Types of factoring

Maturity factoring and financed factoring

According to the time when the factor provides the supplier with finance, factoring can be divided into maturity factoring and financed factoring[①]. Maturity factoring means the supplier cannot obtain the money until the

---

① maturity factoring：到期型保理；financed factoring：预支型保理

documents mature and the buyer makes the payment. Financed factoring means the supplier can immediately obtain the money (minus interest and charges) upon selling its accounts receivable. In financed factoring, the supplier can obtain approximately 85% of the invoice value and the remainder 15% will be settled when the buyer effects payment.

Disclosed factoring and undisclosed factoring

Disclosed factoring means the supplier notifies the buyer of the factoring contract and instructs the buyer to remit money directly to the factor. If the supplier conceals the fact that there is a factoring contract, the money will be cleared between the buyer and the supplier. The buyer does not know the existence of the factoring contract. This kind of factoring is called undisclosed factoring.[①]

Since for a long time financing trade debts was frowned upon by most trade creditors and regarded by most as confession of one's unsound financial position, some suppliers did not want to use factoring publicly. Such a traditional attitude caused some trade creditors to refuse to sell on credit to a firm that is using factoring on the ground that this practice removed one of the most liquid of the firm's assets and accordingly weakened the position of other creditors. Just because of this attitude, some firms may wish to use confidential factoring, allowing the factor to act as an agent in receiving payment from debtors who are not informed of the existence of the factoring arrangement. Nowadays, as more and more firms are engaged in factoring, it is no longer regarded in this light.

Single factoring and co-factoring

Domestic factoring only involves one factor at home and thus is called single factoring, whereas international factoring involves two factors, one at home and the other abroad, and hence co-factoring.[②]

---

① disclosed factoring 公开型保理；undisclosed factoring 隐蔽型保理
② single factoring 单保理；co-factoring 双保理

8.5　Services provided to the exporter by a factor

International factoring is a package of financial services designed to ease the traditional problems of selling on O/A or D/A terms. Services include investigating the creditworthiness of buyers, assuming buyer's credit risk and giving 100% protection against write-offs, collecting and managing receivables and providing finance through immediate cash advances against outstanding receivables.

Credit investigation of buyers

Entrusted by its client (supplier), the factor will first investigate the creditworthiness of the buyers, i. e. the customers of the supplier. In international factoring, it is the import factor that investigates the creditworthiness of buyers in its own country.

Credit investigation generally includes the buyers' registered assets, operation styles, assets to liabilities ratios, recent operational status, etc. Apart from these, the foreign exchange control, the relevant financial policies and the political stability of the buyers' country will affect the safety of receiving the proceeds. An import factor often makes thousands of credit investigations every month, having files immediately available on hundreds of thousands of customers and even subscribing to services providing immediate access to credit information on the customers. The appraisal of the buyers' creditworthiness is based on such investigations. The higher the creditworthiness of the buyer is, the larger the approved credit line will be.

After the import factor approves a credit line to a particular buyer, it will notify its correspondent export factor that will further notify its client. The credit investigation usually has one of the four results.

Approval of all the invoices

One possible investigation result is approving all the invoices. The supplier may sell products to various buyers in the import factor's country. If the supplier has signed sales contracts with the buyers and all the invoices have been approved by the import factor, the import factor will purchase all the receivables. By purchasing the receivables, the import factor assumes the credit risk of all the buyers. If any buyer fails to pay due to its financial inability, the factor will assume the risk of non-payment.

Approval of specific invoices

Another possible result is, after investigating the creditworthiness of the buyers, the factor only agrees to purchase some specific invoices rather than all the invoices. It means that the factor will assume the credit risk of buyers only for the receivables that have been approved.

Declination

If the factor judges the credit standing of the buyers to be unacceptable, it will refuse to purchase the receivables. If the supplier chooses to sell the goods to the buyers and still uses the factor services, the factor will help collect the proceeds but assumes no credit risk of the buyers. The risk of non-payment is borne fully by the supplier.

Limited Approval

If the factor judges the customer to be marginally creditworthy or has insufficient information to make a fully informed judgment, it may agree to purchase the receivables, limiting its obligation to the supplier to a lesser amount. The invoice amount exceeding the limit is treated as a declined risk receivable.

The credit line approved by the factor usually remains valid for one year and after that the line will be investigated and approved again. Within the validity of one year, if the buyer has some obvious changes in its financial status, the factor will make changes on the credit line accordingly.

Credit protection

If the factor has purchased the receivables from the exporter, the factor will pay the exporter when the buyer fails to pay due to financial inability or when a late payment exists. Payment of the net amount of invoices after deducting disputed items, merchandise returns, discounts, allowances, etc. is initiated on the 91st day after the invoice due date. Usually, the factor will automatically initiates collection efforts 15 days after the invoice due date. When the proceeds are collected, they are paid to the exporter usually within the same week. Many exporters want to accelerate their cash flow by borrowing funds secured by their factored receivables. Factors normally will not provide such loans directly to exporters, but their correspondent banks may be called upon to do so against factored receivables.

Collection and management of receivables

Selling goods on O/A or D/A terms is risky if the exporter is not familiar with the buyer, the environment, the related laws and rules, the trade customs and the language of the importing country. Under a factoring arrangement, the export factor collects the receivables through an import factor that will provide high quality services, ensuring the efficiency of collecting the proceeds and at the same time protecting against the possible ruins on the commercial relationship between the importer and the exporter.

Most factors are affiliated entities or departments of large commercial banks and possess sound accounting management systems. By using computer systems, export factors keep contacts with their foreign correspondent factors (import factor) and automatically manage the receivables, including computer automatic bookkeeping, dunning proceeds, clearing, calculating, charging, printing statements and providing the exporter real-time reports on the receivables.

Finance

Under a typical factoring operation, after shipping the goods, the supplier submits the invoice copy to the factor after shipping the goods. Based on the credit line approved by the import factor, the export factor advances the supplier not over 85% of the invoice value. If the buyer goes bankrupt or become insolvent when the invoice matures and the fund advanced is within the approved credit line, the export factor has no recourse to the supplier. If the buyer's non-payment is caused by commercial disputes, the import factor will not assume the risk and the supplier must return the fund advanced to the export factor.

8.6 The role of factoring in international trade

Some people are skeptical about the roles factoring plays in international trade. First of all, one may wonder whether the customers will consider the supplier's financial position unsatisfactory if the supplier uses factoring. Actually, one should not worry about it, for factoring has become so well established that almost all the traders will be dealing with a factor directly or indirectly. As early as in 1998, the total volume of business handled by factoring companies around the world had amounted to over US＄500 billion.

Secondly, one may wonder whether such a payment method can assure the prompt collection of the proceeds. Obviously, it is also in the factor's interest to provide prompt services for its clients in order to keep its clients' loyalty. At the same time, the factor will assume the risk of non-payment by the buyer if the invoice value is within the approved credit line.

Thirdly, one may think a letter of credit is a good payment method for him to use, why using factoring? In fact, not all the customers and potential customers are happy or able to provide letters of credit. If one wants to expand its sales into overseas markets, one must be able to offer more "buyer friendly" terms such as O/A or D/A. Factoring can help offer such terms without reducing security or affecting financing. Thus, factoring is a good supplement to open account and D/A terms.

The supplier

Under international factoring, the supplier can obtain three types of services: (1) The export factor establishes the creditworthiness of existing and prospective buyers and provides up to 100% credit protection; (2) The export factor offers sales ledger administration which reduces the non-productive overheads and frees up the valuable management time; (3) The export factor advances an agreed level of finance to the supplier once the goods have been shipped. The remaining, less the factor's charges, will be paid when the invoice is settled in full.

The advantages of using factoring by the supplier are summarized as follows:

(1) The supplier can expand its sales abroad by offering competitive terms and conditions, such as O/A or D/A.

(2) The supplier can offer open account terms by invoicing the importer and granting deferred payment terms, usually 30 to 90 days after the invoice date.

(3) The supplier is fully protected against credit losses.

(4) It avoids the delays often encountered when arranging letters of credit.

(5) Speedy collection and remittance help improve the supplier's cash flows.

(6) The supplier's administration costs are reduced.

(7) The supplier has access to a flexible source of working capital to help increase export sales.

The buyer

Under international factoring, it is the import factor that guarantees the payment of the buyer to the supplier. Instead of issuing a letter of credit, the import factor establishes a credit line for the buyer. When the invoices are due for payment, the importer pays the import factor which further remits the funds to the export factor.

The advantages to the buyer by using factoring are summarized as follows:

(1) The buyer can buy goods on favorable payment terms such as O/A or D/A.

(2) The buyer does not need to apply for a letter of credit.

(3) The buyer can expand its purchasing power without using its existing credit lines.

(4) The buyer can purchase goods without incurring delays.

(5) The buyer will find it easier to generate new sources of supply.

8.7 Risks faced by factors

Credit risks

In domestic or single factor factoring, the factor is faced with the buyer's credit risk, the supplier's credit risk and the risk of fraud or repeated finance. The buyer's credit risk means, if the buyer becomes insolvent or refuses to pay due to business failure or bankruptcy, the factor will be faced with the loss of the funds that have been advanced to the supplier. The supplier's credit risk means, if the supplier does not fulfill the sales contract with the buyer and causes some commercial disputes, the buyer will refuse to pay, leading to the loss of the factors. Fraud means the supplier used a fake sales contract or both the buyer and the supplier intentionally use a fake sales contract to cheat the factors for advance finance. Repeated finance means the supplier signs factoring contracts with more than one factor and sells its accounts receivable accordingly in order to get advance finance from more banks.

In international or co-factor factoring, the export factor is faced with the supplier's credit risk, the import factor is faced with the buyer's credit risk, and both of them faced with the risk of fraud or repeated finance by the supplier or both of the buyer and supplier.

Operational risks

In domestic or single factor factoring, the factor is faced with the operational risks in signing the factoring contract with the supplier and approving the credit line to the buyer. First of all, if the factor does not strictly examine the accounts receivable, the invoices, the sales contract, there might emerge the cases that the accounts receivable may have defects, the invoices may be reused or even fake, leading to the risk of loss in funds advanced. Moreover, if the factor does not examine the creditworthiness of the buyer and the supplier carefully before approving the credit line or advancing the funds, and do not follow the financial status of the buyer or the supplier, and do not promptly dun the payment of the buyer, the factors will be faced with the risk of loss of funds advanced.

Legal risks

Currently, the legal system in China has no specific relevant laws with respect to factoring transactions. International factoring follows the GRIF while domestic factoring has no rules to follow. Domestic factoring in China has grown rapidly. According to the FCI, domestic factoring turnover in China reached to EUR272,487 million in 2012.

8.8 Factoring in China

In 1993, the Bank of China became the first bank that had joined the FCI, later the Bank of Communications, and as of June 27, 2012, today there are 23 factoring companies in mainland China. Currently, there are 25 factoring companies in China, with domestic factoring turnover of EUR272,487 million and international factoring turnover of EUR71,272 million. Its total factoring turnover is EUR154,550 million, including domestic EUR 119,960 million and international EUR34,590 million.

Table 8.1 FCI Members in China (as of October 22, 2013)

Name of bank
Agricultural Bank of China Limited
Bank of China, H.O.
Bank of Communications
Bank of Dalian Co., Ltd.
Bank of Jiangsu Co., Ltd.
Bank of Nanjing Co. Ltd.
Bank of Shanghai Co., Ltd.
China CITIC Bank
China Construction Bank
China Development Bank
China Everbright Bank
China Guangfa Bank Co., Ltd.
China Merchants Bank Co., Limited
China Minsheng Banking Corporation Limited
Fortune International Factoring Co. Ltd.
HSBC Bank (China) Company Limited

Continued

Name of bank
Hua Xia Bank Co., Limited
Industrial and Commercial Bank of China
Industrial Bank Co., Ltd.
JRF International Factoring Ltd
Ping An Bank Co. Ltd.
Shanghai Pudong Development Bank
Standard Chartered Bank (China) Limited
Sumitomo Mitsui Banking Corporation (China) Ltd.
The Export-Import Bank of China

Source: http://www.fci.nl/fci-members/select-a-member/asia? c=CN, 24 Oct. 2013.

Table 8.2 1994—1999 Global Increase of the Volume of Factoring[①]
(in millions of US dollars)

Nation or area	1994	1995	1996	1997	1998	1999
Total world	274,586	296,139	359,081	488,619	529,575	574,727
United States	55,499	53,051	67,860	76,832	75,550	104,513
United Kingdom	40,321	45,559	55,672	91,917	99,000	103,510
Italy	42,621	47,563	54,548	79,871	88,500	88,264
Japan	22,165	24,661	31,023	41,087	45,802	55,513
Korea	13,269	13,633	21,454	27,575	20,150	15,165
Mainland China	37	35	14	17	13	31
Hong Kong	521	575	853	1,308	1,520	1,805
Taiwan	181	348	540	941	1,180	2,096

Source: FCI, 2000.

The above table shows that the global volume of factoring grew from US $ 274.586 billion in 1994 to US $ 574.727 billion in 1999, increasing by 109.3%. The factoring volume in the United States had been the highest,

---

[①] Factoring Turnover Growth by Country in Millions of USD, see http://www.factors-chain.com

increasing to US $ 104. 513 billion in 1999, accounting for 18. 2% of the global volume. The situation in Britain was similar to that in the United States, but taking the growth speed of factoring volume in the United States into consideration, the volume of factoring in the United States was remarkable. Italy was the largest factoring country in Europe, its factoring volume accounts for 15. 4% of global volume; Japan was the largest factoring country in Asia, accounting for 9. 7% of global volume; Korea was the second largest factoring country. However, the factoring volume in mainland China in 1999 was only US $ 31 million, among which US $ 14 million of domestic factoring and US $ 17 million of international factoring, even much lower than the volumes in Hong Kong area and Taiwan area (US $ 1,805 million and US $ 2, 096 million respectively). Therefore, compared to other countries or areas, the factoring volume in mainland China in 1999 was very low, even lower than that in its start in 1994, when the volume was US $ 37 million.

Table 8. 3   Total Factoring Volume by Selected Countries in the Last 7 Years
(in million of Euro)

Nation or area	2006	2007	2008	2009	2010	2011	2012
Total world	1,133,143	1,300,666	1,324,650	1,283,559	1,648,229	2,015,413	2,132,230
United States	96,000	97,000	100,000	88,500	95,000	105,000	77,543
United Kingdom	248,769	286,496	188,000	195,613	226,243	267,080	291,200
Italy	120,435	122,800	128,200	124,250	143,745	175,182	181,878
Japan	74,530	77,721	106,500	83,700	98,500	111,245	97,210
Korea	850	955	900	2,937	5,079	8,087	8,000
Mainland China	14,300	32,976	55,000	67,300	154,550	274,870	343,759
Hong Kong	9,710	7,700	8,500	8,079	14,400	17,388	29,344
Taiwan	40,000	42,500	48,750	33,800	67,000	79,800	70,000

Source: http://www. fci. nl/about-fci/statistics/total-factoring-volume-by-country-last-7-years, Oct 22, 2013.

In the past 7 years, however, the factoring turnover in mainland China has grown from EUR14, 300 million in 2006 to EUR343, 759 million in 2012, taking up about 16. 1% of the total world factoring volume through FCI in 2012. Meanwhile, the factoring turnover in the United States has been stable till 2011 but dropped in 2012, and the turnovers in the United

Kingdom, Italy and Japan have remained relatively stable without great changes in the past 7 years. The factoring turnover in Korea has increased greatly from EUR850 million in 2006 to EUR8,000 million in 2012, that in Hong Kong SAR has increased greatly from EUR7,700 million in 2007 to EUR 29,344 million in 2012, and that in Taiwan China had first increased from EUR40,000 million in 2006 to EUR79,800 million in 2011 and become stable in 2012.

The reason for the relatively rapid growth of factoring in China is both Chinese banks and enterprises are getting to know more and more about factoring. A few years ago, factoring as a way of trade finance, was a new term to most of exporters or even to some banks. From the growth of the number of FCI members in China, one can see Chinese banks are becoming more and more familiar with factoring. The increased domestic factoring turnover especially means the more and more banks are providing factoring services. Meanwhile, more and more enterprises get to know the factoring services offered by their banks.

Specimen of an FCI interfactor agreement

FCI INTERFACTOR AGREEMENT
(Version June 2002)

AGREEMENT made this _____ day of _____ ,20 _____ ,
by and between _____
and _____ .

WITNESSETH:

WHEREAS, _____ and _____ will from time to time engage the services of the other to act as Import Factor with respect to sale of goods or rendering of services to debtors located in the country (ies) where the Import Factor's services are to be performed;

NOW, THEREFORE, in consideration of the mutual agreements herein contained, it is hereby agreed between the parties as follows:

1. Each of the parties hereby subscribes to and agrees to be bound by all of the terms and provisions of the General Rules for International Factoring ("GRIF"), the edifactoring.com Rules and the Rules of Arbitration, all promulgated by the Factors Chain International as formally revised from time to time, subject to the following modifications:
   _____
   _____
   _____
   _____

2. The services to be performed by _____ or _____ _____ as Import Factor shall be rendered with respect to sellers designated by the parties from time to time and at such commission rates or other compensation as may be mutually agreed upon with respect to each seller.

3. Neither of the parties shall be obliged to engage the services of the other exclusively but each party shall be free to engage the services of any other factoring organisations located in the country (ies) where the parties perform factoring services.

4. This Agreement shall take effect as of the date set out above and shall continue indefinitely, subject to termination by either party on 60 days' prior written notice to the other but such termination shall not apply to, modify or otherwise affect the obligations of the parties hereunder or under the GRIF, the edifactoring.com Rules and the Rules of Arbitration with respect to transactions occurring, accounts receivable transferred or indebtedness incurred prior to the effective date of such termination.

5. Except in relation to assignments of receivables made before 1 July 2002, this Agreement contains all the matters agreed between the parties in relation to the receivables included by Article 3 of the GRIF and all agreements, warranties, representations and other statements made by the Import Factor or the Export Factor to the other before the making of this Agreement and the reliance on any usages or practices are excluded.

IN WITNESS WHEREOF, the parties hereto have caused this instrument to be executed by their respective corporate officers thereunto duly authorised as of the day and year first above written.

By _____
Title:
By _____
Title:

(Printed June 2002)

9 International forfaiting

9.1 Origin and evolution

A variant of forfaiting could be found over 2,000 years ago when Phoenician[①] silk traders sold silk to their Athenian[②] buyers. They sold silk to the buyers on credit basis and received IOUs from the buyers. Since they preferred immediate cash payment, the Phoenician traders cashed them with Levantine[③] financiers. At the maturities of IOUs, Levantine financiers would present them to the Athenian buyers for payment. If the buyer dishonoured, the Levantine financier had the right of recourse to the Phoenician trader for payment. But if the IOU had been conditioned "without recourse", the Levantine financier would have no recourse to the Phoenician trader when the buyer refused to pay.

Forfaiting came to prominence in Europe in the 1950s and the conditions for forfaiting matured in the early 1960s. At that time, Eastern European countries were eager to obtain western particularly West German technology, but they had little hard currency to make payment. Trade credits provided to them by west European exporters usually had a tenor of up to six months, and credits with such a short period was good for imports of commodity, but not good enough for capital goods. On the other hand, West German manufacturers of capital goods were expecting to expand their markets to Eastern European countries. Since they found their exports to Eastern European buyers profitable, they were even willing to wait up to

---

① Phoenician：腓尼基人
② Athenian：雅典人
③ Levantine：黎凡特人

five years for payment of the negotiable instruments which had been guaranteed by a state bank of the relevant Eastern European country.

However, the difficulty encountered by West German manufacturers at that time was they had no access to sufficient funds to offer extended trade credit to their buyers. The growth in the value of their accounts receivable limited their ability to look for more businesses. Under these conditions, banks, as crucial important financial intermediaries, stepped into the gap. Central European financiers, such as Swiss, German and Italian forfaiters, played a key role in the evolution of the forfaiting market. These forfaiters agreed to purchase these trade credit assets from West German manufacturers for cash without recourse, which in turn allowed the manufacturers to continue to expand their trade credit.

Originally, German capital goods exports were the foundation of the market. Since the 1970s such non-recourse trade credit has been used as a method of financing western European capital goods exports not only to Eastern Europe but also to Latin America, Southeast Asia, Middle East and parts of Africa. During the 1970s and 1980s, both the primary and secondary markets for forfaiting grew rapidly. The first forfaiting company Finanz AG was established in 1965, evidencing the formal appearance of forfaiting in the international finance arena. More successful companies during that period were Trade Development Bank, Soditic, Monaval, Hungarian International Bank, Noreco, Fineurop, etc., and the leading West German deposit-taking banks constitutes the forfaiting finance market. Later, specialist forfaiting houses were set up, leading to the further growth of this financing method and the shift of the market from Switzerland and northern Italy to West Germany and more remarkably to London. London played an aggressive role in the forfaiting finance market and gradually came to dominate the trading in the secondary market. In 1984, London Forfaiting Company PLC, the only publicly owned and UK stock market-quoted specialist forfaiting company, was set up.

Why did the forfaiters agree to buy these assets without recourse? Obviously, they did so for profits. At that time, according to the applicable negotiable instrument laws in Europe, a holder of commercial paper at maturity had a right of recourse against all previous parties of the paper and ultimately the drawer in the event of being not paid on the due date. But in order to keep the trade simple, no matter whether they are bills of exchange drawn by the exporter or promissory notes made out by the importer, once the exporter became the bona-fide holder of the negotiable instrument, the exporter could sell it to a forfaiter at a discount and obtained the immediate payment. And this sale was without recourse to the exporter, for the security for the forfaiter was the guarantee of the importer's bank.

International Trade and Forfaiting Association

The International Forfaiting Association (ITFA), as a worldwide trade association for commercial companies, was founded in August 1999. It has more than 140 members from all over the world. The functions of the IFA include developing high quality education for its members, providing assistance and support to the regional committees willing to organize a forfaiting education course and/or seminars, examining matters of a legal nature relevant to the forfaiting market, setting a framework and providing points of reference for transactions in the international forfaiting market, and maintaining a website giving general information on forfaiting and the forfating market to non members. Currently, one of its nine board members is Lixin Guo from Bank of China.

ICC' efforts

With the wide usage of forfaiting by its members, the Interntional Chamber of Commerce is now working on the Uniform Rules for Forfaiting (URF). Currently, the rules are under drafting and will probably come into effect in the near future. Like UCP for documentary credits and URDG for demand guarantees, URF will be the rules to be complied with in dealing with forfaiting when the parties concerned agree to use the rules in their forfaiting agreement. The URF will define and standardize both the primary and secondary forfaiting markets.

9.2 What is forfaiting?

The IFA describes forfaiting as a form of international supply chain financing that involves the discount of future payment obligations on a without recourse basis. It defines forfaiting by six characteristics:[1]

(1) 100% financing without recourse to the seller of the debt.

(2) The payment obligation is often but not always supported by a bank guarantee.

(3) The debt is usually evidenced a legally enforceable and transferable payment obligation such as a bill of exchange, promissory note, letter of credit or note purchase agreement.

(4) Transaction values can range from US＄10,000 to US＄200 million.

(5) Debt instruments are typically denominated in one of the world's major currencies, with Euro and US Dollars being most common.

(6) Finance can be arranged on a fixed or floating interest rate basis.

To make it simple, forfaiting is the purchase by a forfaiter of a series of payment instruments such as bills of exchange, promissory notes or bills of exchange drawn under acceptance credits or other freely negotiable instruments on a without-recourse basis. Without-recourse means that there is no comeback for the forfaiter to the seller of the instruments (the exporter under international trade) if the debtor (the importer under international trade) does not pay.

By purchasing the payment instruments, the forfaiter deducts interests (in the form of a discount) at an agreed rate for the full credit period covered by the instruments. If the debt instruments are bills of exchange, they are drawn by the exporter on the importer and accepted by the importer and most often bear an aval or attached by an unconditional guarantee. The aval or guarantee should have been issued by the importer's bank. In discounting the bills, the forfaiter obtains the right of claiming the debts from the importer and in case of dishonour has the right to claim payment from the guarantor. The forfaiter may either holds the bills until maturity or sells them to another forfaiter on a non-recourse basis. Such selling happens in the secondary market.

---

[1] What is forfaiting? Retrieved on October 30, 2013 from http://www.forfaiters.org/forfaiting/what-is-forfaiting

Parties to the forfaiting transaction

Since the forfaiting transaction may concern two markets: primary and secondary, the parties to the two markets need clarify.

First of all, the forfaiting agreement is the written agreement between the initial seller and the primary forfaiter. The initial seller is the one that first sells the payment claim. It is the exporter or supplier under the international trade settlement. The primary forfaiter is the forfaiting bank that first buys the payment claim from the initial seller.

The secondary forfaiting market is the market where the primary forfaiter sells the payment claims to a buyer. If the buyer sells the payment claim further to another buyer, the transaction also happens in the secondary market. Thus, there are two parties in the secondary market— the seller and the buyer. The seller may be the primary forfaiter or another seller while the buyer is the party who buys the payment claim from the primary forfaiter or another seller.

Required Documents

Debt instruments

Debt documents are the documents evidencing the debt owed by the buyer to the exporter include promissory notes, bills of exchange, letters of credit/standby letters of credit, payment guarantees or open book receivables. In most cases, the debt instrument need bear the unconditional, irrevocable and freely transferable guarantee or the aval of an acceptable bank in the buyer's country. Some top tier corporate or government debt do not need additional guarantee.

Other documents

According to the Draft URF, there may be some documents issued by the primary obligor to supplement or accompany the debt instruments. Other documents include: the documents evidencing the authenticity and binding nature of the signatures of the obligors and the seller, any document that is required to transfer the payment claim and all rights under any credit support document or to be presented when enforcing or exercising rights to receive payment under the payment claim or any credit support document, any credit support documents, any other document specified in the forfaiting agreement or the forfaiting confirmation, which may include documents relating to the underlying transaction; and any document the buyer is entitled to request, for a forfaiting transaction in the primary market or the secondary market.

Aval or guarantee

One of the required documents is the credit support document, which means any document evidencing an obligation of a person rather than the primary obligor to make payment in respect of the payment claim. Usually, it takes the form of aval or guarantee.

Aval is the forfaiters' preferred form of security of payment of a bill or note. For an aval to be acceptable, the avalizing bank must be internationally recognized and creditworthy. The aval may be placed on the face of the note. Sometimes, a guarantee is issued instead of an aval, particularly in some countries that may not recognize an aval as legally binding. In this case, a separate letter of aval or guarantee will be provided. Alternatively, a forfaiter may be happy to accept a blank indorsement by a guarantor on the instrument, or a standby letter of credit. The most important point to note is that any guarantee should be irrevocable, unconditional, divisible, and assignable.

Many U.S. exporters prefer to have the importer's bank open a letter of credit to cover their debt under a supplier's credit, that is, the bank issues a deferred payment or acceptance letter of credit that specifies a series of time drafts which the bank will accept (a form of guarantee) upon presentation of the documents required by the L/C. The letter of credit does not have to be transferable or confirmed by the advising bank in the exporter's country, but must be subject to UCP 600.

Costs

As far as possible, forfaiters will ensure that the buyer, not the seller, incur charges involved in a forfaiting transaction. Forfaiters usually emphasize their flexibility in tailoring deals to suit the exporter's needs. When faced with competition for the contract, exporters may choose to absorb some of the fees or financing cost to make the transaction more attractive to their buyers. Generally speaking, the cost of forfaiting depends on the interest rate relevant to the currency of the underlying contract at the time of the forfaiter's commitment and on the forfaiter's assessment of the credit risks related to the importing country and to the guarantor bank.

First of all, the forfaiter charges for the money received by the seller to cover its interest rate risk. The forfaiter refers to the cost of funds in the Eurocurrency market to calculate the charges to cover the forfaiter's refinancing costs. For instance, the LIBOR (London Interbank Offer Rate)[①] may be applicable to the average life of the transaction.

Secondly, a forfaiter charges for covering the political, commercial, and transfer risks attached to the importing country and the guarantor. This is referred to as margin, varying from country to country, and from guarantor to guarantor.

Additional costs include the days of grace charge and, when necessary, a commitment fee. During the days of grace, the forfaiter also charges interest on the money received by the seller. Days of grace period ranges from none to 10 days on some countries.

Application and tenors

The transactions that can be financed through forfaiting may involve various goods and services. For instance, the London Forfaiting Company's services can be applied to commodities, services, technology, capital equipment, turnkey plants and construction or project. And different applications have different tenors. Finance for commodities such as oil, coal, rice and grain ranges from 90 days to 180 months; finance for services such as engineering, design and maintenance from 180 days to 3 years; finance for technology such as software, computers and communications

---

① the London Interbank Offer Rate: 伦敦银行间拆放款利率

from 180 days to 5 years; finance for capital equipment such as machine tools, generators and tractors from 2 to 7 years; finance for turnkey plants such as power generation and asphalt production from 3 to 7 years; and finance for construction or project such as hospitals, airports and factories from 3 to 7 years.

9.3　The mechanics of a forfaiting transaction

In order to illustrate the mechanics of a forfaiting transaction, this section refers to an example illustrated by Andy Ripley (1996) in his book named *Forfaiting for Exporter: Practical Solutions for Global Trade Finance*.

The underlying trade contract

It was in spring 1996 when a British manufacturing company selling bottling machinery was negotiating a contract to supply a bottling plant to a Czech soft drinks company in Prague. The contract value was £1,000,000.

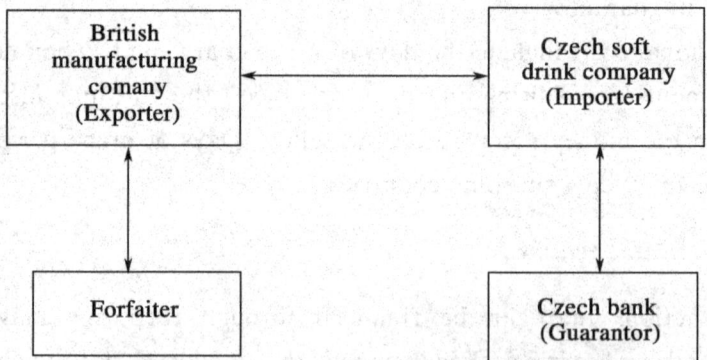

Figure 9.1　Illustration of a forfaiting transaction[①]

The buyer did not have sufficient funds to pay the British manufacturing company on delivery of the plant, and nor did it want to draw on loan facilities at its bank. But it could afford a 10% down payment, and for the rest of the money it required trade credit over two years with four semi-annual installments.

---

① Andy Ripley, *Forfaiting for Exporters: Practical Solutions for Global Trade Finance*, 1996, p. 22

The interest rate that the importer offered was 7% per annum on the outstanding amounts. The Czech buyer also found a local bank to guarantee its payment of the installments. In return, the Czech bank would charge the Czech importer a guarantee fee, which was calculated over the credit period on the outstanding amounts. The British manufacturing company also had its own plans of investment and did not want to have its capital tied up, so it turned to a forfaiter.

On March 1, 1996, the British exporter advised the forfaiter that it expected to finalize a contract with the Czech importer on April and would expect to deliver the plant four months later. From its past experience, the forfaiter estimated that after delivery it usually took two weeks to obtain and finalize the documentation for discount. So, the forfaiter provided the British exporter with an indicative proposal.

The forfaiting proposal

At this stage, an indicative proposal (see Table 9.1) was probably sufficient for the British manufacturing company, as it was not certain whether they would be able to finalize a contract on the terms detailed. However, if required, the forfaiter could offer a firm proposal at this point.

Table 9.1 Sample forfaiting proposal[1]

From: Forfaiting company	To: British manufacturing company
Importer:	Czech Republic soft drinks company
Guarantor:	Czech bank
Re:	Sale of bottling plant
Basis of calculation:	
Currency	Sterling
Required amount	1,000,000
Down-payment	10%
Number of bills	4
Interest paid by importer (per annum)	7%

---

[1] Andy Ripley, *Forfaiting for Exporters: Practical Solutions for Global Trade Finance*, 1996, p.23.

Continued

From: Forfaiting company	To: British manufacturing company
Method of interest calculation	twelfths
Commitment date	1/4/96
Interest/shipment date	31/7/96
Discount date	14/8/96
Commitment fee (per annum)	0.75%
Days of grace	3
Method of discounting	straight discount
Discount rate	6.875,924%
Equivalent semi-annual yield	7.375%
Summery of calculation:	
Currency	£
Contract value	1,000,000.00
Down payment	100,000.00
Principal—terms of reference in market	900,000.00
Interest	78,750.00
Total face value	978,750.00
Discounted value	897,778.02
Total proceeds to exporter	997,778.02
Commitment fee (135 days)	2,715.03
Final proceeds	995,062.99
Bill details:	

No.	Maturity	Principal	Interest	Face value	Net value
1	31/1/97	225,000.00	31,500.00	256,500.00	248,140.67
2	31/7/97	225,000.00	23,625.00	248,625.00	232,044.93
3	31/1/98	225,000.00	15,750.00	240,750.00	216,259.47
4	31/7/98	225,000.00	7,875.00	232,875.00	201,332.95
		900,000.00	78,750.00	978,750.00	897,778.02

By providing such an indicative proposal, the forfaiter indicated its willingness to purchase the debt from the British exporter on the terms quoted in the proposal. Based on the market practice for each country, the forfaiter would indicate the type of negotiable instrument acceptable for the transaction and this would form the basis of one element of the negotiations between the British manufacturing company and the Czech importer. Based on this indicative proposal, the British exporter would continue to negotiate with the Czech importer. Any amendments or changes to the basis of the contract during negotiations would be referred to the forfaiter for them to revise their proposal.

Everything went smoothly as planned and the forfaiting contract was signed on April 1, 1996. The forfaiter then provided the British exporter with a firm offer, setting out a final date by which they must receive the agreed documentation for discount. In practice this final date should cover the scheduled delivery period, the estimated documentation time, and a period to allow for potential delays in manufacture, delivery and processing of documentation. The British exporter accepted the firm offer and was committed to sell the debt to the forfaiter. At the same time, the forfaiter was committed to purchasing the debt from the British manufacturing company without recourse, within the time scale agreed, subject to their receipt of the agreed documentation.

Terms and conditions

Forfaiting is such a flexible financing method that there is no standard format or set terms and conditions. The forfaiter and the exporter mutually negotiate and agree on their own terms and conditions so long as they are not against the laws or statues that govern each party. Typically, terms and conditions of a forfaiting agreement include those on commitment fee, options, methods of discounting, the discount rate, days of grace, number of bills or notes, etc.

Commitment fee

Based on the firm offer, the British exporter finalized the contract with the Czech importer and agreed on April 1, 1996 upon a commitment to deliver the documentation to the forfaiter on July 31, 1996, four months later, and the discount would be on August 14, 1996, two weeks after delivery. The forfaiter promised to purchase the debt (90% of contract value plus interest, i.e. a total of £978,750) from the British exporter.

In many cases, the forfaiter fixes the discount rate when a commitment is agreed upon, thereby running a risk of interest rates increasing over the commitment period. To cover the potential guarantor, country and interest rate risks, the forfaiter usually charges the exporter a commitment fee, calculated on the amount for which the commitment is agreed upon and payable from the date of commitment until the date discount takes place. In this example, the forfaiter quoted a commitment fee of 2715.03 (0.75% per annum calculated on 978,750 from April 1, 1996 to August 14, 1996—a period of 135 days). The timing of the payment of the commitment fee will be agreed upon between the forfaiter and the exporter and depend on the details of each individual transaction.

Option

Option means that the exporter is provided by the forfaiter with an optional period within which the exporter can consider whether he accepts the offer or not. In general, if the exporter accepts the offer within 24 hours, the period is called an option period without any charges to be borne by the exporter. If the exporter accepts the offer more than the time limit stipulated by the forfaiter in his offer, the offer will be revoked. If the exporter accepts the offer more than 24 hours within the time limit, the forfaiter will charge him the option fee and the period is called an option period carrying charges.

Again, in the same example, the British exporter could have agreed upon an option on March 1, 1996, allowing them to cancel the commitment on April 1, 1996 in the event that they did not finalize a contract by that date. An option fee would be negotiated between the forfaiter and the exporter. Using the commitment fee level of 0.75% per annum in this example, this would cost the British company 623.45 (0.75% per annum calculated on 978,750 from March 1, 1996 to April 1, 1996—a period of 31 days).

Methods of discounting

The methods that can be used in calculating the proceeds paid to the exporter by the forfaiter include semi-annual yields, straight discounts, annual yields, simple yields and discount to yields. A straight discount rate takes no account of the true value of money and is applied to the face value of each payment and calculated on a simple basis from the date of discount until the maturity date of each repayment. The reason for a forfaiter to prefer to quote a straight discount rate is its ease to understand.

Discount rate

In the same example, the forfaiter quoted a straight discount rate of 6.875,924% per annum that would give it a rate of return or semi-annual yield of 7.375% per annum.

In calculating their required rate of return, the forfaiter will consider two fundamental points. Firstly, the forfaiter calculates the borrowing costs for the currency and credit period of the transaction together with the margin it requires to cover their perception of the risks involved (i.e. the credit risk, the interest rate risk and the documentation risk). Secondly, the forfaiter takes into account the credit and interest rate risks during the commitment period (i.e. what do they think they will be able to sell the transaction for, once they become holders of the debt).

In our example, the Sterling borrowing costs for the average life of the two year credit period—using the LIBOR—was 6.625% per annum, plus a margin of almost 0.75% to cover the risks detailed above. Moreover, the current secondary market price for the transaction at that time might be 7.125% per annum semi-annual yield, giving a potential profit of 0.25% per annum on the deal assuming interest rates and market sentiment remained unchanged over the commitment period.

First maturity date: 31/1/97

From 14/8/96 (discount date) to 31/1/97 (maturity date) plus three days of grace=173 days

£256,500 (face value) × 6.875,924% per annum × 173/365 = £8,359.33

£256,500 − £8,359.33 (discount cost) = £248,140.67 (net value to exporter)

Days of grace

Days of grace are the number of days a forfaiter adds to each maturity date in calculating discounted proceeds to be paid to the exporter or previous holder of the debt. They can be described as the period the forfaiter believes it will take in order for them to receive payment beyond the actual maturity date. In our example, the forfaiter quoted three days of grace. If payment was received on the actual maturity date, the forfaiter would "earn" three-day interest as an additional profit. If payment was not received until five days after the maturity date, the forfaiter would have a potential two-day interest "loss", as they had waived all rights of recourse to the British company. In practice, the forfaiter or the holder of the debt instrument at maturity could demand delay interest from the Czech importer and/or the Czech bank, depending on the amount and period involved.

Number of bills/notes

The classic forfaiting transaction for capital goods will normally consist of ten non-recourse promissory notes, a note becoming due every six months from the date of shipment. However, there are considerable variations on this format. It may suit the exporter if he or she has no need of cash to hold the notes for a year, receive the payment on the first two notes from the importer and then discount the remaining eight notes for cash with a forfaiter. As discussed above, the number and tenor of bills or notes depend on the specific underlying transaction. In our example, four bills of exchange were used.

Summary of the procedures of forfaiting

Step 1: The importer and the exporter negotiate and the former asks the latter for credit terms.

Step 2: The exporter approaches a forfaiter and asks for an indication of whether the forfaiter is willing to provide this credit and how much it is likely to cost.

Step 3: The forfaiter provides the exporter with an indication of the costs involved. If the exporter accepts, it becomes a firm indication.

Step 4: The exporter goes back to the importer and signs the commercial contract. If required, the importer obtains guarantee from its bank.

Step 5: The exporter presents required documents to the forfaiter for delivery.

Step 6: The forfaiter examines the documents and makes payment to the exporter without recourse.

Step 7: The forfaiter either claims payment from the importer when the instruments mature or sells them to other buyers before maturity in the secondary market.

Step 8: If the importer refuses to pay at maturity, the forfaiter presents the instruments to the guarantor bank for payment.

9.4 Forfaiting vs. other trade financing methods

Forfaiting vs. officially supported export credits

The basic difference between forfaiting and officially supported export credits is that the former is conducted through a forfaiter while the latter through a country's EXIM bank. Forfaiting, as a supplement to those officially supported export credits, offers the exporter some advantages over the EXIM bank's export credits.

A forfaiter allows the exporter a greater flexibility in structuring a deal, particularly when the goods are being supplied from a country where EXIM bank's requirements cannot be met under the existing rules or regulations. Unless it is a very large or complex deal, a forfaiter will be able to indicate within a couple of days whether financing is available or not, while it may take more time for the EXIM bank to come through with a commitment. Moreover, the documentation under forfaiting is concise and straightforward.

Since the forfaiter offers a 100% financing without recourse, the exporter will have no political, transfer, commercial, interest rate and exchange rate fluctuation risks. At the same time, the exporter can receive cash payment while providing trade credit to its customers. Providing trade credit to its customers makes its products more attractive and competitive than its rival's.

Forfaiting vs. factoring

Factoring provides finance with short terms less than 3 months while forfaiting offers the terms from 6 months to 10 years. The goods financed under factoring are mainly consumer goods while the goods financed under forfaiting mostly capital goods. The risk for a factor to assume is only the credit risk of the importer, while the risk for a forfaiter involves political, transfer and commercial ones.

Table 9.2 Comparison between international factoring and international forfaiting

Item	International factoring	International forfaiting
Nature	Assignment of the accounts receivable	The purchase of debt instruments (e.g., promissory notes issued by the importer and guaranteed by the guanrantor bank, bills accepted by the importer and guaranteed by the guarantor bank)
Goods covered	Consumer goods	Traditionally fixed assets such as durable consumer goods, capital equipment, but now more flexible
Credit period	Less than 90 days	Most often from over 180 days to 10 years, depending on the case
Contract value	No limitation	More than US $100,000, now more flexible
Right of recourse	With or without recourse	Without recourse

9.5 Forfaiting in China

Currently, one of its 9 board members of the ITFA is Lixin Guo, a non-executive board member from the Bank of China. At present, it has 10 members from China, including Agricultural Bank of China, Bank of China, Bank of Jiangsu, China Construction Bank Corporation, China

Everbright Bank Co. Ltd., China Merchant Bank Co. Ltd, China Minsheng Banking Corp. Ltd, China Trade Solutions Ltd, CITIC Industrial Bank, and Industrial & Commercial Bank of China.[①]

As early as in the early 1990s, the foreign branches of the Bank of China had started to provide forfaiting for clients. In 2001, the domestic branches of the Bank of China started to offer the forfaiting services. Since 2002, twenty domestic bank branches including Jiangsu Branch, Zhejiang Branch, and Chongqing Branch and some of subbranches began to provide forfaiting services. By the mid-August 2003, the volume of forfaiting in the Bank of China had reached to 20 million US dollars.

Forfaiting offered by Chinese banks is mostly based on the acceptance letter of credit transaction. For example, under an acceptance credit, the exporter (beneficiary of the credit) submits the bills of exchange and shipping documents to the issuing bank, the nominated bank or the confirming bank, if any. The issuing bank, the nominated bank or confirming bank, if any, first accepts the bills of exchange and returns the accepted bills to the exporter and retains the shipping documents. The exporter may hold the accepted bills until maturity and present them to the paying bank for payment. Another choice is to discount the accepted bills with or without recourse with its bank. If its bank is willing to discount the accepted bills without recourse to the exporter, the bank provides forfaiting for its client.

Recently Chinese banks are trying to offer forfaiting for clients on O/A basis. For instance, the Zhejiang Branch of the Bank of China provided forfaiting to a client for an underlying transaction based on O/A 180 days.[②]

---

① http://forfaiters.org
② http://hangzhou.pbc.gov.cn/publish/hangzhou/1250/2012/20120117185812844661958/20120117185812844661958_.html

10 Documents used in international trade payments

Documents here refer to the documentation evidencing the shipment of goods under a sales contract. No matter what payment technique is used, the delivery of goods and the payment of money are based on the documents evidencing the fulfillment of the underlying obligations. Since the documents required in the letter of credit transactions are the most complicated, this chapter mainly discusses the documents under the letter of credit transactions from the perspective of banks.

10.1 Types and functions of documents

Basic documents and additional documents

Based on the functions of documents, documents can be divided into basic documents and additional documents. Basic documents refer to commercial invoices, bills of lading, and insurance policies if the price term requires the exporter to buy insurance. Additional documents are those other than basic ones, including customs invoices, consular invoices, packing lists, certificates of origin, certificates of inspection, etc.

Financial documents and commercial documents

Financial documents refer to bills of exchange, promissory notes, cheques or other similar documents used for acquiring payment while commercial documents refer to commercial invoices and the documents evidencing the title of ownership or other non-financial documents. Basic documents and additional documents all fall into the category of commercial documents.

Among the documents mentioned above, bills of exchange, commercial invoices and packing lists are issued by the exporter, bills of lading or insurance policies are issued by separate professional organizations, and export licenses, certificates of origin or certificates of inspection are issued by relevant governmental or social organizations.

Representing the title to the ownership of the goods

Among all the documents, the marine bills of lading are negotiable instruments and the consignee or holder of the full set of original bills of lading is the owner of the goods that are transported by the carrier. The transfer of bills of lading represents the transfer of the title to the goods. The special role that marine bills of lading play makes it possible for banks to get involved in international trade payments and settlements. Although banks do not deal with goods, services or performance, bank can control the title of goods through controlling the documents.

Evidencing the fulfillment of obligations

Documents also serve as the evidence that the exporter has fulfilled its obligations under a sales contract. The importer effects payment against the documents submitted by the exporter, for the documents have described the details of the transaction.

Under a letter of credit transaction, provided that the documents submitted by the exporter constitute a complying presentation, the negotiating bank will advance the payment to the exporter and then get reimbursed from the issuing bank by forwarding the complying documents.

10.2 Draft(s) drawn under a letter of credit

Some letters of credit require draft(s) while some do not. For instance, a sight payment credit may or may not ask for draft(s), an acceptance credit do require draft(s), and a deferred payment credit never asks for draft(s). In practice, continental European banks often issue deferred payment credits that require no draft (s) to avoid the stamp duty. Under an acceptance credit, however, the draft is indispensable, for the due date is calculated based on its tenor.

Characteristics of drafts drawn under a letter of credit

Requisite form

The draft drawn under a credit must contain all the essential items required by the negotiable instrument law of the place of issue. It is the law of the issuing place that determines the validity of the draft.

Compliance with the credit

The draft drawn under a credit must satisfy the specific stipulations in the credit. In a credit that requires a draft, there is a drawn clause such as "draft(s) drawn under L/C No … " Then, a drawn clause must be incorporated in the contents of the draft, specifying the issuing bank, the L/C number and the issuing date.

Examination of the draft(s) drawn under a letter of credit

Date and place of issue

The issue date of a draft must not be later than the expiry date of the credit under which the draft is drawn and not earlier than that of the relevant transport documents. The place of issue is the place of negotiation, i.e. the place where the exporter is located.

Tenor

Whether the draft is payable at sight, at a fixed time after date, at a fixed time after sight, or at a fixed time after the date of bill of lading, solely depends on the stipulations of the credit. That is, the tenor of the draft must meet the terms of the credit.

Payee

The payee of the draft drawn under a credit may be the beneficiary (including the second beneficiary in a transferable credit) or the beneficiary's bank, i. e., the negotiating bank. If the payee is the beneficiary, the draft is made "payable to ourselves". If the payee is the beneficiary's bank, the draft is made "payable to … bank (the name of the negotiating bank)".

In practice, if the draft is "payable to ourselves," the beneficiary need indorse it blankly when submitting it to the negotiating bank. If the draft is "payable to… bank (the name of the negotiating bank)," the negotiating bank need indorse them blankly when forwarding the drafts to the issuing bank.

Amount

The amount of the draft should not be in excess of that of the credit. The amount in figures should be the same as that in words and must be consistent with those appearing in other documents.

UCP 600 Article 30 states that the words "about" or "approximately" used in connection with the amount of the credit are to be considered as allowing a tolerance not to exceed 10% more or 10% less than the amount to which they refer. If there is no such an indication in the credit, the amount of the draft is not allowed to exceed the amount of the credit. If the amount of the draft exceeds that of the credit, the excess amount should be obtained from the buyer on a collection basis.

Drawn clause and interest clause

A drawn clause includes the name of the issuing bank, the L/C number and the issuing date of the credit. There may be an interest clause, indicating the interest rate and the starting and ending dates of calculating the interest.

Drawee

The drawee of the draft drawn under a credit may be the issuing bank or a bank nominated by the issuing bank. If it is expressed as "drafts drawn on us…," the drawee bank is the issuing bank; if it is expressed as "drafts drawn on… bank (the name of another nominated bank), the drawee bank is the nominated bank other than the issuing bank. Be it the issuing bank or the nominated bank, the drawee of the draft must be a bank. A credit must not be issued available by a draft on the applicant.

Drawer

The drawer of the draft under a credit is the beneficiary or the second beneficiary in a transferable credit.

One of the essential items in a draft is the signature of the drawer. Then, what is the appropriate signature of the drawer? According to UCP

600, a document may be signed by handwriting, facsimile signature, perforated signature, stamp, symbol, or any other mechanical or electronic method of authentication. In practice, the most frequently used one for the draft is the facsimile signature. If a credit requires manual signature, the drawer must sign it by handwriting.

The most frequently found discrepancies with drafts

(1) The draft is presented after the expiry date of the credit.
   (2) The amount of the draft is greater than that of the credit.
   (3) The tenor of the draft is not as shown in the credit.
   (4) The draft is not drawn on the bank specified in the credit.
   (5) The draft is not indorsed or indorsed incorrectly.
   (6) The drawer of the draft is not the beneficiary of the credit.
   (7) There is no signature of the drawer.
   (8) There is no drawn clause as specified in the credit.
   (9) The number of the credit is missing or incorrect.
   (10) The credit requires no draft but the draft is still included in the documents.

Under a credit transaction, two copies of the draft are drawn to ensure that at least one draft reaches the drawee when they are dispatched separately. The first bill is marked with "First of Exchange (Second unpaid)" while the second bill with "Second of Exchange (First Unpaid)".

10.3 Commercial invoices

A commercial invoice is an accounting document by which the seller claims payment from the buyer for the value of the goods being supplied. As the core document in which detailed description of the goods can be found, the commercial invoice can be used for bookkeeping, customs clearance and replacing the drafts in case no draft is required.

Contents of a commercial invoice

A commercial invoice consists of three parts: the heading, the body, and the complementary clause.

Heading

The heading includes the title such as "Commercial Invoice" or "Invoice", the names and addresses of the seller and the buyer, the invoice date and number, the sales contract number, and if available, the bill of lading number, the name of vessel, the port of loading and discharge or transshipment, the shipment date and the delivery terms. It also contains the L/C number and the name of the issuing bank if required by the credit.

Body

The body consists of such items as the name and description of goods, shipping mark, quantity, price and invoice amount, packing, gross and net weight, etc. The description of the goods, services or performance in a commercial invoice must correspond with that in the credit.

According to UCP600, if there is the term "about" or "approximate" before the quantity or unit price in the credit, the quantity or unit price is allowed to be 10% more or 10% less than that stipulated in the credit. Sometimes, the credit itself contains a more or less clause, say "more or less 5%", the quantity or unit price indicated in the invoice should comply with the stipulation.

In the case that the credit contains no "more or less" clause, if the quantity is measured in weight such as kilogram, meter, yard, etc., it allows more or less 5% leeway, but the total amount of the drawings may not exceed the amount of the credit. If the quantity is measured in terms of number of packing units or individual items, such as parcel, barrel, piece, etc., it allows no leeway.

The unit price is sometimes expressed as "$1.80 per yard CIF Liverpool", including the price term. The price term or delivery term may be incorporated in the unit price or indicated separately.

Complementary clause

The complementary clause includes import or export license number, if any, the special statement and the signature of the beneficiary, if required.

According to UCP600 Article 18, a commercial invoice must appear to have been issued by the beneficiary named in the credit, or the second beneficiary in a transferable credit, and it need not be signed. In practice, whether a commercial invoice need be signed or not depends on the stipulation of the credit.

A commercial invoice must be made out in the same currency as the documentary credit. The commercial invoice may show an equivalent in local currency only for information purposes and not as the basis for the manner of settlement.

The most frequently found discrepancies with invoices:

(1) The maker of the invoice is not the beneficiary of the credit.

(2) The buyer's name is not identical to the applicant of the credit.

(3) The description of goods is not consistent with that in the credit.

(4) The quantity of the goods is not within the permitted leeway.

(5) The total amount of the invoice exceeds that of the credit or not in the permitted leeway.

(6) The unit price is not in the permitted leeway.

(7) There is no breakdown of charges, if required by credit, or the calculation is not correct.

(8) There is no signature of the beneficiary but it is required by the credit.

(9) The number of the copies of invoices is insufficient.

(10) The invoices indicate partial shipment which is forbidden by the credit.

(11) The shipping mark and number are not consistent with those on the transport documents.

Other invoices

Proforma invoice

Before concluding a sales contract with the importer, the exporter may issue a proforma invoice to the importer, which can be used by the importer to apply for the import license from the authority of the importing country. The contents of such a proforma invoice include the name of the goods, unit price, measurement, etc.

Customs invoice

Some countries require customs invoices for the importing goods to make sure of the value and origin of the goods, especially to ensure whether there is a dumping.

Although the main contents of customs invoices include the value and origin of the merchandise exported, the form and contents of a customs invoice are determined by the customs of the relative country and they vary from country to country. In general, customs invoices are made out by exporters according to the relative requirements.

Consular invoice

Some countries require consular invoices for the importing goods in order to ensure that there is no dumping of the goods exported. The form of a consular invoice is made by the consulate of the importing country, and the exporter should fill up the form and then have it signed by the consular.

Both customs invoices and consular invoices are considered obstacles to the development of international trade, so their uses are diminishing, though still found.

Certified invoice

A certified invoice may be required to satisfy a specific concern of the buyer in relation to the certification required. The certified invoice has a certification by the beneficiary or a third party as required by the credit. For example, a beneficiary may be required to certify that the contents are correct and comply with the terms of the proforma invoice.

Legalised invoice

A legalized invoice bears the evidence that it has been legalized by the embassy of the import country to meet the requirements set by the control authorities of the import country. A legalized invoice first needs to be legalized by a notary and then by an embassy or a consulate of the import country.

Specimen of a commercial invoice (1)

... CO., LTD.
ADDRESS: ...

COMMERCIAL INVOICE

TO:

INVOICE NO.:
DATE:
LOADING FROM:
TO:
L/C NUMBER:

DESCRIPTION OF GOODS	QUANTITY (MT)	UNIT PRICE (USD/MT)	AMOUNT (USD)
TOTAL			

Specimen of a commercial invoice (2)

	Invoice		Original
	Company's name and address		Company Logo
Customer No.	Invoice Date	Due Date:	Invoice No.
Bill to:			
From:	To:		
B/L No.: B/L Date: Means of Transport:	Payment Terms:		
Freight Terms:	Shipment Date:	Delivery Terms:	

Item	Description	Quantity	Units	Price	Curr/Unit	Amount
Total						

GST Registration No.	Company Registration Number	Net Amount: Tax Amount:
Letter of Credit No.: Dated:		Total Amount:
Amount in Words:		

Telephone: , Fax:

10.4 Transport documents

In international trade, the carrier or its agents issues a transport document that acknowledges that the goods have been received from the beneficiary and states the terms and conditions upon which the carrier undertakes the transport of goods. The means of transport are illustrated in Table 10.1. This section mainly discusses the marine bills of lading.

Table 10.1 Means of transport

Means of transport	Relevant documents
By at least two different modes of transport, e.g., sea/land	Multimodal, combined or through transport Bill of lading
By sea	Non-negotiable sea waybill Charter party bill of lading
By air	Air transport document
By road, rail or inland waterway	Road, rail or inland waterway transport documents
By courier and post	Courier receipt, post receipt or certificate of posting

Marine bills of lading

A marine bill of lading is issued by a carrier or its agent evidencing that the goods have been shipped on board a vessel and will be transported as contracted to the destination. A bill of lading serves as (1) the contract between the carrier and the seller which states the obligation of the carrier to transport the goods from the port of shipment to the port of destination, (2) the title document which evidences the holder's ownership of the goods, and (3) the receipt for goods shipped.

UCP600 Article 20 states in detail the requirements of a bill of lading. According to it, a bill of lading, however named, must appear to indicate the name of the carrier and be signed by the carrier or its agent or the master or its agent. The carrier must sign as carrier, the master must sign as master, and the agent must sign as agent. It means that if it is signed by an agent, it should be indicated that the agent has signed it for or on behalf of the carrier or the master.

Basic parties to a bill of lading

Carrier

It is the party that issues the contract of transport and is responsible for shipping the goods to the destination. It may be the owner of the vessel or the chartered party who rents the vessel.

Shipper/consignor

It is the party who consigns the goods to the carrier. The shipper is usually the seller under the sales contract and the beneficiary of the credit, yet sometimes the credit requires the buyer as shipper. The reason for it may be that the buyer is not the final buyer but a middleman.

Consignee

It is the party who has the right to pick up the goods from the carrier against bills of lading at the port of destination. Usually it is the buyer under the sales contract.

In practice, however, the consignee may be the shipper (seller), the negotiating bank or the issuing bank. When the bills of lading are made out "to the order of shipper," the shipper (the seller) must indorse them blankly before submitting them to the negotiating bank. If the bills of lading are made out "to ... bank (the name of negotiating bank)," the negotiating bank need indorse them before forwarding to the issuing bank. If the bills of lading are made out "to the issuing bank," there is no need for indorsement by the beneficiary or the negotiating bank before forwarding them to the issuing bank.

Notify party

It is the party whom the carrier will notify of the arrival of the goods. It may be the applicant of the credit, the party nominated in the credit or simply left blank if there is no requirement in the credit.

Transferee/holder

The bills of lading are negotiable instruments, so they may be transferred with indorsement and/or delivery. The person to whom the bills of lading are transferred is called the transferee. Against the bills of lading, the transferee is entitled to obtain the goods from the carrier. The holder may be the consignee or the transferee.

Main contents of a bill of lading

The contents of a bill of lading cover all the items on both the front and the back of the document. The main contents on the front include:

(1) the name and address of the carrier,
(2) the name and address of the shipper,
(3) the name and address of the consignee,
(4) the name and address of the notify party,
(5) the place of receipt or the port of loading, the port of discharge or the final destination,
(6) the name of vessel, voyage and nationality,
(7) shipping marks and numbers,
(8) description of goods, weight, measurement and package,
(9) freight and charges,
(10) the place and date of issue, the bill of lading number,
(11) the statement indicating the receipt of the goods, and
(12) the signature of the carrier or its agent.

On the back of a bill of lading are the conditions of the transport contract between the shipper and the carrier, including the liabilities and disclaimers of the carrier.

Types of bills of lading

Shipped on board B/L vs. received for shipment B/L

A shipped on board bill of lading means that the goods have been shipped on board the vessel. According to UCP 600, a bill of lading must indicate that the goods have been shipped on board a named vessel at the port of loading stated in the credit by pre-printed wording, or an on board notation indicating the date on which the goods have been shipped on board. Thus, a shipped on board bill of lading indicates so by a clause such as "shipped on board the vessel named above..." If there is no such a clause printed on the bill of lading, there should be a notation of "On Board" accompanied by the date of boarding on the bill of lading.

A shipped on board bill of lading are considered as an assurance of the buyer's obtaining the goods, there is usually such a stipulation in the sales contract between the buyer and the seller and hence the credit requires a shipped on board bill of lading accordingly.

A received for shipment bill of lading bears no notation of "On Board", and means that the goods have been received by the carrier and ready for shipment. Under a credit, banks do not accept such bills of lading unless stipulated by the credit. However, a received for shipment bill of lading can be transferred into a shipped on board bill of lading when the carrier adds the notation of "On Board" on the face of the instrument.

Clean B/L vs. unclean B/L

A clean bill of lading is one that bears no clause or notation expressly declaring a defective condition of the goods and/or the packing. An unclean bill of lading may have notations such as "rusty of the goods", "breakage of the package", "second hand cases", "used drums", "ship may discharge the goods at the nearest port if unable to reach the destination", "port expenses at destination to be borne by the consignee", etc. Banks will not accept the bill of lading bearing such clauses or notations and only accept clean on board bills of lading. The word "clean" need not appear on the bill of lading, though. But UCP 600 specifies that a transport document bearing a clause such as "shipper's load and count" and "said by shipper to contain" is acceptable.

Straight B/L, blank B/L and order B/L

A straight bill of lading is made out directly to the consignee, i.e. the buyer under a sales contract. It is only the consignee named in the bill of lading that has the right to pick up the goods from the carrier. This kind of bills of lading is seldom used in international trade and only suitable to the precious goods or exhibition goods.

A blank bill of lading is made out to bearer and the bearer of such an instrument may transfer it by mere delivery. This kind of bills of lading is also seldom used, for it is risky. If the instrument was lost or stolen, anyone could be the bearer claiming for the goods.

An order bill of lading is made out to the order of a named party such as "to order", "to order of shipper", "to order of the issuing bank", "to order of the buyer". This kind of bills of lading can be transferred by indorsement and delivery. In practice, however, the most frequently used is "to order" or "to order of shipper". In this case, the shipper (the beneficiary of the credit) should indorse the bills of lading as required before submitting them to the negotiating bank. In some cases, in order to control the title to the goods, the issuing bank may require the bills of lading made out to its own order. However, "to order of the buyer" is seldom used.

Direct B/L, transshipment B/L, and through B/L

A direct bill of lading means that the goods will be transported from the port of loading directly to the port of discharge. If the credit forbids transshipment, banks will only accept direct bills of lading.

According to UCP 600 Article 20 b, transshipment means that the goods will be unloaded from one vessel and reloaded to another vessel during the carriage from the port of loading to the port of discharge stipulated in the credit. Unless otherwise stipulated, banks will not accept transshipment B/L. However, UCP 600 Article 20 c stipulates that "a bill of lading may indicate that the goods will or may be transshipped provided that the entire carriage is covered by one and the same bill of lading." Moreover, even if the credit prohibits transshipment, if the goods have been shipped in a container, trailer or LASH barge as evidenced by the bill of lading, the bill of lading indicating that the transshipment will or may take place is also acceptable.

From the viewpoint of the owner of the goods, direct bills of lading are preferred to transshipment bills of lading, for transshipment will increase costs and probably cause damage to the goods, and the arrival time of the goods will probably be delayed due to unexpected reasons. Thus, only when there is no direct shipment between the port of loading and the port of discharge will transshipment be used.

A through bill of lading means that the goods will be transported by two or more transport means, but the first of which is ocean transport, such as ocean-land, ocean-river, ocean-air or ocean-ocean, etc. A through bill of lading is issued by the first leg ocean carrier.

Long form B/L vs. short form B/L

A long form bill of lading contains the terms and conditions of carriage, i.e., the detailed items on the rights and liabilities of the carrier and the shipper. This form of bills of lading is widely used in practice.

A short form or blank back bill of lading only contains the essential items on the face, but the detailed clauses on the rights and liabilities of the carrier and the shipper are omitted. UCP 600 specifies that a bill of lading must appear to contain the terms and conditions of carriage. If it is a short form or blank back bill of lading, it must make reference to another source containing the terms and conditions of carriage.

Liner B/L vs. charter party B/L

A liner bill of lading sets out in full the contract between the bill of lading holder and the carrier, whereas a charter party bill of lading tends to be in a short form setting out some basic provisions. UCP 600 states that a bill of lading must appear to contain no indication that it is subject to a charter party. If it is not specified in the credit, banks will accept the charter party bill of lading, but will not examine the charter party contracts.

Container B/L

A container bill of lading means that the goods will be transported in containers and the bill of lading usually bears the notation of containerized. A container bill of lading is in the form of received for shipment bill of lading, so it is important to see the notation of "On Board".

On deck B/L

An on deck bill of lading means that goods are loaded on deck. UCP 600 states that a transport document must not indicate that the goods are or will be loaded on deck. On deck bills of lading offer no assurance of the safety of the goods during the course of transportation. But UCP 600 further specifies that a clause on a transport document stating that the goods may be loaded on deck is acceptable.

Advanced B/L and ante-date B/L

At the request of the shipper, the carrier will probably issue bills of lading before the goods are actually shipped on board the vessel, because the date of shipment and the expiry date of the credit will mature before the goods are actually shipped. Issuing this kind of bills of lading will render the carrier in a position of "issuing fake documents."

On the contrary, at the request of the shipper, the carrier will probably issue the bills of lading with the issuing date before the actual date to ensure them in compliance with the requirement on shipping date in the credit. It is also risky for a carrier to do so.

The most frequently found discrepancies with a bill of lading

(1) The consignee's name is not as per the credit.

(2) The notify party differs from that of the credit.

(3) The description of goods is not consistent with that in the credit.

(4) Unclean B/Ls are submitted.

(5) The port of loading or discharge is not as per that required in the credit.

(6) Less than full set 3/3 original B/Ls are submitted.

(7) There is no evidence that freight has been paid and the amount of freight paid is not listed when required by the credit.

(8) There is no "On Board" notation while the bills of lading are received for shipment bills of lading.

(9) "On Board" notation is dated after the latest shipment date required by the credit.

(10) The bills of lading are stale.

(11) The bills of lading are marked "On Deck".

(12) The bills of lading are charter party bills of lading.

(13) The bills of lading have not been indorsed when required.

(14) The shipping mark, the number of packages, the gross weight and

the net weight are not consistent with those on other documents.

(15) The issuer of the bills of lading is not a carrier or an agent of carrier.

(16) The date of bills of lading is later than the date stipulated in the credit.

(17) The date of presentation is later than the date stipulated in the credit.

(18) On board notation is not dated.

Other transport documents

Transport document covering at least two different modes of transport

A multimodal transport document is a transport document that covers at least two different modes of transport. If the journey will involve travel over land, then sea, then land (i.e., land/sea/land), the transport document is usually issued as a combined, through or multimodal transport bill of lading.

Non-negotiable sea waybill

Non-negotiable sea waybills are consigned to a named party, which in documentary credit operations will generally be the applicant. It is not a negotiable document and does not convey the title to the underlying goods.

Charter party bill of lading

Maritime carriers may either own their own vessels or hire (charter) them from shipowners. In the latter case, the hiring arrangement is called a charter party. It is a bill of lading containing an indication that it is subject to a charter party. Unless otherwise stipulated in the credit, banks will not accept a charter party bill of lading. According to UCP 600 Article 22 b, if a credit permits the beneficiary to submit a charter party bill of lading, banks will not examine the charter party contracts, even if they are required to be presented by the terms of the credit.

Airway bill

An airway bill or AWB is issued by an air carrier or its agent evidencing that the carrier or its agent has received the goods and will transport them to the destination. If it is issued by the carrier, the signature of the carrier must be identified as the carrier. If it is issued by the agent, the signature of the agent must indicate that the agent has signed for or on behalf of the carrier. An airway bill serves as both the cargo receipt and the transport contract, but not as the title to the goods. Thus, unlike a bill of lading, an airway bill is not negotiable and cannot be used as the title to the goods. The consignee can pick up the goods only by evidencing that he himself is the consignee of the goods.

Railway bill

A railway bill is a cargo receipt issued by a railway carrier, serving as a transport contract between the consignor and the carrier. The original railway bill goes with the goods and the copies are issued to the shipper to be used for settlement.

Specimen of a marine bill of lading[①]

1. Shipper insert Name, Address and Phone		B/L No.	
2. Consignee insert Name, Address and Phone		XX 集装箱运输有限公司 XX CONTAINER LINES TLX: FAX: ORIGINAL Port-to-Port or Combined Transport BILL OF LADING	
3. Notify Party insert Name, Address and Phone (It is agreed that no responsibility shall attach to the Carrier or his agents for failure to notify)		RECEIVED in external apparent good order and condition except as otherwise noted. The total number of packages or units stuffed in the container, the description of the goods and the weight shown in this bill of lading are furnished by the Merchants, and which the carrier has no reasonable means of checking and is not a part of this Bill of Lading contract. The carrier has issued the number of Bills of Lading stated below, all of this tenor and date, one of the original Bills of Lading must be surrendered and endorsed or signed against the delivery of the shipment and whereupon any other original bills of lading shall be void. The Merchants agree to be bound by the terms and conditions of this Bill of Lading as if each had personally signed this Bill of Lading. SEE clause 4 on the back of this bill of lading [Terms continued on the back hereof, please read carefully] * Applicable Only When Document Used as a Combined Transport Bill of Lading.	
4. Combined Transport* Pre-carriage by	5. Combined Transport* Place of Receipt		
6. Ocean Vessel Voy. No.	7. Port of Loading		
8. Port of Discharge	9. Combined Transport* Place of Delivery		

Marks & Nos. Container/Seal No.	No. of Containers or Packages	Description of Goods (If Dangerous Goods, See Clause 20)	Gross Weight Kg	Measurement
		Description of Contents for Shipper's Use Only (Not part of This B/L Contract)		

10. Total Number of Containers and/or packages (in words) Subject to Clause 7 Limitation					
11. Freight & Charges	Revenue Tons	Rate	Per	Prepaid	Collect
Declared Value Charge					
ex. Rate	Prepaid at	Payable at		Place and Date of Issue	
	Total Prepaid	No. of Original B(s)/L		Signed for the Carrier XX CONTAINER LINES	

LADEN ON BOARD THE VESSEL
DATE   BY
(STANDARD FROM 9801)   CNS 021...
[XX STANDARD FROM 9801]   CNS 021...

---

① Sample bill of lading, 百度文库, retrieved on July 22, 2014 from http://wenku.baidu.com/view/50fc9d7c580216fc700afdc1.html? re=view

Specimen of a charter-party bill of lading

CODE NAME: "CONGENBILL" EDITION 1976

Shipper	... SHIPPING AND TRANSPORTATION CO. LTD.
Consignee	B/L No.
Notify address	BILL OF LADING TO BE USED WITH CHARTER-PARTIES
Vessel　　　　　Port of loading	Reference No.
Port of discharge	

Shipper's description of goods　　　　　　　　　　　Gross weight
...

CLEAN ON BOARD:
"FREIGHT PAYABLE AS PER CHARTER PARTY"

"This shipment of _____ Metric tons was loaded on board the vessel as per of the original _____ lot of Metric tons stowed in _____ with no segregation as to parcels. For the whole shipment _____ sets of Bill of Lading have been issued for which the vessel is relieved from all responsibilities to the extent it would be if one set only would have been issued. The vessel undertakes to deliver only that portion of the cargo actually loaded, which is represented by the percentage that the total amount specified in the Bill (s) of lading bears to the total of the commingling shipment delivered at destination. Neither the vessel nor the owner assume any responsibility for the consequences of such comingling nor for the separation thereof at the time of delivery."

Freight payable as per CHARTER-PARTY dated _____ FREIGHT ADVANCE. Received on account of freight _____ Time used for loading _____ days _____ hours	SHIPPED at the Port of Loading in apparent good order and condition on board the Vessel for carriage to the Port of Discharge or so near thereto as she may safely get the goods specified above. Weight, measure, quality, condition, contents and value unknown. IN WITNESS whereof the Master or Agent of the said Vessel has signed the number of Bills of Lading indicated below all of this tenor and date, any one of which being accomplished the others shall be void. FOR CONDITIONS OF CARRIAGE SEE OVERLEAF
FIRST ORIGINAL　　Freight payable at	Place and date of issue
Number of original Bs/L	Signature

10.5 Insurance documents

According to UCP 600 Article 28 a, an insurance document refers to an insurance policy, an insurance certificate or a declaration under an open cover and must appear to be issued and signed by an insurance company, an underwriter or their agents or their proxies. Any signature by an agent or proxy must indicate whether the agent or proxy has signed for or on behalf of the insurance company or underwriter. Insurance documents evidence the insurer's undertaking to assume its liabilities and serve as a formal contract between the insurer and the insured.

Types of marine cargo transport insurance

Whether the cargo transport insurance is bought by the buyer or the seller relies on the price term agreed upon by them in the sales contract. The most frequently used price terms are FOB, CFR, CIF and CIP. Under FOB and CFR, it is the buyer that buys the insurance covering the transport of the goods while under CIF and CIP it is the seller that does so.

The core contents of an insurance policy are the conditions insured, which define the scope of compensation by the insurer against the damage or loss of the insured goods. Based on the People's Insurance Company of China Ocean Marian Cargo Clause (1981), marine cargo transport risks can be divided into two broad groups: basic risks and additional risks. The latter consists of general additional risks and special additional risks.

Perils of sea

Perils of sea cover natural calamity and accidents. Natural calamity refers to bad climate, thundering and lightening, earthquake, flood, etc. while accidents mean the vessel is grounded, sunk, stranded, in collision, on fire, in explosion, capsized, etc.

Average

The loss caused by perils of sea can be divided into total loss and partial loss. Total loss includes actual total loss and constructive total loss. Partial loss covers general average and particular average.

FPA, WPA/WA and All Risks

Basic risks consist of FPA (free from particular average), WPA/WA and All Risks. FPA does not include the particular average caused by natural calamity while WPA/WA includes the particular average caused by natural calamity. All Risks include FPA, WPA and the losses caused by general additional risks.

Additional risks

Additional risks consist of general additional risks and special additional risks. General additional risks include: theft, pilferage and non-delivery; rain fresh water damage; risk of shortage; risk of intermixture and contamination; risk of leakage; risk of clash and breakage; risk of taint of odor; risk of sweat and heating; risk of hook damage; risk of breakage of packing; and risk of rust.

Special additional risks consist of war risks; failure to deliver; import duty risk; on deck risk; rejection risk; aflatoxin risk; fire risk extension clause; risk of strike, riots and civil commotions; and additional expenses marine war risks.

Examining an insurance policy under a letter of credit

Insurer

It is an insurance company, an insurance underwriter or their agents or their proxies. If an insurance policy is not issued by an insurance company as per the credit, it will be considered a discrepancy by banks.

UCP 600 Article 28a expressly stipulates that an insurance document must appear to be issued and signed by an insurance company or an underwriter or their agents or their proxies. If the insurance document indicates that it has been issued in more than one original, all the originals must be presented. Cover notes will not be accepted.

In practice, the insurance document may be an insurance policy, an insurance certificate or a declaration under an open cover pre-signed by an insurance company, an underwriter or their agent. If a credit requires an insurance certificate or a declaration under an open cover, banks will accept an insurance policy. But if a credit requires an insurance policy, the exporter had better present an insurance policy, but not a certificate or a declaration.

The insured

Under CIF, it is the exporter that buys the insurance for the goods. If there is no specific stipulation in a credit, the insured is the beneficiary of the credit, i.e., the exporter under the sales contract. In practice, depending on the requirements in a credit, the insured may be the buyer or a bank. Sometimes, the negotiating bank or the issuing bank hopes to control the goods by being the insured of insurance cover.

Marks and numbers

Shipping marks and numbers appearing in an insurance policy must be consistent with those on the credit and other required documents. It is not wise to write "Marks & Nos. as per invoice No. 12345" or "Marks & Nos. as per bill of lading No. 56789". The better way is to have the marks and numbers clearly indicated in the insurance policy, or it will be considered a discrepancy by the issuing bank.

Quantity and description of goods

The quantity of the goods should be consistent with that on other documents. The description of goods here may be made in general terms. And the credit number is usually indicated in this part, since some credits require that the credit number appear on all the documents.

Amount insured

The insurance document must indicate the amount of insurance coverage, and the currency should be the same as the credit. The amount insured should be in both figures and words.

In order to calculate the correct amount insured, one should examine the terms on insurance policy carefully. Typically, a credit may requires "… insurance policy for full CIF invoice value plus 10%", suppose the invoice value is USD47,259.00, then the amount insured should be USD 51,985.00. Sometimes, however, the wording of the insurance clause may be expressed as "… insurance policy for 110% cover the CIF value", this wording is quite different and means that, suppose the same invoice value, the amount insured will be USD47,259.00 $\times$ (1 + 110%), i.e.

USD 99,244.00.

According to UCP 600 Article 28, if there is no indication in a credit of the insurance coverage, the amount of insurance coverage must be at least 110% of the CIF or CIP value of goods. If the CIF or CIP value cannot be determined from the documents, the amount of insurance coverage must be calculated based on the amount honored or negotiated or the gross value of the goods shown on the invoice, whichever is greater.

Moreover, one must be careful about the numbers after the decimal points of the invoice value. For example, the invoice value may be USD 47,259.01 or USD47,259.90, but for both of the values, the amount insured must be USD47,260.00, otherwise, the amount insured will be considered inadequate.

Usually, on the invoice appears commission or discount. If there is a commission, the number which has not deducted the commission yet should be used to calculate the amount insured, while if there is a discount, the number which has deducted the discount should be used.

If there is any stipulation on import duty, e.g., "insurance policy for 110% of CIF invoice value, plus 30% to cover import duty", then the insurance policy must be indicated so.

As to the premium and rate, it can be filled as "as arranged".

Transport vehicle

The goods may be transported by sea, by air, by railway, etc. It is so indicated as per the bill of lading, such as "Vessel No. 123", "By s. s. … then by overland transportation to…", "By railway. Wagon No. 123", "By airplane," "By parcel post," etc.

Date of sailing, port of loading and port of discharge

The date of sailing, port of loading and the port of discharge in an insurance policy should be as per the credit and consistent with those in the bills of lading.

The date of the insurance document must be no later than the date of shipment unless it appears from the insurance document that the cover is effective from a date not later than the date of shipment.

Conditions

According to UCP 600 Article 28, a credit should state the type of insurance required and, if any, the additional risks to be covered. If a credit uses imprecise terms such as "usual risk" or "customary risks", banks will accept the insurance document without regard to any risks that are not covered.

When a credit requires insurance against "all risks", banks will accept an insurance document which contains any "all risks" notation or clause. Even if it has no "all risks" in its heading and indicates that certain risks are excluded.

An insurance document may contain reference to any exclusion clause.

An insurance document may indicate that the cover is subject to a franchise or excess (deductible). For example, "a franchise of 10% being applicable on a loss of USD100" means that any loss less than USD10 is payable by the insured not the insurer, while any loss of USD10 and over is payable by the insured and the insured is not liable; "an excess of 10% being applicable on a loss of USD100" means that any loss up to USD10 is payable by the insured, while USD90 is payable by the insurer.

Agent and place of payment

In case of damage or loss of the goods, the agent will examine and evaluate on behalf of the insurer. The place of payment is usually indicated in an insurance policy for the beneficiary to claim for compensation in case of damage to or loss of the goods. If there is no stipulation of the place of payment in a credit, the port of destination will be the place of payment.

Date of issuing the insurance policy

The date of issuing the insurance policy must be no later than the date of shipment, unless the insurance policy indicates that the cover is effective from a date not later than the date of shipment.

Signature of the insurer

An insurance policy must be signed by an insurance company, an underwriter or their proxies, otherwise it will be invalid. Again, any signature by an agent or proxy must indicate whether the agent or proxy has signed for or on behalf of the insurance company or underwriter.

Indorsement

As discussed above, only under CIF or CIP will the exporter need to submit the insurance document. Where the insurance policy is made out "to order", the exporter need indorse it before submitting it to the negotiating bank. If the credit requires special indorsement such as "indorsed to the order of… Co., Ltd.", the exporter must do as shown in the credit. If the credit requires the insured to be another company or a bank, the exporter need not indorse the instrument.

Amendment

If there is any misspelling or wrong clauses found in an insurance policy, only the insurance company is entitled to make any amendment accordingly. Banks have no such rights.

The most frequently found discrepancies with an insurance document

(1) The currency in which the insurance document is expressed is not that of the credit.

(2) The amount of insurance is insufficient.

(3) The merchandise description is not consistent with the credit or invoice description.

(4) The port of loading or place of taking in charge is not in accordance with the credit.

(5) The starting point for the insurance to be effective is not in accordance with the credit.

(6) Specific risks as stipulated in the credit are not annotated in or covered by the document.

(7) Certificates are not countersigned where such countersignature is required.

(8) The insurance policy is not indorsed in terms of the credit.

(9) The effective date for insurance is later than the date of shipment.

(10) All of the originals shown on the insurance document, as issued, are not presented.

Specimen of a certificate of marine insurance under an open cover

                                        Insurance agent's name
                                        and address

                     Insurance agent's Logo

OPEN COVER NO.   ORIGINAL   Certificate no   issued in 2 originals

This is to certify that the shipment mentioned below is insured by this insurance company under a Marine Cargo Policy issued in the name of _____ Co. Ltd and its subsidiaries.

Assured :
Conveyance :
From :
To :

Marks, numbers, goods and manner of packing:

Insured Value (state currency):
Say:
Scope of insurance:
Against "All Risks" as per current Institute Cargo Clauses (A) (01.10.1982) as far as applicable and as per terms, conditions and exceptions of Open Cover No. _____.
Insurance conditions as per L/C: " INSURANCE POLICY/CERTIFICATE IN 2 COPIES FOR 110 PERCENT OF THE INVOICE VALUE SHOWING CLAIMS PAYABLE IN CHINA IN CURRENCY OF THE DRAFT, BLANK ENDORSED, COVERING OCEAN MARINE TRANSPORTATION ALL RISKS, WAR RISKS."

First of 2 originals.

Claims: Claims to be notified to the claims adjuster: ... Co., LTD.
                                                      [Address, Tel and Fax]

In the event of loss or damage:
- The claimant must immediately make a written claim to the Carriers, Port Authorities or other Bailees for any missing packages.
- In no circumstances, except under written protest, should clean receipts be given if the goods are not in a sound condition.
- When goods are carried in Containers the claimant must ensure that the Container and its seals are examined immediately by the responsible official.

- If the Container is delivered damaged or with seals broken or missing or with seal numbers other than as stated in the shipping documents, the delivery receipt must be claused accordingly and all defective or irregular seals must be retained for subsequent identification.
- Any loss or damage must be notified immediately to the claims adjuster at above address for survey.
- Claims will be paid subject to surrender of one negotiable original of this certificate, the remaining originals, if any, thereby becoming void.
- The following documents are to be submitted in support of any claim:
    1. Negotiable original of the Certificate of Insurance
    2. Commercial Invoice and packing list
    3. Original Bill of Lading and/or other original documents relating to the carriage (airway bills, consignment notes, etc.)
    4. Original Survey Report issued the surveyor
    5. Letter of protest against the carriers (see overleaf) and respective replies
    6. Claim statement
    7. Any other document or correspondence in respect of the shipment in question

This Certificate is not valid unless counter-signed by the Assured

Dated: ××/××/12　　　　　　　　　　　　Signed by⋯⋯⋯⋯⋯
⋯authorized
agent for insurance companies:

　　　　　　　　　　　　　　　　　　　　　　⋯
　　　　　　　　　　　　　　　　　　　　　　⋯
　　　　　　　　　　　　　　　　　　　　　　⋯
　　　　　　　　　　　　　　　　　　　　　　⋯

Assured's authorized signature
[Name, address, Tel and Fax]

　　　　　　　　　　　　　　　　　　　[Signature]
　　　　　　　　　　　　　　　　　　　p. p. Managing Director

Specimen of an insurance policy

中国人民保险公司
The People's Insurance Company of China
总公司设于北京　　　一九四九年创立
Head Office: BEIJING　　　Established In 1949

发票号码
Invoice No.

保险单号次
Policy No.

被保险人：
Insured: _____

中国人民保险公司(以下简称本公司)根据被保险人的要求,及其所缴付约定的保险费,按照本保险单承保险别和背面所载条款与下列特别条款承保以下货物运输保险,特签发本保单。

This policy of Insurance witnesses that The People's Insurance Company of China (hereinafter called "The Company"), at the request of the Insured and in consideration of the agreed premium paid by the insured, undertakes to insure the undermentioned goods in transportation subject to the conditions of this policy as per the Clauses printed overleaf and other special clauses attached hereon.

保险货物项目 Description of Goods	包装　单位　数量 Packing Unit Quantity	保险金额 Amount Insured

承保险别　　　　　　　　　　　　　　　　　　　　　　　　货物标记
Conditions　　　　　　　　　　　　　　　　　　　　　　　　Marks of Goods

总保险金额
Total Amount Insured: _____

保费　　　　　装载运输工具　　　　　　　　　　　　　　　　开航日期
Premium _____　Per conveyance S.S _____　Sig. on or about _____
起运港　　　　　　　　　　　　　　　　目的港
From _____　To _____

所保货物,如发生本保险单项下可能引起索赔的损失或损坏,应立即通知本公司下述代理人查勘。如有索赔,应向本公司提交保险单正本(本保险单共有_____份正本)及有关文件。如一份正本已用于索赔,其余正本则自动失效。

In the event of loss or damage which may result in a claim under this Policy, immediate notice must be given to the Company's Agent as mentioned hereunder. Claims, if any, one of the Original Policy which has been issued in _____ Original (s) together with the relevant documents shall be surrendered to the Company. If one of the Original Policy has been accomplished, the others to be void.

中国人民保险公司
THE PEOPLE'S INSURANCE COMPANY OF CHINA
THE PEOPLE'S INSURANCE CO. OF CHINA
... BRANCH
INTERNATIONAL DEPT.

_____
UNDERWRITING MANAGER

赔款偿付地点
Claim payable at _____

日期　　　　　　　　在
Date:_____ at _____

地址
Address: _____

10.6 Other documents

Certificates of origin

A certificate of origin is a statement signed by the appropriate authority, as required by a credit, providing evidence of the origin of the goods.

A certificate of origin falls into one of the three types: GSP Certificate of Origin "Form A", CCPIT Certificate of Origin and the Certificate of Origin made by the exporter itself.

GSP Certificate or Origin Form A

GSP means "Generalized System of Preference", the advantageous duty exemption system offered by developed countries against the imports of some goods from developing countries. The developed countries are called the preferential giving countries and the developing countries are called the beneficiary countries. The aim of the system is to help promote developing countries' exports and industrialization. GSP is based on three principles: (1) non-discrimination, (2) generalized and (3) non-reciprocity.

In order to use a GSP Certificate of Origin, the goods must be made in a beneficiary country, and if there are any imported parts in the products, the imported parts should not take up more than 40% of the finished products. Moreover, the exporter of the beneficiary country must directly dispatch the goods to the preferential giving country. And the most important thing is to provide a GSP Certificate of Origin Form A, which may be issued by the relative authority of the beneficiary country.

CCPIT Certificate of Origin

CCPIT means "China Council for the Promotion of International Trade". When a letter of credit requires that a certificate of origin be issued by such Council or similar chamber of commerce, the exporter in China usually use CCPIT Certificate of Origin.

Certificate of Origin issued by the exporter

When a credit has no specific stipulation on the issuer of the certificate of origin, the exporter may issue the document, evidencing the origin of the products.

What kind of certificate of origin should be presented depends on the requirements of the credit. Banks will accept a certificate of origin as stipulated in the credit. If there is no stipulation on the issuer, banks will accept any certificate of origin that meets the requirements of the credit and not inconsistent with other documents.

Specimen of a GSP Certificate of Origin Form A

<table>
<tr><td colspan="3">1. Goods consigned from (Exporter's business name, address, country)</td><td colspan="3" rowspan="2">Reference No.

**GENERALIZED SYSTEM OF PREFERENCE
CERTIFICATE OF ORIGIN**
(Combined declaration and certificate)

FORM A
Issued in THE PEOPLE'S REPUBLIC OF CHINA
(Country)

See Noted Overleaf</td></tr>
<tr><td colspan="3">2. Goods consignee to (Consignee's name, address, country)</td></tr>
<tr><td colspan="3">3. Means of transport and route (as far as known)</td><td colspan="3">4. For official use</td></tr>
<tr><td>5. Item No.</td><td>6. Marks and number of packages</td><td>7. Number and kind of packages; description of goods</td><td>8. Origin criterion (see notes overleaf)</td><td>9. Gross weight or other quantity</td><td>10. Number and date of invoices</td></tr>
<tr><td colspan="3">11. Certification
It is hereby to certify, on the basis of control carried out, the declaration by the exporter is correct.

____
Place and date, signature and stamp certifying authority</td><td colspan="3">12. Declaration by the exporter
He undersigned hereby declares that the above details and statements are correct that the goods were produced in
____
And that they comply with the original requirements specified for those goods in the Generalized System of Preferences for goods exported to
____
(import country)

Place and date, signature of authorized signatory</td></tr>
</table>

Specimen of a Certificate of Origin of P. R. China

1. Exporter (full name and address)	Certificate No. **CERTIFICATE OF ORIGIN OF THE PEOPLE'S REPUBLIC OF CHINA**			
2. Consignee (full name, address, country)					
3. Means of transport and route	5. For certifying authority use only			
4. Destination port					
6. Marks and Numbers of packages	7. Description of goods: number and kind of packages	8. H.S. Code	9. Quantity or weight	10. Number and date of invoices
11. Declaration by the exporter The undersigned hereby declares that the above details and statements are correct; that all the goods were produced in China and that they comply with the Rules of Origin of the People's Republic of China.	12. Certification It is hereby certified that the declaration by the exporter is correct.			
Place and date, signature and stamp of the exporter	Place and date, signature and stamp of certifying authority			

Inspection certificate

An inspection certificate is a statement issued and signed by the appropriate authority, evidencing that the goods have been inspected and what the results of such inspection are.

In practice, the issuer of an inspection certificate may be a government organization such as China Entry-Exit Inspection and Quarantine (CIQ) or China Certification & Inspection (Group) Co., Ltd. (CCIC) in China, a non-governmental organization such as authentic surveyor, sworn measurer, etc., the manufacturer of the goods or the user or importer of the goods.

The most often seen inspection certificates issued by national inspection organizations in China include: Inspection Certificate of Quality; Inspection Certificate of Quality/Weight; Certificate of Value; Certificate of Origin; Health Certificate; Disinfection Inspection Certificate; Inspection Certificate of Temperature; and Fumigation Certificate.

Packing list and weight list

A packing list contains the details of goods provided by the exporter. A weight list describes the weight of each piece of goods. Both are issued by the exporter and sometimes incorporated in the invoice. All the contents in a packing list or a weight list must be consistent with those on other documents.

Cable copy

A cable copy is presented by the exporter to evidence that the exporter has notified certain parties as required by a credit.

Beneficiary's statement

It is issued by the beneficiary of a credit and declares that the beneficiary has fulfilled the obligations of the sales contract and that the goods are in good conditions, of good quality and packing, etc.

Shipping company's certificate

It is issued by the shipping company, certifying the conditions of the carrying vessel, such as the name, nationality and age of the vessel.

Certificate of analysis

It is issued by the party as stipulated in the credit. It will relate to the analysis of goods as required by the relevant trade and may include details of temperature and chemical content.

Certificate of weight

It is issued by the party as stipulated in the documentary credit. It will relate to the goods net weights of package

10.7 Examination of documents under documentary credits

Upon receipt of the documents submitted under a credit, banks must examine the documents carefully to ensure that all documents are in compliance with the terms and conditions of the credit, the applicable rules of ISBP and UCP 600 and that all documents are consistent with one another. To the negotiating bank, complying presentation is the prerequisite for negotiation and getting reimbursed from the issuing bank. To the issuing bank, complying presentation is the condition for paying the beneficiary or the negotiating bank.

Examination of documents often follows a procedure that includes three parts: (1) Examination of the documents to verify whether they comply with the credit itself, including accepted amendments; (2) Examination of the documents to verify whether they comply with relevant UCP articles; and (3) Examination of the documents verify whether they comply with one another.

Examination of documents with reference to the documentary credit

Documentary credits are transmitted by SWIFT as MT700 message types and they will be in a set format, with fields designated for certain types of data content. Key field data designators are as follows:

Form of credit

The types and characteristics of the documentary credit i. e., irrevocable, transferable, standby, etc is indicated here.

Date of issue

It indicates the date on which the documentary credit is issued.

Applicable rules

The rules that are applicable to the documentary credit may be read as:
"UCP LATEST VERSION",
"EUCP LATEST VERSION",
"UCP URR LATEST VERSION",
"EUCP URR LATEST VERSION",
"ISP LATEST VERSION" or "OTHER".

Applicant

Name of the party that has requested the issuance of the documentary credit is indicated here.

Beneficiary

Name of the party that has presented the documents and expected to obtain the proceeds under the documentary credit is indicated here.

Credit amount

The drawing is in line with the documentary credit amount.

Latest date of shipment

The transport document should be no later than the date stipulated in this field.

Description of goods

The wording of the description of goods on the invoice must correspond to that showed on the documentary credit.

Documents required

This field describes the documentary requirements.

Examination of documents with reference to the UCP

According to UCP600, the issuing bank must examine a presentation to determine, on the basis of the documents alone, whether or not the documents appear on their face to constitute a complying presentation.

In documents other than the commercial invoice, the description of the goods, services or performance, if stated, may be in general terms not conflicting with their description in the credit.

A document presented but not required by the credit will be disregarded and may be returned to the presenter.

A document may be dated prior to the issuance date of the credit, but must not be dated later than its date of presentation.

When the address of the beneficiary and the applicant appear in any stipulated document, they need not be the same as those stated in the credit or in any other stipulated document, but must be within the same country as the respective addresses mentioned in the credit. Contact details stated as part of the beneficiary's and the applicant's address will be disregarded.

The shipper or consignor of the goods indicated on any document need not be the beneficiary of the credit.

Examination of documents with reference to one another

Data in a document, when read in context with the credit, the document itself and international standard banking practice, need not be identical to, but must not conflict with, data in that document, any other stipulated document or the credit.

References

1. About the New York Fed. Federal Reserve Bank of New York. Retrieved 24 July 2014 from http://www.newyorkfed.org/aboutthefed.

2. Anders Grath. *The Handbook of International Trade and Finance*. London and Philadelphia: Kogan Page, 2008.

3. Andy Ripley. *Forfaiting for Exporters—Practical Solutions for Global Trade Finance* International Thomson Press, 1996.

4. Bolero. Bolero.net Retrieved 23 October 2011 from http://www.bolero.net/en/company/overview.aspx.

5. Canadian Imperial Bank of Commerce. *Correspondent Bank Terms and Conditions of CIBC*, Januaryl, 2014. Retrieved 24 July 2014 from https://www.cibc.com/ca/pdf/correspondent-banking/terms-and-conditions.pdf.

6. CHIPS Celebrates 40th Anniversary Milestone. Press Release, New York, April 6, 2010. Retrieved 28 October 2011 from http://www.chips.org/press_releases/pressReleaseDocs/070431.pdf.

7. Christopher R. Seppala. *The ICC Uniform Rules for Demand Guarantees ("URDG") in Practice: A Decade of Experience*, Partner, White & Case LLP, Paris and Legal Advisor, FIDIC Contracts Committee (1), Presented at the ICC Conference, May 15, 2011. See http://www2.fidic.org/resources/contracts/seppala_0601.asp.

8. Comite Maritime International. Rales for Electronic Bills of Lading. 1990. Retrieved 22 October, 2011 from http://comitemaritime.org/Rule-for-Bills-of-lading/0,2728,12832,00.html.

9. Dudley Richardson. (1983). *Guide to Negotiable Instruments and the Bills of Exchange Acts*. London Butterworths, 1983.

10. European Central Bank. About its forerunner TARGET1. *Eurosystem*. 2011. Retrieved 30 October 2011 from http://www.ecb.int/paym/t2/target/html/index.en.html.

11. EDI Overview. EDI Information.com. 2013 - 2014. Retrieved 18 July, 2014 from http://www.ediinformation.com/edi/edi.php.

12. Factors Chain International. *FCI General Rules for International Factoring* (2010 Revision). Factors Chain International, 2014. See http://www.fci.nl.

13. Factors Chain International. Members in China. *FCI*. 2013. Retrieved 24 October 2013 from http://www.fci.nl/fci-members/select-a-member/asia?c=CN, 24 Oct. 2013.

14. Fedwire and National Settlement Services. Federal Reserve Bank of New York. 2011. Retrieved 28 October 2011 from http://www.newyorkfed.org/aboutthefed/fedpoint/fed43.html.

15. Hague-Visby Rules. Wikipedia. 2014. Retrieved 24 July 2014 from http://en.wikipedia.org/wiki/Hague-Visby_Rules.

16. International Chamber of Commerce. Incoterms® 2010. (English Edition). ICC Publication No. 715E, Retrieved 24 July, 2014 from http://store.iccwbo.org/incoterms-2010.

17. International Chamber of Commerce. *Uniform Rules for Collection*, ICC Publication No. 522E, 1995 Edition, 1996.

18. International Chamber of Commerce. *Uniform Customs and Practice for Documentary Credits*. (English leaflet Edition). ICC Publication No. 600Le, 2007 Edition, 2007.

19. International Chamber of Commerce. *International Standard Banking Practice (ISBP) for the Examination of Documents under Documentary Credits*. ISBP 745. ICC Publication No. 745E, 2013 Edition, 2013.

20. International Chamber of Commerce. *International Standby Practices*. ISP 98, ICC Publication No. 590E, 1998 Edition, 1999.

21. International Chamber of Commerce. *Uniform Rules for Demand Guarantees*. ICC Publication No. 758E, 2010 Edition, 2010.

22. International Chamber of Commerce. *Uniform Rules for Contract Guarantees*. ICC Publication No. 325E, 1978 Edition, 1978.

23. *International Convention for the Unification of Certain Rules of Law relating to Bills of Lading ("Hague Rules"), and Protocol of Signature*, Brussels, 25 August 1924. *Admiralty and Maritime Law Guide*. Retrieved 24 July 2014 from http://www.admiraltylawguide.com/conven/haguerules1924.html

24. International Trade and Forfaiting Association. *ITFA*. 24 July 2014. http://itfa.org.

25. Johan Bergamin. *Payment Techniques in Trade Finance*. ING Barings, 1999.

26. John S. Gordon. *Export/Import Letters of Credit and Payment Methods: Making Payments in International Trade*, Second Edition. Global Training Center, Inc, 2002.

27. J. W. Richardson. *The Merchants Guide*, 1998 Edition. P & O Nedlloyd, 1998.

28. London Forfaiting Company Ltd. (July 2014). http://www.londonforfaiting.com.

29. SWIFT. *Annual Review* 2010. Retrieved 25 October 2011 from http：//www. swift. com/about_swift/publications/annual_reports/annual_review_2010/SWIFT_AR2010. pdfhttp：//www. bolero. net.

30. The Data Interchange Standards Association. *An Introduction to Electronic Data Interchange*. The Data Interchange Standards Association，Inc.（DISA），1991.

31. The League of Nations. *Convention Providing a Uniform Law for Bills of Exchange and Promissory Notes*（Geneva，1930），Lex Mercatoria. Retrieved 24 July 2014 from http：//www. jus. uio. no/lm/bills. of. exchange. and. promissory. notes. convention. 1930/doc. html，1930.

32. United Nations. *United Nations Convention on the Carriage of Goods by Sea*，1978 Hamburg，31 March 1978. Retrieved 24 July 2014 from http：//treaties. un. org/pages/ViewDetails. aspx? src=TREATY&mtdsg_no=XI-D-3&chapter=11&lang=en.

33. 电子数据交换. 维基百科. 2011 年 10 月 22 日，参见 http：//zh. wikipedia. org/wiki/电子数据交换.

34. 高德步编著. 国际经贸惯例——规则与公约. 北京：中共中央党校出版社，1995.

35. 固然. 特色独具的福费廷——贸易融资产品综合比较. Foreign Exchange，2001（4）. 44.

36. 杭州中心支行. 浙江中行办理全球首笔 TSU 项下福费廷业务. 中国人民银行杭州支行. Retrieved 24 July 2014 from http：//hangzhou. pbc. gov. cn/publish/hangzhou/1250/2012/20120117185812844661958/20120117185812844661958_. html.

37. 贺培主. 国际结算学. 北京：中国财政经济出版社，2000.

38. 胡小娟. 国际贸易风险管理与案例评析. 湖南：湖南人民出版社，2002.

39. 黄维梁. 出入口实务精要. 香港：万源图书有限公司，1998.

40. 姜学军. 国际结算. 辽宁：东北财经大学出版社，2000.

41. 李向群. 一则关于信用证的案例启示. 中国对外贸易，2001(9).

42. 李玉刚. 出口经典案例分析. 北京：经济日报出版社，2000.

43. 罗晶. 国际保理：企业出口贸易融资的选择. Foreign exchange，2001(3)：42-43.

44. 孟晓峰. 部分国家和地区对 D/P 远期的处理方式. 2014 年 8 月 21 日转引自 http：//info. ipincai. com/WaiMaoZhiDao/WTpUKfAKZrhF-1. html.

45. 如何汇款. 西联汇款. 2013. Retrieved 2012/3/12 from http：//www. westernunion. cn/sc/how_to_send. php.

46. 沈锦旭等. 国际支付与结算（修订本）. 上海：上海外语教育出版社，1996.

47. 石玉川、徐进亮、李贞. 国际结算惯例及案例. 北京：对外经济贸易大学出版社，1998.

48. 苏宗祥. 国际结算. 北京：中国财政经济出版社，1982.

49. 提单样本. 百度文库. Retrieved on July 22，2014 from http：//wenku. baidu.

com/view/50fc9d7c580216fc700afdc1.html? re=view.

50. 王丽丽. 国际结算. 北京:中国金融出版社,1996.

51. 肖罗. 走进国际保理. Foreign exchange,2001(3):44-45.

52. 杨新丰. 银行结算实用手册. 南京:南京出版社,1990.

53. 英国 Bills of Exchange Act 1882. 上传者 xiaosignature. 百度文库. 2014 年 7 月 24 日转引自 http://wenku.baidu.com/link?url=K8GfCq8q4dKZcQW-1dx1LPX7ix8lxVYrX1zhiFCNyJY7Yb3t01uJYdf95NB99-hKrx1rCQa3GiKiRk_gV2Rh3KMVaxPf-Tuk3ddt1XE6QW.

54. 张燕玲,王仲和. 国际结算业务指南. 北京:中华工商联合出版社,1997.

55. 赵威. 国际票据法理论与实务. 北京:中国政法大学出版社,1995.

56. 赵薇. 信用证打包贷款的风险与防范. 改革与开放,1997(8).

57. 张红. 国际结算. 南京:南京大学出版社,1996.

58. 中国人民银行会计司. 支付结算制度汇编——企业、银行正确办理支付结算指南. 北京:新华出版社,1997.

59. 中国现代化支付系统. 百度百科. 2011 年 10 月 30 日转引自 http://baike.baidu.com/view/1035980.html? fromTaglist.

60. 中国现代化支付系统的发展. 中国人民银行. 2011 年 11 月 2 日转引自 http://www.pbc.gov.cn/publish/zhifujiesuansi/903/2010/20100910134943002421899/20100910134943002421899.html.

61. 周明. 跨境支付:国际卡组织的主战场. 中国信用卡(专业)(China Credit Card) 2010(8).